3.50

By Robert Lynd

IN DEFENCE OF PINK

THINGS ONE HEARS

ESSAYS ON LIFE AND LITERATURE

BOOKS AND WRITERS

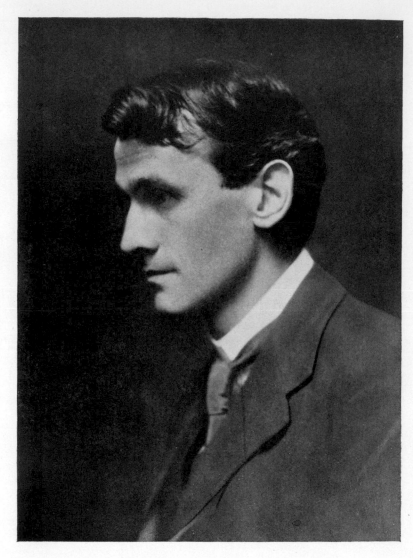

ROBERT LYND, 1917

Robert Lynd

BOOKS AND WRITERS

With a foreword by
RICHARD CHURCH

LONDON
J. M. DENT & SONS LTD

Foreword

IT is a great thing to be able to say of a man that he was universally loved, although he never attempted to conceal the idiosyncrasies of his character. It can be said of Robert Lynd, both as a man and as a writer. For over fifty years he was an active professional writer, and principally a critic who never compromised because it might have been expedient to do so, and never concealed the principles on which he based his standards of judgment. Yet he never made an enemy. The reason for this is that he expressed his views, and particularly his adverse views, in terms of a benevolence that was so patently sincere and natural that anger and chagrin disappeared before it. Equally in his personal contacts with fellow writers, football fans, cab drivers, and the rest of the world, his attitude, if this word can be used in connection with him, was one of shrewd kindness. This endeared him to everybody with whom he came into contact, and at the same time it kept him detached and wholesomely feared. The ambitious young tyro, the successful veteran, the bitter failure, who represent the three types of egotism in all human activities, were restrained from their monomanias in the presence of Robert Lynd. His quiet demeanour, his half-inaudible, rapid remarks, his side-glances out of a pair of extraordinarily handsome and wistful eyes, his stooping figure and Fra Angelico profile—all these attributes combined to invest him with an unquestioned authority, an office which he was never known to claim.

It is that office, however, which presides in his writing, no matter how casual the moment and how playful the mood. It is the unconscious office of a personality. Its gentleness, tolerance, humour, scepticism, united to make a sort of dalmatic which he wore as unconsciously as his beloved Dr. Johnson wore the cloak of gruffness. His qualities were taken somewhat for granted, as is the habit in Fleet Street, while his essays, articles, and critiques were pouring out day by day during his long professional life. Now that his work can be seen in bulk, as in

v

this volume and in the more general collection in Everyman's Library, these qualities cohere and present not only a distinct personality but also a philosophy. The personality must remain a legend that partially survives in his literary remains. The philosophy is one which represents the fine flower of European humanism.

The circumstances of the modern world appear to be combining to tread that flower into the ruins of past civilizations. Something new, perhaps something even more splendid, may be in store for mankind, but the breaking up of the ground to prepare for the growth is a terrible experience, as we know to-day. We see the combined forces of classical humanism and of Christianity, the two upholders of the freedom and dignity of the individual, being attacked in such a way that they cannot retaliate to defend themselves without denying their own principles. Shall the Christian turn the other cheek or not? Shall the humanist forswear freedom of thought and action in order to present a united front against the powers of materialism? These are questions which paralyse the mind and body of western Europe. The wise man sees them as eternal questions which have always coiled like serpents in the bosom of every religion and every philosophy by which loving-kindness has been organized into a way of life, both for the individual and for society as a whole.

Robert Lynd's work, day in and day out, has been a running commentary upon these questions, examining their validity, and referring them back always to the base from which they sprang, that loving-kindness which for himself Lynd knew to be the source of his own life and his relationship with the world around him.

That world was a wide one, for his interests were not imprisoned within his profession, as happens with so many folk. He loved men, women, children, birds (particularly birds!); he loved town and country, village life and solitude, football crowds and Fleet Street pub; there was no limit to the range of his interests, so long as their circumstances offered him some facet of the drama of life. To heighten that drama, to give it form and coherence, Lynd turned to literature, which he looked upon, nevertheless, as a moon reflecting the vital glory of the sun of daily life. For this purpose he believed that since literature was a mirror of life, its purpose was lost if the surface should be ruffled or broken by obscurity, perverseness, or any other forms of aberration affecting literary technique and the sanity of thought and conduct.

In so far as Lynd demanded from writers that sanity, he was a classicist: in so far as he was willing to accept an infinite variety in the presentation of that sanity, he was a romantic. In this present volume of literary essays, selected from the last twenty-five years' work, we see Lynd as a liberal humanist, standing between those two extremes, a characteristic figure set firmly, and on principle, in the centre of his own tolerance. It is a stance which to-day appears to attract more hatred and derision than any other. For that reason, Lynd's work becomes a challenge to many of the tendencies of the mid twentieth century. But Lynd was never a man to care for fashions. Examples of that indifference will be found here in his essays on Henry James, James Joyce, and Mr. T. S. Eliot. He was always sceptical of mystification and esotericism in literature, and their counter-parts in life, chicane and secretiveness. His belief was that 'the safe rule in writing is to say what one precisely means, even if it appears to destroy the shape of the sentence. If the sense does not give the sentence good shape, then all the high-sounding words in the dictionary will not do so.' Behind that literary axiom stand all the virtues of healthy protestantism, but none of its fervours and insularity. Lynd in himself was like that, and I believe that this quality in his work will give time an excuse for endowing it with permanence.

1952.   RICHARD CHURCH.

Contents

PART III. *CRITICISM AND CRITICS*

CONTENTS   xi

Illustrations

Acknowledgments

Many of these essays appeared over the signature 'John o' London' in *John o' London's Weekly*.

The publishers are indebted to the following for permission to reproduce photographs:
Central Press Photos: George Bernard Shaw; Howard Coster: Arnold Bennett; Messrs. Constable & Co. Ltd.: Katherine Mansfield; Henry Grant: Robert Lynd and Sylvia Lynd; E. O. Hoppé: Thomas Hardy; F. Ledger: Anthony Trollope; Man Ray and the New York Museum of Modern Art: James Joyce; National Portrait Gallery: George Eliot; Picture Post Library: Victor Hugo and George Meredith; The Society for Cultural Relations with the U.S.S.R.: Leo Tolstoy and Ivan Turgenev. The portrait of Henry James by J. E. Blanche is from the artist's *Portraits of a Lifetime*, published by Messrs. J. M. Dent & Sons Ltd. The illustration of Herman Melville is from Metcalf's *Journal of a Visit to London and the Continent*, copyright by the President and Fellows of Harvard College (1948) and reproduced by permission of the Harvard University Press and Messrs. Cohen and West.

I
Among the Immortals

Whitman: Man and Poet

(1947)

WHEN Walt Whitman resigned from the editorship of
the *Brooklyn Freeman* in 1849 he bade a characteristic farewell
to his readers: 'To those who have been my friends, I take
occasion to proffer the warmest thanks of a grateful heart. My
enemies—and all hunkers generally—I disdain and defy the same
as ever.' In spite of his frequently expressed love for even the
lowest of human beings, indeed, Walt was never patient of those
who did not appreciate him. In one of his poems in *Drum Taps*
he addresses 'a certain civilian,' obviously an obtuse person:

Go lull yourself with what you can understand, and with piano tunes,
For I lull nobody, and you will never understand me.

His fellow Americans, it must be admitted, were slow to recognize his genius, and in 1868—thirteen years after the publication
of the first edition of *Leaves of Grass*—he declared sorrowfully in
a letter to Moncure Conway: 'In my own country, so far, from
the Press and from authoritative quarters, I have received but
one long tirade of impudence, mockery, and scurrilous jeers.'
Emerson, it is true, wrote him an early letter of encouragement:
but it was in England and Ireland that he was first applauded with
some lustiness by Swinburne, W. M. Rossetti, Edward Dowden,
and others. That this gave him great pleasure is clear from his
writing to Conway: 'I may here confess to you that to be
accepted by these young men of England and treated with the
highest courtesy and honour touches me deeply.'
It is not surprising that so defiant a voice aroused opposition
among his own countrymen, for he defied in his verse not only
the accepted canons of poetry but the accepted notions of
morality and decency. His celebration of sex in those pre-
Freudian days led Carlyle to describe him as the parish bull with
a pen in his hand, and he wrote of love between man and woman
like a physiologist rather than a poet. I do not think he ever
wrote a real love poem in his life. His poem, 'A Woman

3

Waits for Me,' is addressed not to a nonpareil among women but to women in general.

> It is I, you women, I make my way;
> I am stern, acrid, large, undissuadable, but I love you.

There is more love-poetry in a page of Browning than in all the verse Whitman ever wrote.

Friendship meant more to him than the love of any woman, and he proclaimed that it was his purpose to establish 'the institution of the dear love of comrades.'

In *Calamus* his rhapsodies on friendship were expressed in such fashion as was soon to bring upon him all the usual accusations of perversity with which dull minds delight to defame genius. Whitman's own answer to such charges was given in a letter written two years before his death to John Addington Symonds:

> About the questions on *Calamus*, etc., they quite daze me. . . . That the *Calamus* part has even allowed the possibility of such construction as mentioned is terrible. I am fain to hope that the pages themselves are not to be even mentioned for such gratuitous and quite at the time undreamed and unwished possibilities of morbid influence —which are disavowed by me and seem damnable.

That, surely, is conclusive, coming from one of the most candid and defiant autobiographers who ever lived.

I fancy, however, that Whitman's verse would have shocked most readers even if it had not sung the body electric or written *Calamus*. Some of it still seems dreadful, as, when in answer to the child's question, 'What is the grass?' he writes:

> I guess it must be the flag of my disposition,
> Out of hopeful green stuff woven.
> Or I guess it is the handkerchief of the Lord,
> A scented gift and remembrancer designedly dropt.

And again:

> And now it seems to me the beautiful uncut hair of graves.

Verse such as this would have brought ridicule even on the most diminutive of minor poets.

I remember the rapture with which I read Whitman fifty years or so ago. It was mainly as a prophet, I fancy, that he then intoxicated me; but there was not only prophecy but the

poetry of prophecy in his grand effusions. Here was a message
of the greatness of the individual that added a cubit to one's
stature as one read.   Here was a vision of the future of mankind,
marching towards a Promised Land greater than any hitherto
conceived, under the leadership of an America populated by
God-like sons and daughters.   Here were the scriptures of
liberty.   Even to-day my pulse beats a little faster as I read the
close of the poem addressed to Europe in the mid-century years
of revolution:

Not a grave of the murder'd for freedom but grows seed for freedom,
    in its turn to bear seed,
Which the winds carry afar and re-sow, and the rains and the snows
    nourish.

Not a disembodied spirit can the weapons of tyrants let loose,
But it stalks invisibly over the earth, whispering, counseling, cautioning.

Liberty, let others despair of you—I never despair of you.
Is the house shut? is the master away?
Nevertheless, be ready, be not weary of watching,
He will soon return, his messengers come anon.

Reading lines like these, one forgets all Whitman's poetic
gaucheries, aware only that here is a man with the divine breath
in his lungs who is under compulsion to speak.

Whitman, indeed, was an inspired man—only intermittently
inspired, it is true, and never for long enough to enable him to
write a perfect or nearly perfect poem—and for his particular
kind of inspiration free verse was the natural medium.   His
poetry is not for the most part the poetry of reverie, but the
poetry of affirmation addressed to men for their good.   Like a
great evangelist, he has always his audience in mind—'You,' the
reader—and he speaks to it in a rhythmic oratory which seems
often to come from a borderland between prose and verse.
How near his verse is to prose and his prose to verse is shown
by his publishing one famous passage as verse in *By Blue Ontario's
Shore* and printing it as prose with a few alterations in the preface
to the first edition of *Leaves of Grass*.   Here is the passage in
its verse form:

I have loved the earth, sun, animals, I have despised riches,
I have given alms to every one that ask'd, stood up for the stupid and
    crazy, devoted my income and labor to others,

Hated tyrants, argued not concerning God, had patience and indulgence
    toward the people, taken off my hat to nothing known or unknown,
Gone freely with powerful uneducated persons and with the young,
    and with the mothers of families.

If you possess the Nonesuch Whitman, turn to page 575 and you
will find these lines transformed from a personal confession to
an injunction to the poets of the future: 'Love the earth,' etc.,
instead of 'I have loved the earth,' etc. I, for one, prefer the
prose version.

It is significant, I think, of Whitman's defects as a poet that
very few of those who praise him quote passages for their sheer
poetic beauty. He is more often quoted in illustration of his
faith than as a master of phrase and imagery. Yet how beautiful
words ordinary enough in themselves sometimes become under
the stress of his passionate feeling! In 'Out of the Cradle
Endlessly Rocking,' how moving is the reminiscence of the boy
on the seashore listening to the song, the aria, of the widowed
bird calling to his mate:

The aria sinking,
All else continuing, the stars shining,
The winds blowing, the notes of the bird continuous echoing,
With angry moans the fierce old mother incessantly moaning,
On the sands of Paumanok's shore gray and rustling,
The yellow half-moon enlarged, sagging down, drooping, the face of
    the sea almost touching,
The boy ecstatic, with his bare feet the waves, with his hair the
    atmosphere dallying,
The love in the heart long pent, now loose, now at last tumultuously
    bursting.
The aria's meaning, the ears, the soul, swiftly depositing,
The strange tears down the cheeks coursing,
The colloquy there, the trio, each uttering,
The undertone, the savage old mother incessantly crying,
To the boy's soul's questions sullenly timing, some drown'd secret
    hissing,
To the outsetting bard.

Whatever it may be, this cannot be labelled prose. Those
participle endings of the lines are the device of a poet, as the
participle endings in the opening of Mr. T. S. Eliot's *Waste Land*
are. Whitman himself had no doubt that he was giving the

world a new kind of poetry.   Writing—with no mock modesty —an anonymous review of his own work, he declared: 'The style of these poems . . . is simply their own style, just born and red.   Nature may have given the hint to the author of *Leaves of Grass*, but there exists no book or fragment of a book which can have given the hint to them.'   Unfortunately, even if it is true that he had no ancestors as a poet, he has had followers; and is there anything drearier in literature than Whitmanesque free verse written by a well-meaning disciple?

Will the young of the present generation respond to Whitman's rhythmic recitatives, I wonder, as many of the young did fifty years ago?   Will his glorying in democratic individualism appeal to an age that has turned to democratic socialism?   But there are many fashions of democracy and Whitman's is now out of favour.   I think that Europe would breathe a freer air to-day if it absorbed something of the spirit of Whitman when he wrote: 'I swear nothing is good to me now that ignores individuals.' The line may not be poetry, but it is a piece of eternal and quickening truth.

The Return of Henry James

(1947)

HENRY JAMES, we are told, is coming back. There are three Henry Jameses, however, according to Philip Guedalla's memorable witticism—James I, James II, and the Old Pretender —and it will be interesting to see which of them turns out to be the rival of Trollope in the bookshops. I should be inclined to back James I—the James who wrote *Daisy Miller* and *The Portrait of a Lady*.

It is true that in these early stories the heroines are not very solidly built. One sometimes feels that, if one of them stood on a weighing machine, the hand of the machine would scarcely move.

What a delightfully diaphanous heroine he created, for example, in Francie Dosson in that early short novel, *The Reverberator*—one of the most amusing of his writings! This is a comedy of manners in which a newly rich American widower and his two daughters, visiting Paris, come into contact with a Europeanized American family where the daughters have married into the French aristocracy; and the fun reaches its climax after Fanny with the *nouveau riche* father becomes engaged to the son of the Europeanized house. She is a girl almost imbecile in her innocence—imbecile enough to give away the family secrets of her in-laws-to-be to a vulgar American gossip-writer who publishes them in his paper, gloating over the fact that one of them is a kleptomaniac and that another of them has a lover.

The scene in which her prospective sisters-in-law and their French husbands, horrified by this ignoble publicity, take Fanny to task for her appalling misdeed, but cannot persuade her that she has done anything wrong, is a delicious invention of the comic spirit. A little pathetic, too, for the imbecile Fanny is as honest and courageous as she is beautiful. The story ends

HENRY JAMES

happily but rather lifelessly, for one does not quite believe in Fanny's fiancé. Still, I think that any one who has never read Henry James and wonders whether he is worth reading would do well to try *The Reverberator*.

The Portrait of a Lady is the most famous of the early novels, and, though too long, it is certainly a good one. The beauty of its setting in England and Italy enchants the imagination. I see that in a recent book, *The Question of Henry James*, a collection of critical essays by various writers, Mr. William Troy raises the question whether the gardens described in the story may not have a symbolic value. He writes:

> Is it merely an accident . . . that . . . all the great climaxes in Isabel Archer's career—from her refusal of the English lord to her final flight from Caspar Goodwood—are made to occur in a garden? If an accident it was a fortunate one, for the garden-symbol provides a wonderful point of concentration for the widest possible number of associations—the recollection especially of the famous garden in which one of Isabel's ancestresses was also confronted with the fruit of the tree of knowledge of good and evil.

I do not know whether that will sound like nonsense to you. It sounds like nonsense to me. I cannot see what rational pleasure is to be got from transforming gardens into garden-symbols.

There are critics, however, who, in their dislike of the obvious, perpetually look for meanings beneath the surface and discover them with enthusiasm even when they are not there. Such, it seems to me, are all those critics who try to persuade us that *The Turn of the Screw*, the most popular story of James's second period, is not what it seems to be—the story of a heroic governess who combats the powers of darkness to protect the two children left in her care—but that the governess is really 'a neurotic case of sex-repression,' and that the ghosts she fights against are not ghosts at all but 'merely the hallucinations of the governess.'

I do not know who first set this theory afloat. I suspect Henry James of having many years ago pulled somebody's leg or having said something periphrastically evasive which put whoever heard it on a false scent that has been eagerly followed by critics—especially by those with a taste for psycho-analysis—ever since. Thus, Mr. Edward Wilson, one of the best known

of American critics, accepts the 'neurotic hallucination' interpretation, though he admits: 'Nowhere does James unequivocally
give the thing away: almost everything from beginning to end
can be read equally in either of two senses.' If this is true,
what a wretched writer Henry James must have been! But I
hold that it is not true. There is no hint of neurosis in the
language in which the governess tells her terrifying story;
dramatically it is the speech of a perfectly sane woman. That
the ghost of Peter Quint is no hallucination is shown by the fact
that the housekeeper recognizes him when he is described by
the governess who had never seen him alive. Besides this,
James in a preface speaks of the two apparitions as 'my demons,'
'my demon spirits,' and adds: 'What, in the last analysis, had I
to give the sense of? Of their being, the haunting pair, capable,
as the phrase is, of everything—that is, of exerting, in respect
to the children, the very worst action small victims so conditioned
might be conceived as subject to.' Well, as we recently saw,
there are critics who believe that *Paradise Lost* does not mean
what Milton said it meant, so that we need not be surprised to
find critics who believe that *The Turn of the Screw* does not mean
what Henry James said it meant. I think whoever it was was
right who advised such critics to read and re-read Hans Ander-
sen's story, *The Emperor's New Clothes*. It is they—not the
governess—who are the victims of hallucination.

That James in his later period began to write an increasingly
obscure prose that attracted many readers, not in spite of its
obscurity, but because of it, must be admitted. There are
readers who enjoy being puzzled by authors and solving the
puzzles—the old-fashioned Victorian Browningites and Mere-
dithians, for example—and Henry James afforded them this kind
of pleasure in his later work. They did not notice that at the
same time he was becoming more remote from life, as when in
The Papers he made London newsboys with the latest editions
of the evening papers under their arms cry: 'Mysterious Dis-
appearance of Prominent Public Man'—a mouthful of words
such as was never heard from a paper-seller in the Strand. His
dialogue ceased to be an echo of natural speech and became the
singular language of the inhabitants of the Jamesian brain. His
sentences, too, became so wordy and unstraightforward that
they slowed down the reader in his effort to follow the meaning.

Take, for example, the opening of the story called *Mora Maltravers*:

They were such extraordinary people to have been so odiously stricken that poor Traffle himself, always, at the best—though it was, indeed, just now at the worst—what his wife called horribly philosophic, fairly grimaced back, in private, at so flagrant a show of the famous, the provokedly vicious 'irony,' the thing he had so often read about in clever stories, with which the usually candid countenance of their fate seemed to have begun of a sudden to bristle.   Ah, that irony of fate often admired by him as a phrase and recognized as a truth so that if he himself ever wrote a story it should certainly and most strikingly *be* about that—he fairly saw it leer at them now, could quite positively fancy it guilty of a low wink at them, in their trouble, out of that vast visage of the world that was made up for them of the separate stony stares or sympathizing smirks presented by the circle of their friends.

Now that is quite intelligible, but it takes two or three times as long to grasp its meaning as would a passage of equal length in Dickens or Tolstoy.

One cannot help speculating as to what it was that turned James from a writer of lucid prose into a writer so obscure that only his out-and-out disciples could find their way through the maze of his sentences.   I sometimes wonder whether, like the later Joyce, he ultimately found himself with nothing much to say and concentrated his genius on elaborating a new way of saying it.   Or was his obscurity simply the result of his ceasing to write his stories and dictating them to a secretary, thus reproducing in his prose the longwindedness and qualifying subtleties of his conversation?   In a delightful new book, *The Legend of the Master*—a compilation by Mr. Simon Nowell-Smith of notes on Henry James by friends and acquaintances—there is a quotation from Mrs. Wharton in which she tells us that James's 'slow way of speech, sometimes mistaken for an affectation . . . was really the partial victory over a stammer which in his boyhood had been thought incurable.'   May it not be that this suppressed stammer came ultimately to affect his dictated prose as it affected his conversation?

Mrs. Wharton gives an amusing account of how he bewildered an old man in Windsor by the entangled sentences in which he asked the way to the King's Road.   Reading this, one feels that his later style, far from being an artifice, was a natural expression of his personality.   His art was an echo of his talk, of which Mrs. Wharton writes:

> To James's intimates . . . those elaborate hesitations, far from being an obstacle, were like a cobweb bridge flung from his mind to theirs, an invisible passage over which one knew that silver-footed ironies, veiled jokes, tiptoe malices, were stealing to explode a huge laugh at one's feet.

Obviously this was talk only for the alert of mind, the chosen few, who thought it the best talk in the world as they thought his later novels about the best novels in the world.   James, however, might have talked and dictated more simply if he could, for he longed to be a popular writer.

He once said to W. W. Jacobs: 'Mr. Jacobs, I envy you. . . . You are popular.   Your admirable work is appreciated by a wide circle of readers: it has achieved popularity.   Mine never goes into a second edition.   I should so much have loved to be popular!'

Only a minority of readers, I am afraid, will ever think novel-reading worth the effort that is necessary to the enjoyment of the later novels of Henry James.   I do not belong to that minority.   I can enjoy the autobiographical books, *A Small Boy and Others*, and *Notes of a Son and Brother*, partly in spite of their style and partly because of it; but I like fiction chiefly as a relaxation, and it is not always easy to relax when reading Henry James at his most difficult.

To read about him, on the other hand, in *The Legend of the Master*, is an immense pleasure.   He was as truly a character, though not as great a character, as Dr. Johnson.   As regards his later work as a novelist, H. G. Wells caricatured him as a hippopotamus picking up a pea—doing with consummate genius something that was not worth the trouble.   This, I am sure, is in accord with the popular verdict.   And I doubt whether it will ever be reversed while grass grows and water runs.

George Meredith Restored
(1948)

IT was time for someone to put Meredith back on his pedestal again, and in his book, simply called *Meredith*, Mr. Siegfried Sassoon has to my mind, succeeded in doing so. I do not always agree, however, with the excuses he makes for the lapses Meredith is accused of as a man.

If you are shocked, for example, to learn that this hero of Radicalism at one time earned part of his income by writing vehement Tory leading articles for a newspaper, you will not think it a particularly impressive defence to say that this 'was merely an expedient which enabled him to pay tradesmen's bills,' and that one of the articles was written for him by 'that paragon of Liberalism, John Morley.' And, if it is immoral to write against one's convictions, is it not rather irrelevant to suggest that instead of blaming Meredith for doing so, we should sympathize with the poor man 'with that awful partisan stuff to be pumped out every Thursday'?

I agree that it is foolish to blame Meredith, especially as in his early life his Radical convictions may not have been so deeply rooted as they became in later years. In any case, his life as a whole is the best evidence of the greatness and nobility of his character. In comparison with this his faults seem trifling.

The snobbery of which he has been accused seems shocking mainly because we expect too much from greatness—especially from a great man famous for his philosophic laughter at humbug. And it certainly was petty of Meredith to be so ashamed of being the son of a tailor that he made a false entry about his birthplace in a census paper and, instead of putting down his occupation as 'author,' said 'Has private means.' But it is only fair to remember that, as Mr. Sassoon tells us, he made no secret of his parentage to his friends, such as FitzGerald and Maxse. I myself fancy that he had been ridiculed in his schooldays as a 'son of a snip' whose airs and graces were too fine for a trades-man's son, and that this is why he was nicknamed 'Gentleman

Georgie.' If so, one can understand how the memory rankled, even when he was able to laugh at such sensitiveness as he did in *Evan Harrington*, a delightful satire on snobbery.

The truth is, I am sure, that Meredith was never more than a bit of a snob. The way in which he writes of his tailor grandfather in the first chapter of *Evan Harrington* suggests to me that he was proud of his ancestor even if not of his trade:

Mr. Melchisedec, whom people in private called the great Mel, had been at once the sad dog of Lymport and the pride of the town. He was a tailor, and he kept horses; he was a tailor, and he had gallant adventures; he was a tailor, and he shook hands with his customers. Finally he was a tradesman, and he never was known to send in a bill. Such a personage comes but once in a generation, and, when he goes, men miss the man as well as their money.

It is significant that Meredith gave this fictitious 'great Mel' the actual Christian name of his grandfather—significant, surely, of the very reverse of the secretive kind of snobbery.

I have no wish to portray Meredith as an angel, but I feel sure that, if we knew all the facts, we should find that there is a fairly good answer to most of the charges that have been made against him. He is blamed for not going to see his first wife when she was dying, but there is no evidence that this was owing to his inability to forgive her for having run away from him. After all, he wrote about her without a trace of vindictiveness in *Modern Love*—that poem which is partly a novel just as some of his novels are partly poems. Nor did he blame her in his conversation with his friends. His explanation of the broken marriage was: 'No sun warmed my roof-tree; the marriage was a blunder'—a marriage between a young man of twenty-one and a widow of thirty—and he hinted at a taint of madness in her family.

As for his relations with the son of this first marriage, Meredith has been blamed for the estrangement that came between them. Yet if you read Meredith's letters to and about his son, Arthur, you will find that he was a devoted parent. He was certainly not indifferent to the welfare of the boy then at school in Germany, to whom, though himself not a Christian, he wrote:

The Christian teaching is sound and good. . . . Belief in the religion has done and does good to the young: it pilots them through

GEORGE MEREDITH

the perilous sensual period when the animal appetites most need control. . . . If your mind honestly rejects it, you must call on your mind to supply its place from your own resources. . . . Let nothing flout your sense of a Supreme Being, and be certain that your understanding wavers whenever you doubt that it leads to good. We grow to good as surely as the plant grows to the light. The school has only to look through history for a scientific assurance of it. And do not lose the habit of praying to the unseen Divinity. Prayer for worldly goods is worse than useless, but prayer for strength of soul is that passion of the soul which catches the gift it seeks.

When Meredith signed this letter 'Your loving father,' I do not believe that this was a mere form of words.

Mr. Sassoon's book, however, is not written in a controversial spirit. It is for the most part a straightforward survey of a great writer's life and work. One myth about Meredith's early struggles is rejected at the outset. 'The journalistic legend that he started his career as a writer with one guinea, which he invested in a sack of oatmeal, has long since been confuted as nonsense.' His mother, the tavern-keeper's daughter, seems to have left him enough money to pay for his apprenticeship to a solicitor; and, though the trustees are said to have mismanaged the property, he cannot himself have been a pauper when, a youth of twenty-one without a job, he married the daughter of Thomas Love Peacock. The fact that two years later he was able to pay £60 in order to have his first book of poems published is evidence that he had some small private means from the start.

This book included the first version of 'Love in the Valley,' and, though Meredith afterwards described it as 'worthless, immature stuff of a youth in his teens, who had not found his hand,' it was praised by such eminent reviewers as W. M. Rossetti and Charles Kingsley, and Tennyson wrote to say that he went about the house repeating its ['Love in the Valley's'] cadences to himself.

This early recognition by leading contemporaries, however, brought him no pence from the public. *Richard Feverel*, which he published at the age of thirty-one, was from a selling point of view a failure, and it was nearly twenty years before a second edition was called for.

'My name is celebrated,' said Meredith to an interviewer towards the end of his life, 'but no one reads my books. As for

Englishmen, I put them to flight because I bore them. . . . No, my countrymen do not value me; at the most they will value me after my death.'

There is a good deal of exaggeration in this, but it is undeniable that Meredith was never a popular author in the sense in which Dickens and Thackeray and Trollope and George Eliot were. His books brought him fame but not riches. At the same time, he was never a tragic example of genius left to starve. Several of his novels were serialized. Incredible though it seems, *The Egoist* was accepted as a serial by the *Glasgow Herald*.

There is no more fundamentally honest book in English literature than *The Egoist*. It is as though Malvolio had seen himself as he really was. There is no other comedy of pretentiousness in the language to match it, and it may be doubted whether Meredith could have written it so well if he had not been able to draw from himself as a model. Once, when talking to Lady Butcher, he praised laughter as a corrective to complacency, and said that 'a woman should train herself to look at herself from outside, and to learn, or rather teach herself, to laugh at herself.' As a writer, if not as a man, Meredith adopted his admirable advice to women, and learned to laugh at himself to such purpose that, while we read *The Egoist*, we, too, are compelled to laugh at ourselves. By his genius he has converted an individual egoist and humbug into a universal type, and has laughed wisdom—in so far as it can be laughed—into human nature.

Meredith, however, will survive in fiction, not only as a derider of the egoist in man, but because he invented a new and beautiful kind of comic fiction. 'Never did man wield so shrieking a scourge upon vice,' he wrote of Molière in the *Essay on Comedy*, and he himself wielded a sufficiently shrieking scourge on the vice of self-importance—but in the same essay he also wrote of Comedy as 'the sweetest of diversions, the wisest of delightful companions.' He regarded Comedy as a cousin not only of philosophy but of poetry, and, as a result, he wrote novels of an unprecedented kind, that were half satire and half lyric. Like Thomas Hardy, he liked to think of himself as an immortal poet rather than as an immortal prose-writer, and it was an essentially poetic imagination that expressed itself in his prose. To reconcile poetry and satire is a much rarer feat than to reconcile poetry and tragedy, since it is possible only to a writer who can at once belittle human beings and ennoble them. Meredith was that extraordinary thing—a comic and satiric writer who endowed his characteristics with a dignity worthy of the tragic buskin.

A critic once complained that his women are all eight feet high, and, though this is hardly fair, Diana of the Crossways is not the only one of his heroines who seems to have been nursed on Olympus. These heroines of his have a beauty, a gravity, and a wisdom beyond the common. They are fit to be the comrades of the greatest, and all the loveliest things in nature seem to have been created as a setting for them. We can never think of Diana without seeing her among Swiss mountains at dawn on that morning on which 'a linnet sang in her breast, an eagle lifted her feet. The feet were verily winged . . . to be a girl again was magical. She could fancy her having risen from the dead. . . . All her nature flew and bloomed; she was bird, flower, flowing river.' And we can never think of Clara Middleton in *The Egoist* without remembering how she found Vernon Whitford asleep beside the double-blossom wild cherry-tree and how she

turned her face to where the load of virginal blossom, whiter than summer cloud on the sky, showered and drooped and clustered so thick as to claim colour and seem, like higher Alpine snows in noon-sunlight, a flush of white. From deep to deeper heavens of white her eyes perched and soared. Wonder lived in her. Happiness in the beauty of the tree pressed to supplant it.

Beauty born of all the loveliest things in nature has passed into the faces of all Meredith's heroines as of no other novelist's. That alone will be enough to ensure the revival of his fame as soon as the reaction against Victorianism has spent itself.

Some critics hold that the difficulty of reading him will prevent Meredith from ever becoming a popular writer. But the difficulty of reading him has been greatly exaggerated. *Harry Richmond* is as easy to read as *Lorna Doone*, and school children can enjoy *Evan Harrington*. There is little except the epigrams to puzzle an ordinary reader in *Richard Feverel*; and even *The Egoist*, if you skip the prelude—and there is no reason why you should not skip the prelude—is a reasonably straightforward comedy.

B

As for his verse, he was probably wrong in thinking that it would outlast his novels.   Much of it is poetry of thought rather than of the heart, and, as poetry of thought, it is often difficult and incoherent.   Meredith has not a sufficiently wide range of emotions to be a great poet.   He does not share the sorrows of his fellows as the great poets do.   You have only to compare Shelley's 'Skylark' with Meredith's 'Lark Ascending' in order to realize the difference between a poet who speaks for us as he sings and a poet who only speaks *to* us.   In 'The Lark Ascending,' as in 'The Woods of Westermain,' Meredith comments on life rather than transfigures it.

There are at least two of his poems, however, in which he does identify himself with us and escape from the sage's chair into the music of common experience.   In 'Love in the Valley' he wrote the most beautiful poem of youthful love in the English language; and in 'Dirge in Woods' he gave a new image and a new music to the ancient theme of the fleetingness of human life.

These poems have already found their way into the permanent anthology of English poetry.   Whatever else of Meredith's verse is forgotten, these, it is safe to prophesy, will endure.

Towards the end of his life, his novels were popular enough to encourage his publishers to issue a sixpenny edition of four of them.   Obviously, then, though he was never an author for that fabulous person, the tired business man, he was not the failure he sometimes imagined himself.   Mr. Sassoon thinks that his sense of failure may have been due to the fact that 'his poetry had never found many readers.'   His *Modern Love*, first published in 1862, was not reprinted for thirty years; and in 1883, when most of his greatest novels had already appeared, he was obliged to publish his third book of verse, *Poems and Lyrics of the Joy of Earth*, at his own expense 'with full expectation of losing money on it.'

If you agree with Mr. Sassoon's estimate of the poems, you will have to admit that Meredith had good cause for feeling resentment at his treatment by the reading public.   Of *Modern Love* he writes: 'I am tempted to reckon it second to the Sonnets of Shakespeare.'   'Love in the Valley' he rates as 'one of the very greatest sustained love lyrics in English poetry.'   'The Lark Ascending' is 'one of the poems in the English language of which it can be said that they are matchless of their kind.'   Of

the 'Hymn to Colour' we are told: 'The thing is a perfect whole
. . . it is one of his grandest poems, and in some ways his
greatest.'

Those who sit down to read Meredith for the first time should
be warned, I think, against beginning with the more difficult
examples of his verse and prose. Only a graduated Meredithian
is likely to find 'The Empty Purse' a poem, or *One of Our
Conquerors* a novel, lucid to his understanding. In reading *The
Egoist*, again, it is wise for the beginner to skip the first chapter
if he finds himself puzzled by it; the rest is straightforward
enough. *Harry Richmond*, *Evan Harrington*, and *Richard Feverel*
present very few difficulties except to those who enjoy skimming
books rather than reading them. By the time he has finished
these the reader will be able to decide whether it is worth his
while to go on to the dazzling *Diana of the Crossways* and the
other novels.

If he is lucky he will find in the novels draughts of prose
that are as rapturous as poetry, heroines that seem to call for
celebration in verse, nature as it is seen in hours of enchantment,
the comedy of human pretentiousness exhibited by an expert and
philosophic showman—all these in a combination never known
before or since in English literature. No other English novelist,
surely, has been master to the same degree of the extremes of
ecstasy and derision. He did not believe, we are told, in the
immortality of the soul, and he had no desire for an immortality
of fame. I should not be surprised, however, if he finds himself
possessed of both in spite of this.

Trollope the Readable

(1947)

IN a letter from Paris to his father and mother, Stevenson, then a young man of twenty-seven, wrote: 'Do you know who is my favourite author just now? How are the mighty fallen! Anthony Trollope. I batten on him; he is so nearly wearying you, and yet he never does; or, rather, he never does until he gets near the end, when he begins to wean you from him, so that you're pleased to be done with him as you thought you would be sorry. I wonder if it's old age? It is a little, I'm sure. A young person would get sickened by the dead level of meanness and cowardice; you require to be a little spoiled and cynical before you can enjoy it. . . .

'I have just finished *The Way of the World*. . . . All the heroes and heroines are just ghastly. But what a triumph is Lady Carbury! That is real, sound, strong, genuine work: the man who could do that, if he had the courage, might have written a fine book; he has preferred to write many readable ones.'

I confess that I had never heard of Trollope's having borrowed the title of Congreve's best play for one of his novels; and, looking through a recent biographical work, *The Trollopes*, in search of some facts about it, I found no mention of it, and realized that Stevenson must have been referring to *The Way We Live Now*—a novel of which the authors of *The Trollopes* wrote:

Society as seen in *The Way We Live Now* was utterly corrupt. . . . Corruption was not confined to the upper circles: Trollope hit out fiercely at publishers and critics—all were venal, all dishonest. The roots of his wrath were a tangle of past and present. In Lady Carbury could be traced features of the mother ten years dead and sixteen years silent, so long forgotten that kindly time disguised his unfilial use of her.

'It was a bitter, wrathful book,' declared the biographers, 'marred by careless writing and by an awkward welding of themes which in so ample a book could have been skilfully combined; yet these defects could not spoil one of the greatest Victorian novels.'

I have never read *The Way We Live Now*, but am now resolved to get hold of it if it is anywhere in print.

What interested me chiefly as I read Stevenson's letter, however, was the contrast between Stevenson's judgment of Trollope and the reasons usually given to-day for the revival of Trollope's popularity. Nearly all the articles I have read explaining why Trollope has become in recent years the most talked of Victorian novelist next to Dickens suggest that, living in an unstable world, we take a particular pleasure in being carried back imaginatively into the Golden Age of Victorian stability largely populated by churchmen, statesmen, and landed gentry with £20,000 a year. One would almost gather at times that Trollope's world seems a desirable world to the modern anxiety-haunted reader.

Yet Stevenson thought it a ghastly world; and I see that Mr. Michael Sadleir is quoted on the dust-cover of the new World's Classics edition of *Mr. Scarborough's Family* as saying that this is 'a novel of property, and perhaps the bitterest and most cynical of the kind that nineteenth-century literature can show.' It, like *The Way We Live Now*, belongs to Trollope's latest period; but who would maintain that even in the earlier novels, such as *Barchester Towers*, Trollope depicted a world that a contemporary of Mr. Attlee's would care to return to? One would rather read about Mrs. Proudie and Mr. Slope than live and move and have one's being in the same circle.

The simple explanation of the present vogue of Trollope seems to me to be that a large public has discovered that he has in an exceptional degree the gift of being readable—that he not only is a good narrator, but can create interesting characters and interesting situations. It is often said that he has no prose style, and he was certainly no gourmet in his choice of language. But is it not a little unreasonable to condemn a style in which the writer succeeds in telling a story better than nearly everybody else? Henley once spoke of Dumas as 'the seventy-times-seven-to-be-forgiven'; and Trollope may justly be forgiven for sentences often commonplace and sometimes faulty in view of the uncommon effects he achieves with them. 'Readable' has, with modern reviewers, become a not very complimentary

adjective meaning 'only just readable.' Trollope, however, is
not only just readable: he is supremely readable—as readable as
the most readable novel of the moment coming fresh from the
publishers.

No one, I am sure, would call *Mr. Scarborough's Family* one of
Trollope's best novels. But how supremely readable are its
best chapters and how sufficiently readable is the rest! It is as
absorbingly interesting at the outset as the report of a scandalous
family lawsuit of the kind that sets everybody talking. Here
Trollope takes a skeleton from the cupboard for our delectation,
and seldom has there been a better showman of a skeleton than
he. And how brilliantly he portrays old Mr. Scarborough, the
wealthy and unscrupulous old squire who enjoys nothing more
than outwitting the laws of man and is generally thought to be
equally inimical to the law of God!

The family scandal breaks out when he discovers that his elder
son, Mountjoy, a captain in the Guards, has gambled so recklessly
that, when he succeeds to the estate, which is entailed, he will
be left all but penniless as a result of his having raised enormous
sums on post-obits from the money-lenders. Mr. Scarborough
thereupon discloses proof that Mountjoy is illegitimate, having
been born before marriage took place, and joyfully cheats the
Jews out of their money by making his son's signatures to his
promises to pay not worth the paper they were written on.
His second son, the more worldly-wise Augustus, now becomes
the true heir, and Mountjoy, a comparative pauper, is barred
from his clubs as a man who has disgraced himself by being
unable to pay his card debts.

Both the money-lenders and Mountjoy, however, are convinced that the old man is up to some trickery; and Mountjoy
is even angrier at the slur cast on his mother than at being
disinherited. Meanwhile, old Scarborough, a dying man, who
has been carved up by the surgeons and is given only a few
weeks to live, approaches death cheerfully as he reflects on his
cleverness in robbing the money-lenders of their gains. There
is one drop of bitterness in his cup, however. His second son
is a thoroughly hateful young man who makes it quite clear that
he is waiting, impatiently and cold-bloodedly, for his father's
death, and the old man hates him as he deserves to be hated.

This is a sordid enough basis for a story about stable Victorian

ANTHONY TROLLOPE

society; and the two characters who come nearest to winning our affections are the wicked old squire and Mountjoy, the ruined gambler. We like the old squire because of his stoical courage, and because with all his egoistic trickeries he is capable of kindness. We agree with one of his doctors who said of him to Mountjoy: 'I have always regarded your father as a most excellent man; but thoroughly dishonest.'

As for Mountjoy, he is not a gambler of the vile sort, like the cousin who lies and cheats through *Sir Harry Hotspur*. He is a manly man who is at the same time a pitiable victim of his ruling passion. Trollope, I think, showed remarkable insight in his study of gamblers. How well he describes the cravings of the gambler as he tells how Mountjoy, having promised his father to reform, revisits London with fifty pounds in his pocket:

He went up to London late in the afternoon, and spent an uncomfortable evening in town. It was absolutely innocent as regards the doings of the night itself, but was terrible to him. There was a slow drizzling rain, but none the less after dinner at his hotel he started off to wander through the streets. With his greatcoat and his umbrella he was almost hidden, and as he passed through Pall Mall, up St. James's Street, along Piccadilly, he would pause and look in at the accustomed door. He saw men entering whom he knew, and knew that within five minutes they would be seated at their tables. 'I had an awfully heavy time of it last night,' one said to another as he went up the steps; and Mountjoy, as he heard the words, envied the speaker. Then he passed back and went again a tour of all the clubs. What had he done that he, like a poor Peri, should be unable to enter the gates of these Paradises? He had now in his pockets fifty pounds. Could he have made absolutely certain that he would not have lost it, he would have gone into any Paradise, and have staked his money with that certainty.

Mountjoy, indeed, was, so far as this one vice was concerned, irreclaimable.

The subsidiary plot of the story, in which another heir to an entailed estate is the chief figure, is not so engrossingly readable as the story of the Scarboroughs; but it never ceases to be readable, and the rich uncle's scheme for disinheriting an heir, whom he has come to dislike, by marrying Miss Thoroughbury provides us with some good farcical comedy. The heir, however, is rather a weed and hardly deserves the hand of the girl who might have redeemed Mountjoy, or so he thought in his devotion to her. She is a girl much proposed to, and we are always glad to get back from the scenes of her proposals to the less edifying atmosphere of the Scarborough family.

While old Scarborough or his son is on the stage there is never a dull moment, even though Trollope strains our credulity when he endows Scarborough with a foresight and ingenuity that enable him not only to diddle the money-lenders but ultimately to diddle Augustus out of his expected inheritance. Though a far from moral character, the old twister is very good company —in a novel.

Mr. Scarborough's Family is not one of the important novels of the nineteenth century. It is empty of the poetry of life. It has none of the exuberant humour, large-heartedness and fantastic puppetry of Dickens. It is deficient in the literary graces of Thackeray. It does not give us a picture of a dignified but faulty world as Trollope's own *Barchester Towers* and *Phineas Finn* do. Yet on a level somewhat above that of a report of an unusually interesting family lawsuit—though here the scandal never gets into court—it has that gift of being extraordinarily readable of which Stevenson wrote.

It is interesting to note, by the way, that, with all his alleged cynicism, Trollope was not—at least, not always—cynical about lawyers. Both here and in *Sir Harry Hotspur* the lawyer is conspicuously honest in a not too honest world.

George Eliot
(1928)

AMONG women novelists George Eliot has for the moment
at least been left behind in the race for fame by Jane Austen and
the Brontës. She had lost her position as a favourite writer
even with the later nineteenth-century critics. In *The English
Novel* Saintsbury devoted less space to her than to Charles
Kingsley, and showed little interest in her books except in so
far as they were examples of 'the way in which the novel—once
a light and almost frivolous thing—had come to be taken with
the intensest seriousness—had in fact ceased to be light literature
at all.'

There was a time when she was regarded as the greatest
English novelist since the death of Dickens. To-day who among
the writers, old or young, gives any sign of wishing to replace
her on that eminent pedestal? Mr. Norman Collins, in that
brilliant *tour de force* of his youth, *The Facts of Fiction*, though
affirming that her heroines are better drawn than those of any
other woman novelist, damns her in the sentence: 'If you like
the manner of the female preacher and continuation-school
teacher, you will like George Eliot.' That, I think, expresses
what many people feel about her novels to-day.

One would have thought that, even if she has sunk in the
estimation of critics, she might at least attract the biographers
in this age of biography. She was one of the great Victorian
rebels, revolting against orthodox religion, outraging the moral
code of her time by living with a man to whom she was not
married, and in her sixty-first year making a startling marriage
with a man twenty-one years younger. Add to this the fact
that she did not begin writing fiction till she was thirty-six years
old, and you will surely conclude that so unusual a career has in
it the makings of an interesting story. Yet for some reason or
other the personality of George Eliot, impressive though it was,
had little of that fascinating quality that makes biographers eager
to write about Shelley and other famous rebels. Perhaps if her

marriage to George Henry Lewes—for it was a marriage in everything apart from its not having been celebrated in a church or registry office—had turned out to be a tragic failure, she would have been a figure exciting more sympathy and that passionate enthusiasm of defence which is so often a kind of posthumous compensation for those who have lived disastrously. As things were, however, she was exceptionally happy in her life with Lewes, and, more than this, she was one of the most respectable women who ever flouted the laws of respectability. She might even be described as one of the most sinless sinners who ever lived.   All this tends to make her sufficiently eventful life seem somewhat uneventful.

There is this, too, to be remembered—that, compared with most of her fellow novelists, she lived a life of monotonous seclusion.   Hence, no great variety of stories and gossip accumulated about her.   One feels at times that the chief things that impressed her contemporaries in regard to her, apart from her books, were that she was a prophetess and that she was plain.

Mr. Gerald Bullett's biography, *George Eliot*, should do something towards winning the affection of his readers for this noble and tender-hearted woman and towards persuading them to consider afresh her claim to be a great novelist.   Marian Evans —to give George Eliot her real name—was the daughter of a Warwickshire estate agent who is said in his strength and gentleness of character to have borne some resemblance to Adam Bede and Caleb Garth.   Her early seriousness, or rather the solemnity with which she expressed her seriousness in word and deed, leads Mr. Bullett to say of her: 'Nature and circumstance had conspired to make her a prig'; but this is hardly fair to a burning religious sincerity that renounced the normal pleasures of life so that at the age of eighteen, when on a visit to London, she refused to go to the theatre with her brother and preferred to spend her evenings reading Josephus's *History of the Jews*.   After all, about this time she wrote to an aunt regretting her 'lack of humility and Christian simplicity,' and prigs do not criticize themselves in this fashion.

Two years later, when she was living with her father in Coventry, she came to know the Brays, a local family in whose house she met Robert Owen, Harriet Martineau, and Emerson. In this new intellectual atmosphere she became more and more doubtful of the claims of orthodox Christianity, and renounced church-going with the same conscientiousness with which she had earlier renounced the theatre. This caused an estrangement from her father, but ultimately—and we like her the better for it—father and daughter became reconciled and she went to church with him on Sundays for the rest of his life.

When he died she was in her thirtieth year, without having yet made any contribution to literature except a translation of Strauss's heretical *Life of Jesus*. Two years later her friendship with the Brays put her in touch with John Chapman, the free-thinking and rather free-loving proprietor of the *Westminster Review*, who invited her to become his assistant editor. In her new circle she met Herbert Spencer, who described her as 'the most admirable woman, mentally,' whom he had ever met, and there were reports that they were to be married. Spencer, however, as we learn from his autobiography, seems never to have contemplated marriage. 'The clue to his decision,' says Mr. Bullett, 'is perhaps in that fatal qualification "mentally," for he will not have us suppose him unappreciative of physical beauty. In later life he declares beauty to have been a *sine qua non* for him—"as was once unhappily proved when the intellectual traits and the emotional traits were of the highest."'

Accepting the view of Charles Bray that George Eliot was 'not fitted to stand alone,' but always required 'someone to lean upon, preferring what has hitherto been considered the stronger sex to the other and more impressionable,' Mr. Bullett suggests that 'her heart as well as her mind' was at this time at the disposal of her amorous employer, who reduced her to tears of despair, however, by discoursing on 'the incomprehensible mystery and witchery of beauty.'

It was in the same year in which this occurred that Herbert Spencer took George Henry Lewes to call on her; and it is interesting to note that Spencer had before this expressed his attitude to the marriage tie in the sentence: 'I do not conceive the most perfect happiness attainable in marriage while the legal bond continues; for, as we can never rid ourselves of the consciousness of it, it must always influence our conduct. But the next best thing is to banish it from our minds, and let husband and wife strive to act towards each other as they would were there no such tie.' How odd it is to find the solemn Spencer approximating in his view of marriage to that of Congreve's witty Millamant! Whether his opinions on the subject influenced George Eliot we do not know. We do know, however, that, even after she had become 'Mrs. Lewes' at the age of thirty-five, she never was an advocate of free love, and, indeed, was perturbed by the fear that her example might be cited as an argument for sexual licence.

As a boy I frequently heard that the reason why George Eliot and Lewes did not marry was that he was unable to get a divorce from his wife, who was a drunkard. There is no support for this legend, however, in Mr. Bullett's book. Lewes, we are told, who had 'libertarian opinions,' shared both his home and his wife with Leigh Hunt's son, Thornton, who became the father of two children by her. His doctrines, however, when put into practice, did not make for happiness, and when he met George Eliot he was a profoundly miserable man, aching for sympathy. 'It is clear,' says Mr. Bullett, 'that she did not love him at sight,' and, indeed, he was ugly enough to justify Carlyle in calling him 'the Ape.' It was a considerable time after their first meeting that she wrote of him with increasing warmth as 'a man of heart and conscience wearing a mask of flippancy.' Nineteen years later she looked back on what she called 'our blessed union' with no regrets, describing it as 'the prime blessing that has made it all possible to me.'

Lewes is still remembered as the leading English biographer of Goethe, but he made his most important contribution to literature on the day on which he finally persuaded George Eliot to try her hand at fiction—a suggestion previously made by Herbert Spencer. It had always, we are told, 'been a vague dream of hers that some day or other she might write a novel,' but she had lost hope of ever being able to do so, 'just as I desponded about everything else in my future life.'

There was no need for pessimism, however. The first of the stories afterwards collected into the volume entitled *Scenes from Clerical Life* was enthusiastically accepted by *Blackwood's Magazine*, and with the book of which it formed a part George Eliot may be said to have awakened to find herself famous, Dickens (who guessed that the author was a woman) being among her most ardent admirers.

How her fame grew may be measured by the fact that a later

GEORGE ELIOT

admirer, Lord Acton, said of her that she 'justly seemed the most illustrious figure that had appeared in literature since Goethe.'

It may be that George Eliot is a novelist whose gifts are more likely to be appreciated by the adult than by the adolescent. She has none of the extravagance, the gusto, the superlative excitement, the uncontrollable sense of fun, that make the young feel that life is not only worth living but worth reading about. I do not think she ever created a hero whom a normal boy would wish to resemble or a heroine with whom a normal boy would fall in love, as normal boys used to fall in love with Diana Vernon and Beatrix Esmond. We are not swept off our feet as we read her, and when we are young we prefer authors who sweep us off our feet.

Ouida was a midget novelist in comparison with George Eliot, but she could sweep us off our feet in those days—at least in *Under Two Flags*. The very title of George Eliot's first book, *Scenes of Clerical Life*, was enough to suggest to eager-hearted schoolboys that here was an author for their parents rather than for themselves.

Probably it was her deficiency in gusto that made Henley dislike her and led him to denounce her heroes as 'governesses in revolt whom it has pleased her to put forward as men.' There are plenty of good male characters in her books, but the heroes and lovers are not the most lifelike of them. In *Felix Holt the Radical*, for example, Felix is a bundle of fine qualities in homespun rather than a man of flesh and blood. In *Middlemarch* again the artist lover whom Dorothea Brooke ultimately marries is a much less lifelike portrait than the withered clergyman who is her first husband.

At first, I confess, I was prejudiced against Dorothea herself, or rather against George Eliot's presentation of her. Having been led by the prelude to expect to meet an English provincial St. Theresa, and been reminded of the saint's walking forth one morning as a little girl 'hand-in-hand with her still smaller brother to go and seek martyrdom in the country of the Moors,' I thought that George Eliot somewhat falsified Dorothea and added an incredible touch or two of self-righteousness—in order, perhaps, to avoid making her inhumanly perfect. Thus, when Dorothea and her sister, Celia, are dividing their dead mother's jewels and Dorothea with her ultra-Puritanical suspicion of ornament will accept none of them but a ring and a bracelet, Celia asks her: 'Shall you wear them in company?' and Dorothea replies—'rather haughtily,' we are told—'Perhaps. I cannot tell to what level I may sink.' I for one cannot believe that the Dorothea whom we get to know later would ever be sunk to the level of that answer.

Again, when Dorothea with her love of good works uses her influence with Sir James Chettam to persuade him to build decent cottages for his tenants and is told that he takes an interest in her plans only because he loves her, she declares that she can have nothing more to do with the plans or the cottages. 'Poor Dodo,' says Celia. 'It is very hard; it is your favourite *fad* to draw plans.' '*Fad* to draw plans!' exclaims Dorothea. 'Do you think I could care about my fellow creatures' houses in that childish way? I may well make mistakes. How can one ever do anything nobly Christian, living among people with such petty thoughts?'

Did any young woman burning with the ardour of a devotee ever express herself in such fashion? George Eliot wrote fairly stilted letters in early life, and even the finest human beings may have a dash of egotism in their composition; but I cannot believe that the Dorothea who sacrificed herself with such idealism to the Rev. Mr. Casaubon ever talked like a traditional Pharisee.

It is after she has married the middle-aged pedant, a dried-up well of humanity, under the impression that 'here was a modern Augustine who united the genius of doctor and saint' that our hearts begin to ache in sympathy with her. How she longs to learn Latin and Greek so that she may be able to read aloud to her scholar-saint 'as Milton's daughters did to their father,' and to be of use to him in composing his great life-work, the *Key to All the Mythologies*!

She had looked forward to being Eve in some Eden of saintly scholarship, but to her dismay she found that Casaubon was incapable of sharing her real interests with her, and that instead of the spiritual and intellectual companionship of which she had dreamed she must resign herself to a life of spiritual and intellectual loneliness. It is a tragedy of isolation in which he, too, suffers, for the delight that he had anticipated in his marriage to a young and beautiful woman eludes him. He is too old and too firmly set in his monkish habits. He is only human enough to be jealous.

It is a remarkable achievement on the part of an author to write an engrossing novel with this ill-assorted married couple as its most memorable theme. Yet with such insight does George Eliot portray them—their consciences, their helpless longing to do what is right, their broken hopes, their fears, their misunderstandings—that we feel we know them more intimately in some ways than any other hapless pair in Victorian fiction. And, realistically though they are drawn, they are drawn without a moment's failure of charity.

At the age of twenty-nine Arnold Bennett made an entry in his diary: 'Essential characteristic of the really great novelist: a Christlike, all-embracing compassion.' George Eliot's compassion extends to Mr. Casaubon even when he is attempting to compel his wife to make him a promise that would enslave her to him after his death and when he leaves a will robbing her of his fortune if she should marry his Bohemian cousin, Will Ladislaw. We feel glad when, throwing over the fortune, she finds happiness with Ladislaw; but, compared with Casaubon, he is a puppet beside a portrait; so it is not he, but the mean-minded, middle-aged scholar, the double failure in scholarship and in marriage, who wins the greater sympathy. One will never forget that last pathetic scene in his life when, waiting in the shrubbery for his wife to bring him word that she promises to obey him even when he is dead, he dies before she arrives to announce her decision.

Middlemarch, however, is not the story of merely one unhappy marriage. There is a second and scarcely less interesting story of married life in ruins—the story of young Lydgate, the idealistic doctor with a passion for reform, and his pretty young wife, Rosamond, who by her petty worldliness wrecks him as an idealist and turns him into a commonplace fashionable success. Here, too, are characters drawn in a profound understanding of human nature; and, though Rosamond ought to be indicted, and up to a point is indicted, we have a good deal of sympathy with her as with a pretty animal behaving according to its nature. The third love-story in the book, in which Mary, with her sweet, unselfish character, makes a man of feckless Fred Viney, is more ordinary, but it has the great merit of introducing us to Mary's father, that stalwart old worker, Caleb Garth.

It is a world crowded with excellent portraits, indeed, in which we move as we read *Middlemarch*—Dorothea's delightful, rambling old uncle, Mr. Brooke; her sister Celia; her fine country gentleman of a lover, Sir James Chettam, who ends by marrying Celia; the easy-going, generous clergyman, the Rev. Mr. Farebrother, who adds to his tiny income by playing whist, and the greedy relations of old Featherstone congregating near his death-bed in the hope of inheriting his money. And for excitement we have a hypocritical leader of Dissent committing indirect murder in order to get rid of a blackmailer.

George Eliot seems to have alienated many people who suspected her of wanting to preach to them. Preacher or not, however, she proved herself in *Middlemarch* to be a great story-teller—a story-teller, too, with happy gleams of humour.

As for her preaching, let us remember her own statement in a letter to Charles Bray: 'If art does not enlarge men's sympathies, it does nothing morally. I have had heart-cutting experience that *opinions* are a poor cement between human souls; and the only effect I ardently long to produce by my writings is that those who read them should be better able to *imagine* and to *feel* the pains and the joys of those who differ from themselves in everything but the broad fact of being struggling, erring human creatures.'

William Hazlitt

(1947)

THERE has been some interesting discussion lately about the prospects of young writers of talent in an increasingly Socialistic State. A very important question is how the young writers will be able to preserve their freedom of speech when everything, or nearly everything, has been nationalized. Some people, however, seem to be more concerned with the question of how they will be able to earn a living; and Rupert Brooke's suggestion that the State should subsidize a considerable number of selected writers (as well as practitioners of the other arts) without imposing any conditions on them has been a good deal talked about.

It seems to me that the problem of providing the good writer with an income would be unlikely to present any more difficulties in a Socialist State than it did under the various regimes of the past. It is true that the writer with private means would vanish; but the majority of good writers for centuries have lived by giving pleasure to their patrons, and the Russian experiment proves that they can do so even under Socialism when their patron is the public.

I do not believe that the good writer of the future will find it half so hard to earn an income by his books as did the good writers, for instance, of Wordsworth's day. Think of the constellation of men of genius who wrote at that time, and inquire how many of them, out of the books they published, made as good an income as a small shopkeeper's. Wordsworth himself had to be found a Government job; Coleridge lived largely on his friends; Shelley would have starved but for having private means; Keats, if he had lived, could never have supported Fanny Brawne by his poetry alone; Charles Lamb's *Essays of Elia* earned him only £30 when published in book form, and even this was never paid to him; and Hazlitt, though he did not die destitute as has sometimes been said, certainly died hard up. Scott and Byron and Moore were more fortunate; but the genius of the age was more commonly rewarded with fame than with pounds, shillings, and pence—fame, too, within a comparatively small circle.

How Hazlitt remained a struggling author all his life is made clear in P. P. Howe's biography. Hazlitt's original ideas of authorship, it must be admitted, did not promise a future of affluence. As a schoolboy of about fourteen he meditated writing a work to be entitled *Project for a New Theory of Civil and Criminal Legislation*, and at the age of eighteen he was planning an *Essay on the Principles of Human Action*. Two years later he was still engaged on this essay, but then gave it up in despair. He wrote in later life of his disappointment:

After trying in vain to pump up some words, images, notions, apprehensions, or observations, from the gulf of abstraction in which I had plunged myself for four or five years preceding, (I) gave up the attempt as labour in vain, and shed tears of helpless despondency on the blank, unfinished paper.

He then decided to become a professional painter like his brother John; but his genius craved for fuller expression than it could achieve on canvas. His ambition outran his accomplishment, and he ultimately realized with sorrow that he could not be a second Titian. 'I flung away my pencil in disgust and despair,' he has told us. 'Otherwise I might have done as well as others, I dare say, but for a desire to do too well.' He took his brushes up again, however, and continued to paint till, at the age of thirty-four, he got his first regular job in journalism as Parliamentary reporter for the *Morning Chronicle*.

That, unpromising though it may seem, was the beginning of Hazlitt as the writer of genius we know. Before long he was contributing articles on all manner of subjects—the drama, art, politics, and things in general—though, according to Miss Mitford, his editor 'used to execrate "the d——d fellow's d——d stuff" for filling up so much of the paper in the very height of the advertising season.' Hazlitt was still far from prosperous, however. 'It is quite painful,' Crabb Robinson wrote at the time,

to witness the painful exertions for a livelihood which H is condemned to make, and how strongly it shows that a modicum of talent outweighs an ample endowment of original thought and the highest powers of intellect, when a man does not add to that endowment the other of making it turn to account. How many men are there connected with newspapers who live comfortably with not a tithe of H's powers as a writer.

Hazlitt, however, was not born for good fortune. Apart from the fact that he was never rewarded according to his merits, he was the possessor of a demon that fought against his happiness. He was like the Saul who flung a spear at David. He separated from both of the women whom he married, and he seems to have quarrelled at some time or other with all his friends. I doubt whether any one who knew him well ever praised him without reservation. Coleridge wrote:

His manners are ninety-nine in a hundred singularly repulsive; brow-hanging, shoe-contemplating, strange . . . he is, I verily believe, kindly-natured; is very fond of, attentive to, and patient with, children; but has a jealous, gloomy and an irritable pride.

Leigh Hunt drew a similarly black and white portrait:

I have often said I have an irrepressible love for Hazlitt on account of his sympathy for mankind, his unmercenary disinterestedness, and his suffering; and I should have a still greater affection for him if he would let me; but I declare to God I never seem to know whether he is pleased or displeased, cordial or uncordial—indeed, his manners are never cordial.

Even Lamb's noble tribute to him when he wrote: 'I think W. H. to be in his natural state one of the wisest and finest spirits breathing,' contains the reservation 'in his natural state,' as though Hazlitt had black moods for which he was scarcely responsible and which called for forgiveness like the temper of a passionate but fundamentally generous-hearted child.

Hazlitt's very virtues, it must be remembered, brought upon his head floods of malignant calumny of a kind to destroy the temper even of a fairly good-natured man. It was not his faults, but his 'unmercenary disinterestedness' as a democrat and defender of the French Revolution that incited the thugs of reaction to assault him. 'I could swear (were they not mine),' he wrote of the essays in *Table Talk*, 'the thoughts in many of them are founded as the rock, free as air, the tone like an Italian picture. What then? Had the style been like polished steel, as firm and as bright, it would have availed me nothing, for I

am not a Government tool.'   His *Characters of Shakespeare's Plays*
was damned for the same reason.

Our anti-Jacobin and anti-Gallican writers soon found out that I
had said and written that Frenchmen, Englishmen, men were not
slaves by birthright.   This was enough to *damn* the work.   Such has
been the head and front of my offending.

It is evidence of the power and permanence of Hazlitt's love
of liberty that 'probably his last written words' were an expression of joy at the success of the minor French Revolution of
1830.   'The Revolution of the Three Days,' he wrote from his
sick room, 'was like a resurrection from the dead, and showed
plainly that liberty, too, has a spirit of life in it; and that hatred
of oppression is "the unquenchable flame, the worm that
dieth not."'

Hazlitt was a great hater.   There has never been another
essayist of comparable genius so prone to hate and to confess his
hatred.   The fire in his soul that gave birth to his hatreds,
however, was the same fire that burned in him as a lover of
many of the things that make life worth living—a fine picture,
the enchantment of a landscape, a good book, great acting, the
wisdom of a profound thinker, walking, liberty, and the energy
and skill of a manly game.   He is the essayist of ecstasies and of
raptures, and this without a tinge of insincerity—a rare achievement in an essayist of the kind.

A recent writer has questioned the authenticity of the tradition
that Hazlitt's last words were: 'Well, I've had a happy life';
but certainly he could look back on great feasts of happiness—
happiness such as he experienced in youth especially before the
world had 'grown old and incorrigible.'

It might be said that Hazlitt was born with a superlative gift
for enjoyment, but that, as he grew older, enjoyment and dis-
illusionment took their turns with him.   In his essays the sun
shines on the past oftener than on the present or the future.   It
was a long-past walk on the road to Llangollen on his way to
visit Coleridge that he wrote: 'Besides the prospect which
opened beneath my feet, another also opened to my inward sight,
a heavenly vision, on which was written in letters large as Hope
could make them these four words: Liberty, Genius, Love,
Virtue: which have since faded into the light of common day
and mock my idle page.'   The pleasures of hope became more

and more illusive with the years, and were faint by the time he wrote 'On the fear of death':

My public and private hopes have been left a ruin. . . . I should like to leave some sterling work behind me. I should like to have some friendly hand to consign me to the grave. On these conditions, I am ready, if not willing, to depart. I shall then write on my tomb —Grateful and Contented. But I have thought and suffered too much to be willing to have thought and suffered in vain.

Two of these conditions at least were satisfied. Lamb was there at the end, and, as for having left some sterling work behind him, it is clear that a growing number of people regard him as having done so, since three biographies of him have appeared in the present century.

P. P. Howe's is a book full of good matter, devotedly collected and set in order; but Hazlitt the man, in his exultations, his wraths, and his sufferings does not quite come to life in it. If Howe had lived to rewrite it I think he would have made more use of *Liber Amoris* as a revelation of the sombre fires that burned in Hazlitt's soul. *Liber Amoris* is not important as literature; but we know Hazlitt better when we have read it. Good men in the last century wished it had never been written as they wished Keats's letters to Fanny Brawne had never been written. For my part I cannot see how it is possible to read either without a deepening of sympathy and understanding.

Keats in his Letters

(1947)

ONE of the things about which the present generation differs widely from the Victorians is the need for reticence. Respectable Victorians regarded it as indecent, not merely to write obscenely, but to publish the whole truth about the illustrious dead if the publication seemed to them likely to be derogatory.

A belief in the decency and duty of reticence did not, of course, make its first appearance during the reign of Victoria. After all, Hannah More was concerned some time before that lest Boswell should be over-realistic in his biography of Johnson. Still, I think it must be admitted that the nineteenth century was particularly addicted to the *de mortuis nil nisi bonum* attitude to biography. Tennyson seems to have regarded biography itself as a violation of the sanctities of private life, and Thackeray, dreading that this might happen, left instructions that no biography of him was to be written.

As a result of this attitude, the two-volume Victorian biography frequently was little more than a funeral oration in two volumes. And this naturally led to a violent reaction, in the course of which good men were 'debunked' without mercy and reticence was thrown overboard.

The new school of biography flourished, partly through the desire for truth and partly because it is a human weakness to gloat over the faults, real or imaginary, of those who are our betters. I have known men who were never more gleeful than when attributing some purely conjectural vice to one of the mighty dead, explaining in that way why he was deaf or blind or remained unmarried. Perhaps it was the resolve to crush this instinct that was at the root of the excessive reticence of the Victorians which turned many a biographical tome into a tombstone.

So hostile were some of the finest Victorians to the revelation of a man's private life that there was a protesting outcry even over the publication of Keats's letters to Fanny Brawne.   Buxton Forman has told us that, when he made up his mind to publish these in 1878 he was 'fully alive to the risk of vituperation,' and that half the press regarded their publication as 'an outrage unheard of.'   What is particularly astonishing in all this to the reader to-day is that the critics protested largely on the ground that it was cruel to expose Keats as a man, sick unto death, wracked with the torments of a hopeless passion.   These letters, which now seem to many of us to be among the most beautiful love-letters ever written, were looked on as somehow disgraceful and unmanly; and when Sir Sidney Colvin wrote his monumental life of Keats, Fanny Brawne, poor girl, had taken the place of the *Quarterly* as the enemy of Keats's life, happiness, and genius. She was a siren, a vampire, a woman unworthy of his love.

I remember, when Colvin published his biography, challenging this view and arguing that, far from Keats's genius having been ruined by his love for Fanny Brawne, it was the passion for this 'minx' that 'transformed him, in a few months, from a poet of doubtful fame into a master and an immortal.'   The evidence for this seemed to me overwhelming.   Keats first met Fanny Brawne in 1818, and he became engaged to her in December. In the following month he wrote *The Eve of St. Agnes*.   In April 1819 he wrote *La Belle Dame Sans Merci*, *Ode to Psyche*, *Ode to a Grecian Urn*.   In May he wrote *Ode to a Nightingale*.   In June he wrote *Lamia*, part one.   Then came the *Bright Star* sonnet, work on *The Fall of Hyperion*, and *Ode to Autumn*.   At an earlier date Keats had written in a letter: 'I have the same idea of all our passions as of Love: they are all, in their sublime, creators of essential beauty'; and this was surely true of his love for Fanny Brawne.

When I made these points in a review, Sir Sidney wrote to me to say that, if I were right, this would knock the bottom out of his biography—or some such phrase—and that he intended to publish an answer to me.   The only answer he ever published, however, was in the preface to the third edition of his biography, where he wrote: 'Now it is, of course, true that most of Keats's best work was done after he had met Fanny Brawne.   But it was done—and this is what is really unquestionable—not because of her but in spite of her.'   And he maintained that not to see this is 'to misunderstand Keats's whole career.'

I do not think I have ever come upon a more questionable use of the word 'unquestionable'; and I can see no explanation of Sir Sidney's logic except that in his sympathy with Keats's sufferings he disliked Fanny as though she were the only cause of them and, in his dislike, came more and more to look on her as Keats's destroying angel. It is symptomatic of his hostility to Fanny, I think, that, in quoting Keats's last letter but one to Charles Brown, he omits the deeply moving appeal: 'My dear Brown, for my sake be her advocate for ever.' I wonder why he omitted that sentence. Was it a mere accident of abbreviation? Or did he feel that, after his indictment of Fanny, he dared not quote a sentence in which Keats himself was a witness in her favour?

The Letters of John Keats are among the greatest letters ever written by an English poet, and it is an interesting fact that nearly all the best English letters were written by poets. In fact, Horace Walpole is the only prose-writer who has written letters that will stand comparison with those of Gray, Cowper, Byron, Charles Lamb (for he, too, was a poet), and FitzGerald. It is also interesting to remember that all these men were unmarried or lived most of their lives as bachelors.

Keats, to my mind, excels the others as an autobiographer. He reveals the depths of his soul and lays bare the twin passions of his life—the passion of a poet and the passion of a lover—to an extent that none of the others do. The first letters that have survived date from his earliest twenties, when we find him writing to Reynolds: 'I cannot exist without Poetry—without eternal Poetry—half the day will not do—the whole of it.' About the same time he wrote to Leigh Hunt:

I have asked myself so often why I should be a poet more than other men, seeing how great a thing it is—how great things are to be gained by it, what a thing to be in the mouth of Fame—that at last the idea has grown so monstrously beyond my seeming power of attainment that the other day I nearly consented with myself to drop into a Phaeton. Yet, 'tis a disgrace to fail even in a huge attempt; and at this moment I drive the thought from me.

To Haydon he writes:

I hope for the support of a High Power while I climb this little Eminence, and especially in my years of more momentous Labour. I remember your saying that you had notions of a good Genius presiding over you. I have of late had the same thought. . . . Is it too daring to fancy Shakespeare this Presider?

Even at this early date he seems to have accustomed himself to the thought of death. 'I am never alone,' he writes,

without rejoicing that there is such a thing as death. . . . I have two brothers; one is driven by the 'burden of Society' to America; the other, with an exquisite love of life, is in a lingering state. My love for my brothers, from the early loss of our parents, and even from earlier misfortunes, has grown into affection 'passing the love of women' . . . I have a sister, too, and may not follow them either to America or to the grave. Life must be undergone, and I certainly derive some consolation from the thoughts of writing one or two more poems before it ceases.

Poetry to Keats was a religion. 'I am convinced,' he declares, 'more and more every day (except the human friend philosopher) a fine writer is the most genuine being in the world. Shakespeare and the *Paradise Lost* every day become greater wonders to me. I look upon fine phrases like a lover.' And again: 'I am convinced more and more every day that fine writing is, next to fine doing, the top thing in the world. The *Paradise Lost* becomes a greater wonder.'

One cannot help thinking of him as other than a man burnt up by the ardour of his imagination. His sorrows as well as his joys are the result of this. 'I carry all matters to an extreme,' he writes to Bailey—'so that, when I have any little vexation it grows in five minutes into a theme for Sophocles.' Life tortured him long before he met Fanny Brawne, and told her: 'A person in health as you are can have no conception of the horrors that nerves and a temper like mine go through.'

When Keats first met Fanny Brawne he was nearly twenty-three years old and she was close upon nineteen. Not long before this he had declared that he had never been in love. Even a month after he had met Fanny he wrote to his brother: 'I hope I shall never marry. . . . The roaring of the wind is my wife and the stars through the window-pane are my children.' His chief ambition was still to perform the great work he was sent into the world to do. 'I am ambitious,' he declared, 'of doing the world some good if I should be spared, that may be the work of maturer years. . . . The faint conceptions I have of

poems to come bring the blood frequently into my forehead.'
His first impression of Fanny was that she was 'beautiful and
elegant, graceful, silly, fashionable, and strange,' and that she
was a minx—'not from any innate vice but from a penchant
she has of acting stylishly.'

That Fanny was something better than a minx and that her
love for Keats was unselfish seems to me to be proved by her
engaging herself to one who was an impecunious poet with no
prospect of being able to support her—an unknown youth whose
work had brought him more derision than praise.   Keats's love
of her certainly was a source of exquisite happiness as well as of
exquisite pain.   'I have been astounded,' he wrote in one of
his letters to her, 'that men should die martyrs to religion—I
have shuddered at it.   I shudder no more—I would be martyred
for my religion—love is my religion—I would die for it—I
would die for you.   My creed is love and you are its only tenet.'

In his feverish state he was often tortured with jealousy as we
see in the letter in which he wrote: 'My greatest torment since
I have known you has been the fear of you being a little inclined
to the Cressid'; and, as his health grew worse, his jealousy drove
him to utter cries of anguish.   'I appeal to you,' he wrote to
her, 'by the blood of that Christ you believe in: Do not write
to me if you have done anything this month which it would have
pained me to have seen.   You may have altered—if you have
not—if you still behave in dancing rooms and other societies as
I have seen you—I do not want to live—if you have done so I
wish this coming night may be my last.   I cannot live without
you, and not only you but *chaste you; virtuous you.*'

In his fits of jealousy he demanded that Fanny should abjure all
ordinary pleasures as he himself was forced by his debilitating
illness to do.   'Your going to town alone,' he once wrote to her,
'was a shock to me—yet I expected it—*promise you will not for
some time till I get better.*'   Let us remember along with these
miseries of love the ecstasy of devotion in which he wrote: 'I
will imagine you Venus to-night, and pray, pray, pray to your
star like a heathen.'   Let us remember, too, the letter in which
he wrote: 'You are always new.   The last of your kisses was
ever the sweetest: the last smile the brightest: the last movement
the gracefullest.   When you passed my window home yesterday,
I was as filled with admiration as if I had then seen you for the

SYLVIA LYND, 1902

first time. . . . I never felt my mind repose upon anything with complete and undistracted enjoyment—upon one person but you. When you are in the room my thoughts fly out of the window; you always control my whole senses.'

All this seems to me to give us good reason for regarding Keats's devotion to Fanny not as a disaster, but as the greatest piece of good fortune that ever befell him both as a man and as a poet.   With him the height of love more than compensated for the depth of despair.   'I think,' he wrote to Brown when he was leaving England to die in Italy, 'without my mentioning it you would be a friend to Miss Brawne when I am dead.   You think she has many faults—but for my sake, think she has not one'—a passage, it is only fair to say, that Colvin quotes.

Then there is the last simple farewell letter to Mrs. Brawne:

I dare not fix my mind on Fanny, I have not dared to think of her.   The only comfort I have had that way has been thinking for hours together of having the knife she gave me put in a silver case—the hair in a locket—and the pocket-book in a gold net.   Show her this.   I dare say no more.

There is nothing more heart-rending in the history of poets than is contained in these letters and nothing more revealing of a beautiful spirit in the toils of tragic circumstance.

The Innocence of Shelley

(1933)

ONE is sometimes tempted to wish that as little were known about Shelley's life as about Shakespeare's. I agree with those who desire to know all that can be discovered about the life of a great writer, believing that a poet of genius is himself as interesting as any character a poet of genius has ever invented. Shelley, however, seems to arouse in those who love him the spirit of controversy. As J. A. Symonds put it: 'Those who ought to meet in love over his grave have spent their time in quarrelling about him and baffling the most eager seeker for the truth.' Even to-day it is not easy to discuss the facts of his life in such a way as not to incite some ardent partisan to accuse one of misunderstanding one of the noblest of men.

The difficulty arises from the fact that there were two Shelleys. There was Shelley the angel who dreamed of bringing down heaven to earth; and there was Shelley the baffled human being who became impatient when he found that he could not put his dream into practice. His father, Sir Timothy Shelley, is described by Dowden as a man who 'had a wrong-headed way of meaning well and doing ill.' Sir Timothy's well-meant schemes were on the side of respectability; Shelley's on the side of revolution. It was the lot of both of them, however, to see their best intentions coming to other people's grief.

Shelley might be described as a born experimentalist. As a boy, it is said, he had 'a passion for playing with fire,' with the result that on one occasion he set fire to his father's butler. He alarmed his family with his experiments in chemistry and electricity.

When he was at Oxford, again, his rooms had the appearance of an untidy laboratory, with acid stains everywhere and holes burnt in the carpet, and his friends were in constant terror that he would one day blow himself up or set the college on fire.

It may seem surprising at first sight that the most ethereal of the nineteenth-century poets should have been the most scientific in his interests, and Shelley was sufficiently ahead of his time even to have a passionate faith in the future of flying. He believed that a balloon had only to appear over Africa in order to secure the emancipation of the last slave. He was equally devoted to what is now called psychic science. He made various attempts to get into communication with the spirits of the dead, and was ready to sit up all night among the bones in the vault at Warnham Church in the hope of seeing a ghost. This, perhaps, however, was the effect less of scientific curiosity than of reading sensational sixpenny novels.

His reading led him to experiment with literature as well as with science. He published a novel, *Zastrozzi*, while he was still at Eton, and wrote a second one, *St. Irvyne*, for which he optimistically hoped to secure a good press by means of bribery. 'Pouch the reviewers,' he wrote to one of his friends on the subject; '£10 will be sufficient I should suppose. . . .'

Even the incident in his life that has subjected him to the most hostile criticism—his desertion of his first wife, Harriet West-brook—might be described as the end of an experiment in philanthropy. Shelley had not married Harriet for love, but because he wished to save her from the despotism of parents and schoolmistresses. A boy of nineteen, at war with authority since the authorities of University College had expelled him for atheism, he saw in Harriet, a girl of sixteen who hated going back to school, a victim of tyranny like himself. With the best possible intentions he carried her off to Scotland and married her though he was conscientiously opposed to marriage. Harriet was a pretty, vivacious, intelligent girl, and the marriage might conceivably have been a happy one if her elder sister, Eliza, had not come to live with her. Shelley unfortunately conceived a violent detestation of Eliza, and resented even her natural desire to caress his infant daughter, Ianthe. He wrote to Hogg:

I certainly hate her with all my heart and soul. It is a sight which awakes an irrepressible sensation of disgust and horror to see her caress my poor little Ianthe. I sometimes feel faint with the fatigue of checking the overflowing of my unbounded abhorrence for this miserable wretch. But she is no more than a blind and loathsome worm that cannot see to sting.

Here irritability had got the better of philanthropy, as it did in the same period towards the end of Shelley's friendship with the schoolmistress, Elizabeth Hitchener.   Shelley's experiments in benevolence led only to his being convinced that he was housed with female demons.   Even Harriet, partly perhaps because she refused to suckle her child, lost his sympathy and seemed to him merely a 'noble animal,' unfit to be the partner of his life.

Possibly, however, Shelley and Harriet would have separated, even if Eliza had not made his home hateful to him.   When he fell in love with Godwin's daughter, Mary, Harriet's happiness was doomed.   Once more Shelley did his utmost to live up to the highest principles.   A youth of twenty-one, he eloped with Mary, a girl of sixteen, to the Continent, but he could not bear the thought of making Harriet unhappy.   He wrote to her, therefore, inviting her to go and live with Mary and himself on the assumption that this would be an ideal solution of the tangle in which they found themselves.   It was one of his characteristics that he could seldom see any point of view except his own, and, even while deserting Harriet, he was aware of nothing incongruous in borrowing money from her and in assuring her that he felt no anxiety about her coming safely through the ordeal of giving birth to the baby that was yet to be born.   There is nothing in literary biography more astonishing than the high-minded egoism shown by Shelley at this crisis—an egoism more than ever obtrusive since Dr. Hotson's discovery of the lost Harriet letters.

Mr. Oliver Elton has said that Byron was an egoist, but that he sometimes seemed to be sorry.   He compares Shelley's egoism to that of a child, on the other hand, who cannot even realize that it has wounded a playmate.   When Harriet drowned herself in the Thames two years later, he earnestly declared that the responsibility was not his.

The fact remains that it is impossible to read the life of Shelley without realizing that he was one of the noblest and most unselfish of men.   He was not, it may be admitted, a normal human being of his century.   He was like a character out of Morris's *News from Nowhere*, lost among the conventions of nineteenth-century England, and innocently surprised to find that the standards of Utopia caused disaster when put into practice in an unreformed world.   There was no humbug in this. All Shelley's friends have testified to his sincerity and goodness of heart.

Hogg undoubtedly portrays Shelley with all his eccentric habits, his obsessions and illusions and his general incompatibility with common life. But these are merely the trappings of a divine man of genius. Hogg's life of Shelley would have been eternally interesting if it had contained nothing but the famous passage in which he describes his first sight of Shelley and Mary together. He and Shelley had called on Godwin, who was not at home. They waited for him in a room:

'Where is Godwin?' he asked me several times, as if I knew. I did not know, and to say the truth, I did not care. He continued his uneasy promenade; and I stood reading the names of old English authors on the backs of the venerable volumes, when the door was partially and softly opened. A thrilling voice called 'Shelley!' A thrilling voice answered 'Mary!' And he darted out of the room, like an arrow from the bow of the far-darting king. A very young female, fair and fair-haired, pale indeed, and with a piercing look, wearing a frock of tartan, an unusual dress in London at that time, had called him out of the room. He was absent a very short time—a minute or two; and then returned. 'Godwin is out; there is no use in waiting.' So we continued our walk along Holborn.

'Who was that, pray?' I asked; 'a daughter?'

'Yes.'

'A daughter of William Godwin?'

'The daughter of Godwin and Mary.'

That scene is surely of a piece with Shelley's own poetry.

For the rest, if there seems to be any disharmony between certain phrases of Shelley's life and the poems, we must blame the facts, not the biographers. Critics may say that his poetry, like his life, was an expression of his belief in the impossible, and then make use of the facts of his life as a comment on the philosophy of his verse. We have only to read 'The Euganean Hills,' however, or 'Adonais,' or 'Episychidion,' to be swept up into high places of the imagination where biography cannot reach or criticism disturb. It is in Shelley himself, after all, and not in Hogg or the others, that we find the immortally beautiful true portrait of Shelley, his ardours, his hopes, his sufferings, and his loves.

Matthew Arnold has been severely criticized for describing

Shelley as an ineffectual angel. Obviously, the author of the 'Ode to the West Wind' is not ineffectual as a poet, and as a visionary he has had an influence on many Englishmen in succeeding generations. At the same time there seems to me to be a sense in which Matthew Arnold was right.

Shelley was the most eccentric, the most heretical, of the great English poets in his opinions and in his life. It was almost enough that a belief should be established to convince him that it was not only untrue but monstrously wicked. Where other poets would have seen useful or at least harmless windmills, he saw cruel and oppressive giants. As a result we see him in his life and writings again and again as a rebel in religion, in morals, in politics, and—he took this very seriously—in diet.

Perhaps it was his behaviour over his first marriage that particularly stamped him in the eyes of many people as an ineffectual angel. Clearly, he eloped with Harriet Westbrook, a schoolgirl of sixteen, for reasons that may be regarded as angelic. He regarded her as the victim of parental tyranny, and, though only nineteen years old himself, he eloped with her to Scotland. How odd, however, were his grounds for thinking she was brutally treated! 'Her father,' he wrote to Hogg, 'has persecuted her in a most horrible way by endeavouring to compel her to go to school.' The knight, having rescued the captive princess from the ogre, once more showed the angelic side of his nature by going through the marriage ceremony with her in Edinburgh. To do this he had to violate his passionately held principles; for he was a convinced disbeliever in marriage. 'Yes,' he had written to Hogg three months before, 'marriage is hateful, detestable. A kind of ineffable, sickening disgust seizes my mind when I think of this most despotic, most unrequired fetter which prejudice has forged to confine its energies.' Harriet was more conventional, however, and Shelley unselfishly gave way to her 'prejudices.'

Shelley's extraordinary attitude to life is clearly revealed in the story of his relations with Hogg, his bosom friend, when Hogg was accused of making love to Harriet soon afterwards. Many people look on Hogg as a hypocrite and a villain; and undoubtedly he was a queer enough customer for anything. His treatment of some of Shelley's letters, recently published in their original form, shows that he did not stop short of forgery.

To omit sentences from published letters is in some cases legitimate, if the omission does not create a false impression; but Hogg alters letters and sentences to his own advantage. His editor thinks that he did this for Shelley's sake. But consider. Shelley, heart-broken by his friend's treachery and dreading to see him again at the time, wrote: 'Follow us not. Dare to be good. Dare to be virtuous. Seize once more what once thou didst relinquish, never, never again to resign it.' Hogg printed this as: 'Cannot you follow us?—why not? But I will dare to be good—dare to be virtuous; and I will soon seize once more what I have for a while relinquished, never, never again to resign it.' Forgery on this scale takes one's breath away. Shelley on another occasion wrote: 'I don't think you sinless.' Hogg altered this to: 'I do not think you infallible.' An editor must be a whole-Hogger to palliate such things.

These letters are more interesting, however, for the light they throw on Shelley, than for the light they throw on Hogg. Here we see an idealistic young doctrinaire in a dilemma. Believing in the principle of free love, Shelley could not logically condemn Hogg for falling in love with Harriet. He wrote to him quite candidly: 'I hope I am not prejudiced . . . I attach little value to the monopoly of exclusive cohabitation. You know that frequently I have spoken slightingly of it . . . this *I* would not value.' At the same time, he had to consider Harriet's happiness as well as his principles, and Hogg had made Harriet desperately unhappy. Writing of the possibility of a *ménage à trois*, he said:

It is the consideration what men have chosen to make of this, from which I *perhaps* am not quite free, what you *certainly* retain, what Harriet (the last, the greatest complication) still cherishes, still cherishes, as a prejudice interwoven with the fibres of her being— this is the point; that, if you lived with us you would be driven to this last consummation of your love for Harriet. . . . You would again deceive yourself. You would fancy it was virtue.

How far a natural jealousy influenced Shelley as he wrote these passionate and despairing letters, it is hard to guess. 'Your crime has been *selfishness*,' he tells Hogg; and, again: 'I admit the distinction you make between mistake and crime. I heartily acquit you of the latter, but how terrible has been your mistake. . . . You never could think it *virtue* to act as you

c

desired. . . . I said you were insincere? I said so because I
thought so.' Yet even amid his reproaches and remonstrances,
he cannot help remembering how much Hogg's friendship means
to him; and, indeed, it was to prove the most lasting friendship
of his life. 'Think not,' he writes, 'that I am otherwise than
your friend, a friend to you now more fervent, more devoted
than ever, for misery endears to us those whom we love. You
are, you shall be my bosom friend, you have been so—but in
one instance, and there you have deceived yourself.'

It has been thought that this astonishing correspondence had
its origin, not in Hogg's behaviour to Harriet, but in one of
Shelley's frequent hallucinations—that there is no serious basis
of fact, indeed, in the Hogg-Harriet story. I find it hard to
believe this. So close a friend as Hogg could soon have dissipated
a mere hallucination.

Hogg seems to me to have had a peculiar gift for falling in
love with those with whom Shelley fell in love. A youthful
idolater, he saw women through his friend's eyes. A number
of letters here show that, after Shelley married Mary, Hogg
carried on an amorous correspondence with her; and he afterwards married one of Shelley's women friends, Jane Williams,
the widow of the man who was drowned with Shelley.

Hogg must certainly have had many good points to retain
Shelley's love till the end; but whether he was merely a flirt or
worse, he was obviously an odd fellow with some singular
notions of morality.

I doubt, indeed, whether Hogg will ever appear to the
majority of readers other than a very curious mixture. But
Shelley was undoubtedly vehemently excitable and abnormal; he
was also in many respects a theorist rather than a practical man,
and some of his theories were, in the judgment of fairly wise
men, unsound. Yet his essential goodness—his pursuit of the
ideal life as he saw it—makes one think of him as noble beyond
the common. Byron said of him that he was 'the most gentle,
the most amiable, and the least worldly minded person I ever
met,' and added: 'I have seen nothing like him, and never shall
again, I am certain.' His generosity with money and other forms
of assistance was almost boundless. It is easy to see the comic
side of some of his eccentricities, and who could help laughing
at the extravagances of this marvellous youth of genius?

At the same time, the more one reads of him, the more one is aware of the angel in him, with or without the reservations of Matthew Arnold in describing him as 'a beautiful and ineffectual angel, beating in the void his luminous wings in vain.' Certainly, one reflects, not in vain in his poetry, and not always in vain in his life. All the same, I think there is a good deal of truth in Arnold's lovely image.

Burns the Universal Brother

(1943)

How many of you, I wonder—those of you, at least, who were born outside Scotland—read Burns nowadays. Southern critics have, in recent years, paid little attention to him. I have met Englishmen who said that the language in which he wrote is too difficult for them. They affirmed that, little Latin though they learnt at school, they could translate Horace more easily than some of the verses in 'To a Louse. On Seeing One on a Lady's Bonnet at Church'—such a verse, for example, as:

> My sooth! right bauld ye set your nose out,
> As plump and grey as onie grozet;
> O for some rank, mercurial rozet,
> Or fell, red smeddum,
> I'd gie you sic a hearty dose o't,
> Wad dress your droddum!

I have urged them to read something simpler, like 'To a Mouse. On Turning Her Up in her Nest with the Plough, November, 1785,' but even there they confess to an inability to understand such phrases as 'a daimen icker in a thrave,' 'foggage green,' and 'cranreuch cauld.' Perhaps someone will one day invent Basic Scots and translate Burns into it for the weaker brethren south of the Border. I am afraid, however, that in the course of the translation Burns's verse would lose nine-tenths of its magic.

I myself was more or less brought up on Burns. At least, I spent my infancy in a nursery in which my nurse, during the intervals when she was not singing 'The Protestant Boys' and 'The Boyne Water,' used to croon—not in the modern fashion of crooning—'Ye Banks and Braes of Bonnie Doon.' This was my first experience of disinterested melancholy. I did not know very clearly what the poem meant, but the lines:

> How can ye chant, ye little birds,
> And I sae weary fu' o' care?

made me feel pleasantly sad. And when I came to the close of the song with:

> And my fause lover stole my rose,
> But, oh! he left the thorn to me,

I was initiated into the heart-break at the heart of things.

Thus I was fortunate enough to think of Burns from the beginning not as a difficult, but as a simple and natural, writer. And apparently a vast number of people have been equally fortunate, since, according to Sir Patrick Dollan who has just edited a Burns anthology, called *Songs of Liberty*, more than 100,000 copies of Burns's poems 'were printed and sold each year prior to the outbreak of this catastrophic war.' How many poets can boast of so large and perpetual an audience? Milton? Wordsworth? Shelley? I doubt whether any of them is popular on this scale.

The truth is, Burns was a popular poet in a sense in which no great English poet has been. Like Rudyard Kipling, he wrote verse that appealed to an enormous number of people who cared little for poetry in general. Mr. T. S. Eliot has praised Kipling as a very great verse-writer who occasionally became a poet, and Burns might be described as a great poet who was also a great verse-writer. And by verse I mean such lyrics as 'A Man's a Man for a' That' and 'My Wife's a Winsome Wee Thing.' Kipling, however, for all his genius, never became a writer for the people, appealing equally to the peer and the peasant. Burns is as likely to be quoted by a ploughman as by the Moderator of the Church of Scotland. He had, it must be admitted, the great advantage of having at hand some of the greatest melodies on earth to which to set his verses. But other poets have had the same store of music to draw upon if they could have used it. Tom Moore in Ireland composed his verses to airs as lovely, but he never became a people's poet as Burns is a people's poet.

He failed to do this because he was not, as Burns was, a representative man. Burns might be described as Everyman both in his strength and in his weaknesses. He was at once a sinner and a preacher, a singer of the heroic life and a celebrator of the easy-going joys of the tavern. He was torn by passions and repented of them. He was a pagan Puritan, as self-indulgent

as Falstaff—and as likable—but with a strain of the moralist in
him that Falstaff lacked.   The very variety of his nature put him
on a brotherly footing with men of all sorts and conditions.   He
could express the ideals—if you can call them ideals—of the
village Lothario in 'Anna of the Gowden Locks' and other poems,
and at the same time in his 'Epistle to a Young Friend' preach
religion and morality more effectively than any minister of
the Kirk:

> The sacred lowe o' weel-plac'd love,
> Luxuriantly indulge it;
> But never tempt th' illicit rove,
> Tho' naething should divulge it:
> I waive the quantum o' the sin,
> The hazard o' concealing:
> But och! it hardens a' within,
> And petrifies the feeling! . . .
>
> The great Creator to revere,
> Must sure become the creature;
> But still the preaching cant forbear,
> And ev'n the rigid feature:
> Yet ne'er with wits profane to range,
> Be complaisance extended;
> An atheist's laugh's a poor exchange
> For Deity offended!

Burns has been taken to task for this 'double life' that we find
in his verse, and I have seen him accused of hypocrisy in his more
virtuous utterances.   Robert Louis Stevenson, if I remember
right, described Burns's fits of remorse as 'unmanly repentance.'
But surely the whole secret of Burns lies in the fact that, like
most human beings, he was compact of good and evil, and that
he has expressed so many of the varying moods of fallible humanity
with honesty and genius.   Men have not been unknown who
drank whisky to excess in what for the moment was a paradise
of boon-companionship, and also gravely warned their nephews
against following in their footsteps.   Burns was human enough
to want to see his nephews—if he had any—growing up to be
better men than himself.

I see that Sir Patrick Dollan calls one section of his anthology
'Songs of Fellowship,' and in 'Auld Lang Syne' Burns wrote the

greatest song of fellowship in the English—if I may call it so—
language. Nowhere where English is spoken has this song failed
to penetrate. Mr. Micawber, you will remember, was puzzled
by the vocabulary, not knowing what 'gowans' were or what a
'willie waught' was; but he and Mrs. Micawber and David
Copperfield sang it none the less heartily on that account, and
'were really affected.'

Others of Burns's songs have gone the round of the world—
'My Love is Like a Red, Red Rose,' 'Ae Fond Kiss' and 'Green
Grow the Rashes, O' among them. Some of them owe a great
deal to their musical setting; but others need no music to set
off the magic of their verse. No love-lyric more beautiful in its
simplicity has been written since the Elizabethan Age than 'The
Silver Tassie':

> Go fetch to me a pint o' wine,
> An' fill it in a silver tassie;
> That I may drink before I go,
> A service to my bonnie lassie.
> The boat rocks at the pier o' Leith;
> Fu' loud the wind blaws frae the Ferry;
> The ship rides by the Berwick Law,
> And I maun leave my bonnie Mary.
>
> The trumpets sound, the banners fly,
> The glittering spears are ranked ready;
> The shouts of war are heard afar,
> The battle closes deep and bloody;
> It's not the roar o' sea or shore
> Wad mak me langer wish to tarry;
> Nor shout o' war that's heard afar,—
> It's leaving thee, my bonnie Mary.

And Burns felt more deeply than most of the Elizabethan
lyrists. It is because his feeling was as profound as it was
universal that he has won the hearts as well as the literary
enthusiasm of millions of human beings. His love of national
freedom, his radicalism, became exalted into music as he wrote
of them. His bitter hatred of hypocrisy, most powerfully
expressed in 'Holy Willie's Prayer,' sprang from the same
passionate zeal for 'the things that are more excellent.'

He was touched more deeply than common mortals are by

the griefs as well as the joys that common mortals know; and
in the last verses of 'To a Mouse' his autobiography becomes the
autobiography of a multitude:

> But, Mousie, thou art no thy lane,
> In proving foresight may be vain:
> The best laid schemes o' mice and men
>   Gang aft a-gley,
> An' lea'e us nought but grief an' pain,
>   For promis'd joy.
>
> Still thou art blest, compar'd wi' me!
> The present only toucheth thee:
> But, och!   I backward cast my e'e
>   On prospects drear
> An' forward, tho' I canna see,
>   I guess an' fear!

Such lines, it may be thought, have become commonplace
with repetition; but the very fact that so much of Burns has
become commonplace and is still able to move us is a measure
of his genius.

I hope that Sir Patrick Dollan's selection will fall into the
hands of many young English and American as well as Scottish
readers, and that they will find his vocabulary less forbidding
than they feared.   He is certainly one of the most human, if not
one of the greatest, poets—at his best, the minstrel, not only of
a nation, but of mankind.

Sir Walter is still Readable

(1947)

ONE of the compensations for a prolonged illness is that, when the temperature is not too high and when the wrists are not too feeble to hold a book with comfort, the invalid has exceptional leisure for reading. This is particularly welcome to one whose professional work includes the reviewing of books and who is therefore bound to devote a great part of his time to reading, not the books that he would prefer to read, but a medley of books, good, bad, and indifferent, which have just been sent out by the publishers. The reviewer who has to do so much reading as a duty can seldom, when in good health, enjoy a long spell of reading purely for pleasure. He enjoys reading many of the books he reviews, of course, but there is a special pleasure in reading not under compulsion. This luxury has been mine for some months now as a result of a fairly tolerable illness.

One of the first books I read during this time was *Ivanhoe*. It happened to be in my bedroom, and, as a clever writer had just been affirming that Scott is 'simply unreadable,' I thought I might as well put to the test so bold an assertion about one of our grandfathers' demigods. I had not read *Ivanhoe* since I was a schoolboy; indeed, I had re-read comparatively little of Scott in recent years, preferring Dickens as a perpetual standby— Dickens of whom Arnold Bennett once said to me: 'Can't read him.'

I had not got far into *Ivanhoe* when, to my great delight, I discovered that, for me at least, Scott was as readable as ever. The book seemed to have lost none of its freshness since I first read it at the age of thirteen when I bought twenty-five volumes of the Waverley Novels one by one in a paper-backed edition at 4½d. each. That I was entranced by them is shown by the fact that in the next few years I had bought a cloth-bound edition of the novels for twenty-five precious half-crowns. I had begun reading them on the advice of my father, who assured me that

I should find them quite as exciting as the ephemeral reading matter to which I was largely addicted; and for a time there was no author in the world for me to equal Sir Walter.

It is possible, I admit, that Scott's greatness was overestimated in the nineteenth century. Some people spoke of him as though he were as supreme among the novelists as Shakespeare among the poets; and he himself was until fairly recently believed to have written, in the course of an anonymous appreciation of his novels in the *Quarterly Review*: 'The characters of Shakespeare are not more exclusively human, not more perfectly men and women as they live and move, than those of this mysterious author.' Fortunately for Scott's reputation for good sense, it is now known that, though partly for a joke he wrote this review for the *Quarterly*, the extravagant eulogies were added to the article by the editor.

To say that Scott is not a prose Shakespeare, however, is not to dispraise him. Hazlitt wrote a wise essay pointing out the absurdity of comparing Scott with Shakespeare; yet he was one of Scott's most enthusiastic admirers. He began a review of *The Pirate* with the sentence: 'This is not the best nor is it the worst (the worst is good enough for us) of the Scotch novels' —a sentence which shows that at least he never found Scott unreadable. And later in the review came the paragraph:

Whatever he touches we see the hand of a master. He has only to describe action, thought, scene and they everywhere speak, breathe, and live. It matters not whether it be a calm seashore, a mountain tempest, a drunken brawl, the 'Cathedral's choir in gloom,' the Sybil's watch-tower, or the smugglers' cave; these things are immediately those that we should see, hear, and feel. He is Nature's secretary. He neither adds to nor takes away from her book; and that makes him what he is, the most popular writer living.

It is proof of Scott's power of enchantment that he could wring such praise even from a Radical like Hazlitt, who not only was prejudiced against his toryism but had heard his character spoken of with contempt. Whatever Scott may have been like as a man, however, Hazlitt insisted that as an author he could not but be admired for 'the magnanimity and freedom from bigotry and prejudice shown in the drawing of the characters in his books.'

In that 'magnanimity,' I think, we have one of the secrets

of the spell that Scott has cast for more than a century on a multitude of readers. In ordinary life it is a common experience to be equally charmed by good stories and by the story-teller who narrates them. We have often, it seems to me, a similar experience in reading books. To read Scott with pleasure is to feel that one is in the best of company—the company of a good-natured, high-spirited man, chivalrous, humorous, in love with life, with goodness, and with courage, steeped in the lore of the past, and yet with an ever eager interest in the world about him, and magnanimous not least in his desire to entertain his fellow mortals. He is the ideal host in his books as he was at Abbotsford.

Some readers may reply to this: 'What you say may be true, but the fact remains that he is long-winded and therefore a bore.' I confess that I did not find him so in reading him again. I remember skipping a good deal when I read him in my boyhood; but now I was seldom tempted to skip even a paragraph. There is much less superfluous descriptive stuff than is generally believed; and the chief examples of his long-windedness occur, it seems to me, not in his landscapes but in some of his dialogue, as when Jeanie Deans's father talks theology or some other character takes to jabbering law. The frequent Scottish dialect, no doubt, slows down the narrative for many southern readers; but one might as well find fault with the medieval English of Chaucer.

If Scott is less read now than fifty years ago, this is due, in my opinion, not to faults and weaknesses in his work, but to a change of fashion. The historical novel that he invented—at least he was the first man of genius to write a historical novel—had a huge progeny in the nineteenth century, and it was probably developed as far as it could be along its original romantic lines. From Dumas and Victor Hugo down to Stevenson, Weyman, and Conan Doyle, many memorable writers had made it a vehicle of entertainment. But the entertainment of one age often spells boredom for the next; and many people nowadays find a more 'realistic' kind of historical novel or even books which are a mixture of history, biography, and fiction more readable then Sir Walter Scott.

Let us then agree that it is foolish to put Scott in a class with Shakespeare and that he could not have created a Hamlet or a

Macbeth; but let us at the same time not damn him on this account. If this were ground for damnation we should be compelled to damn a good many famous authors from Homer down to Anthony Trollope. There is a considerable gulf between being un-Shakespearian and being unreadable. I myself find Scott so readable that I went on with *Old Mortality* in bed the other night till my eyes ached and, when I woke in the morning, I was strongly tempted to resume where I had left off instead of reading the daily papers. That seldom happens to me in reading a novel nowadays—to me who am a glutton for newspapers.

In *Old Mortality* Scott breathes the breath of life into a dead world—the world of the underground movement of the Scottish Covenanters—and keeps the reader keyed up with apprehension about the fate of his characters. Here and there the dialogue of the lovers may strike the modern reader as a little stilted; but it should be remembered that conversation was not so unbookish in the second half of the seventeenth century as it is to-day. Here and there a sentence is loosely worded; but, though Scott had a faulty style, it was an exceptionally good style for narrative, humorous, and descriptive purposes. His heroes and heroines had not that uniqueness of personality that the great heroes and heroines of drama and fiction have—he himself said of the hero of *Waverley*: 'The hero is a sneaking piece of imbecility, and if he had married Flora she would have set him upon the chimney-piece, as Count Borolawsky's wife used to do with him'—but his heroes for all that may be more like the heroes of real life than the D'Artagnans and the Alan Brecks, and their adventures stir us as deeply, if not more so. I remember one of the great writers of our own time once saying to me unexpectedly: 'The only novels I read are Scott's. The psychology is so much better than in modern novels.'[1]

And there is nothing of the cardboard and limelight in the scene-painting in these novels of action. The storming of the Tolbooth in *The Heart of Midlothian* is as real to us as we read as though we were present at it. How memorable is one scene after another in the novels—the tournament in *Ivanhoe*, the adventures of Jeanie Deans with the robbers and the insane

[1] This was said to Robert Lynd by Bernard Shaw when we were in Adelphi Terrace for luncheon with him one day after the First World War.—S. L.

Madge Wildfire on her way to London, the rescue of the drowning buccaneer in *The Pirate*! Add to this the skill with which Scott makes the atmosphere tense by the introduction of characters about whom hangs a mystery, from the Disinherited Knight to Norma of the Fitful Head, and you will realize what a variety of ingredients go to make the Waverley Novels readable.

If the young English reader who does not know Scott shrinks from the dialect in the Scottish novels, let him begin with *Quentin Durward* and *Ivanhoe*, and see whether it is the fault of Scott or of some of his critics that he is often pronounced dull. Dull? I am longing to read *Redgauntlet* again. And *The Antiquary*. And *The Bride of Lammermoor*. There are greater novels, no doubt, of a different kind; but I do not know of any better or more readable novels of the same kind.

The Fame of Blake

(1947)

CRABB ROBINSON tells us that Wordsworth said to him one day after reading some of Blake's *Songs of Innocence and Experience*: 'There is no doubt this poor man was mad, but there is something in the madness of the man which interests me more than the sanity of Lord Byron or Walter Scott.' Blake has always been highly appreciated by his fellow poets— by Coleridge, Southey, Lamb, Landor, and Swinburne among them; and in more recent years W. B. Yeats acclaimed him, not only as a great lyric poet, but as a great mystic who 'stands among the mystics of Europe beside Jacob Boehme and the makers of the Kabala, as original as they are and as profound.' 'He is,' Yeats went on, 'one of those great artificers of God who uttered great truths to a little clan.'

Between the wars Mr. Geoffrey Keynes's masterly edition of the *Writings of William Blake* and Miss Mona Wilson's *Life of William Blake*, published in noble form by the Nonesuch Press, were evidences of the intense devotion of members of the little clan—a growing clan by then—to the genius of the master, and to-day the devotees probably rank Blake higher both as poet and as artist than he has ever been ranked before.

As regards his poetry, we find Professor Saurat writing of him: 'In fact, he is the greatest of English poets after, say, Chaucer, Spenser, Shakespeare, and Milton.' It is a judgment that amazes me and with which I must disagree, but it is significant of the growth of Blake's reputation in modern times.

Those who love Blake may be divided into two categories— those who are content to enjoy his lyrics and are hopelessly out of their depth in his longer poems, and those who find even more beauty and wisdom in his prophetic writings than in his lyrics. Professor Saurat belongs to the second group. 'I hope,' he says of his anthology, 'that the perusal of this book will induce some to believe that Blake achieved his highest in some passages of the long epics and that the short poems are only his exercises before reaching his full strength.' He is not a Blakian, however, who regards the master as being verbally inspired. 'A very great poet,' he writes, 'but, so often, a very bad poet. A child—and a nuisance. And he raved and he ranted—and he told lies.'

Taking this view of Blake, he has made in his book 'an attempt to choose those passages in which he wins through and to isolate them from the deleterious rubbish. The test,' he adds, 'is literary. There is none other.' I wonder, however, whether in his appreciation of Blake, Professor Saurat has not been influenced by the fact that Blake's philosophy is in tune with some popular theories of modern times as much as by literary considerations. He himself insists that the lyric,

> I laid me down upon a bank where love lay sleeping,

'contains the seed of all our twentieth-century psycho-analysis,' and notes that Blake's 'imaginings of the compulsion to be chaste producing thorns and thistles is . . . in keeping with our own feeling that all repression is evil and that sins of omission are much more deadly than sins of commission.'

I am sure Blake is especially valued to-day by many people for his teaching on the subject of repression. Like many great and good men, he did not believe in a morality that consists chiefly in not doing this and that. He denied that the good life could be achieved by mere unimaginative obedience to a series of 'Thou shalt nots,' and glorified the energy of Satan himself above the negative sanctity of the Pharisees. He seems to have been blind to the fact that chastity, as with the saints or even with people who are less than saints, can, like the other virtues, be a positive and not a negative virtue; and it would be easy to extract from his writings a philosophy of free love. On the other hand, he could become a moralist of the moralists, as when he wrote:

> The whore and gambler, by the State
> Licensed, build the nation's fate.
> The harlot's cry from street to street
> Shall weave Old England's winding sheet.

If he believed in the theory of free love, he seems never to have put it into practice as Shelley did. It is said that at one time he proposed to bring a concubine into his home, but that his wife wept at the prospect and that was the end of it. There has never, indeed, been a more faithful husband in the history of genius.

Nor was he an enemy of morality, except in the sense that he believed that morality was not enough, and that he rated spiritual higher than merely moral values. His philosophy on the subject has been summarized by W. B. Yeats like this:

Sin awakens imagination because it is from emotion, and is therefore dearer to God than reason which is wholly dead. Sin, however, must be avoided, because we are prisoners and should keep the rules of our prison house. For 'you cannot have liberty in the world without what you call moral virtue and you cannot have moral virtue without the subjection of that half of the human race who hate what you call moral virtue.'

But let us recognize that these laws are but 'the laws of prudence,' and do not let us make them 'the laws of God,' for nothing is pleasing to God except the glad invention of beautiful and exalted things. He holds it better indeed for us to break all the Commandments than to sink into a dead compliance. Better any form of imaginative evil— any lust or any hate—rather than an unimaginative virtue, for 'the human imagination alone' is 'a divine vision of fruition' 'in which man liveth eternally.'

This is good doctrine to address to the 'unco-guid' but dangerous teaching for those who do not share Blake's spiritual faith or view.

Some of Blake's affirmations in his famous *Proverbs of Hell* —and Blake, it should be remembered, did not mean by hell what you and I mean—contained teaching that is equally dangerous for the unwary. Take, for example: 'The road of excess leads to the Palace of Wisdom.' This may contain a germ of truth, but how untrue it is of life in general! The road of excess branches into many paths, some of which may lead to the Palace of Wisdom, but others obviously lead to the hospital, the jail, the home for dipsomaniacs, or an early grave. Again, it is true only in some cases that 'he who desires and acts not breeds pestilence.' To say so is, if we use words in their ordinary sense, to say that the man or woman who resists a strong temptation to steal or to give way to ill temper is doing his soul an injury. Blake's proverbs, however, like the oracles of old, need to be interpreted before we can find such truth as they contain. The meaning of the last proverb I have quoted, for example, becomes clearer when it is read in the light of the further saying, 'Sooner murder an infant in its cradle than nurse unacted desires.' Here 'nurse' is the significant word. Even so, the sentence, if interpreted literally, is obvious nonsense. It is simply an imaginative expression of revolt against negative morality, like so much in Blake's writings.

Blake's teaching, indeed, is in great measure only for those who can breathe the air of the mystical and spiritual heights where he was at home. Blake declares:

> I am more famed in Heaven for my works than I could well believe. In my brain are studies and chambers fitted with pictures which I wrote and painted in ages of eternity before my mortal life; and those works are the delight and study of Archangels.

And it must be confessed that he spoke a language at times more likely to be intelligible to archangels than to common mortals.

That is why most of us turn oftenest, not to the prophetic books, but to the lyrics in *Songs of Innocence*, written with a pen dipped in sunshine, or to those in the contradictory *Songs of Experience*, written in the knowledge of the miseries of man. No poet before Blake, so far as I know, ever wrote a series of beautiful poems and afterwards wrote another series of equally beautiful poems answering them, as it were. In his two series, 'Infant Joy' in the first is balanced by 'Infant Sorrow' in the second, a happy 'Holy Thursday' has as its complement the 'Holy Thursday' that begins:

> Is this a holy thing to see
>   In a rich and fruitful land,
> Babes reduced to misery,
>   Fed with cold and usurous hand?

Similarly, there are two versions of 'The Chimney Sweeper,' two of 'The Nurse's Song,' two of 'The Little Boy Lost,' and 'The Lamb' gives place to 'The Tiger.'

It is, I fancy, in the *Songs of Joy* that the common reader finds the Blake he most loves—in poems like 'Night,' which begins:

> The sun descending in the west,
> The evening star does shine;
> The birds are silent in their nest,
> And I must seek for mine.
> The moon, like a flower
> In heaven's high bower,
> With silent delight,
> Sits and smiles on the night;

and which ends with the vision of the lion and the lamb at peace:

> And there the lion's ruddy eyes
> Shall flow with tears of gold:
> And pitying the tender cries,
> And walking round the fold:
> Saying: 'Wrath by His meekness,
> And, by His health, sickness,
> Are driven away
> From our immortal day.
>
> 'And now beside thee, bleating lamb,
> I can lie down and sleep,
> Or think on Him who bore thy name
> Graze after thee, and weep.
> For, washed in life's river,
> My bright mane for ever
> Shall shine like the gold,
> As I guard o'er the fold.'

That was a new voice and a new music in English literature. It is for the sake of such loveliness, I fancy, that the longer poems of Blake have been kept alive. It is for their sake that many readers—and wisely—will read Professor Saurat's anthology, to see whether the genius of Blake in his prophecies seems to them even more resplendent than in those simpler songs of the Golden Age.

Henry Fielding

(1947)

WHEN I was a boy in Belfast and frequented the Linen Hall Library, the reader himself picked from the shelves the books he wished to take away with him. There was one locked book-case, however, containing books from which the borrower had to make an application to the librarian—books of doubtful morality, presumably, not to be left lying about with a possibility of their getting into the 'wrong hands'—and there, imprisoned behind wire netting, were handsome editions of the novels of Richardson and Fielding.

Tom Jones may seem a harmless and even a healthy book to-day, when standards both of conduct and of speech have altered; but the Victorian elders felt more responsible for the morals of the young than their modern successors do, and many of them no doubt were uneasy lest so attractive a young scapegrace as Tom should mislead their sons by his example. J. M. Dent once told me that he had had qualms about admitting the book into Everyman's Library, and how it was only after he had consulted the scholarly congregationalist divine, Dr. R. F. Horton, on the matter and obtained his approval that he decided to do so.

There is no need to be censorious of the Victorians and their dread of the influence of doubtful books on the young. Fielding himself would to some extent have agreed with them. In one of his best essays in *The Covent Garden Journal* he recommends to his readers 'a total abstinence from all bad books,' and adds:

> I do therefore most earnestly entreat all my young readers that they would cautiously avoid the perusal of any modern book till it has first had the sanction of some wise and learned man; and the same caution I propose to all fathers, mothers, and guardians. 'Evil communications corrupt good manners' is a quotation of St. Paul from Menander. *Evil books corrupt at once both our manners and our taste.* (The italics are Fielding's.)

And Fielding, in speaking of 'bad books,' was not referring merely to the scribblers of his own time. He included two acknowledged authors of genius in his condemnation. After praising Shakespeare and Molière for the use they made of their talents, he went on:

There are some, however, who, though not void of these talents, have made so wretched a use of them that, had the consecration of their labours been committed to the hands of the hangman, no good man would have regretted their loss; nor am I afraid to mention Rabelais and Aristophanes himself in this connection. For, if I may speak my opinions freely of these two last writers and of their works, their design appears to me very plainly to have been to ridicule all sobriety, modesty, decency, virtue, and religion of the world.

Even when we have agreed that books may have an influence either for good or for evil, however, it is not easy to agree which are the good and which the bad books. A book that merely inflames the bodily passions of one reader may inflame the heart of another reader with charity. There is such a thing as a bad reader as well as a bad book.

If we judge literature from a moral point of view—as Fielding himself did—all that we can reasonably ask of a book is that it shall enlarge the sympathy of the ordinary reader, give him a healthy view of life, or fortify his spirit. Dr. Johnson would not apparently have admitted that *Tom Jones* passed any of these tests. Boswell tells us that he quoted with approval a saying of Richardson's that 'the virtues of Fielding's heroes were the vices of a really good man,' surely a foolish and even meaningless judgment. Boswell himself seems to me to have gone to the heart of the matter with much greater wisdom. 'I will venture to add,' he wrote,

that the moral tendency of Fielding's writing, though it does not encourage a strained and rarely possible virtue, is ever favourable to honour and honesty, and cherishes the benevolent and generous affections. He who is as good as Fielding would make him is an amiable member of society and may be led on by more regular instructors to a higher degree of ethical perfection.

Buoyant with vitality, he was evidently a man who made others feel that it was a good thing to be alive in the same world with him. Lady Mary Wortley Montagu in one of her letters gives us a vivid impression of him as a practitioner of the virtue of enjoyment. 'His happy constitution,' she says, (even when he had with great pains half demolished it), made him forget everything when he was before a venison pasty or even a flask of champagne, and I am persuaded he has known more happy moments than any prince upon the earth. His natural spirits gave him rapture in his cook-maid, and cheerfulness when he was fluxing. There was a great similitude between his character and that of Sir Richard Steele. He had the advantage both in learning, and, in my opinion, in genius; they both agreed in wanting money in spite of all their friends, and must have wanted it if their hereditary lands had been as extensive as their imaginations; yet each of them was so formed for happiness it is a pity he was not immortal.

In spite of the charm of his character and its exuberant vitality, however, Fielding has left no legend behind him as Pope and Swift, Johnson and Goldsmith and many others of the great writers of the century have done. Living in an age of gossip, he is the theme of few anecdotes, and his conversation, good as it must have been, had no Boswell to record it. Yet he did not live in obscurity. He was at Eton with the great Chatham and remained intimate enough with him to consult him as to the advisability of publishing *Tom Jones*. He lived for years in the blazing light of the theatrical world. He won immediate fame as a novelist. He was a famous figure in the small London dominated by Dr. Johnson. He was the friend of Hogarth and Garrick. He ended his life as the most humane, efficient, and progressive magistrate in London. All this we know, but we do not know Fielding the man in the details of his daily life and conversation as his contemporaries knew him.

At the age of eighteen Henry made a romantic beginning in an attempt to abduct a fifteen-year-old heiress at Lyme Regis; but there was little romance in the long story that follows of his career as a hack-writer for the stage. The most interesting thing we know about Fielding's career as a dramatist is that his attacks on Sir Robert Walpole were the direct cause of a censorship of plays and—whether a censorship is a good thing or a bad one—what a benefit it turned out to be to English literature! It drove Fielding out of the theatre, where he was only a man of talent, and impelled him to seek a new literary outlet in fiction in which he proved to be a man of genius.

Journalism and study for the Bar occupied him for some years before the publication of Richardson's *Pamela or Virtue Rewarded* in 1740 tickled him by its solemnity and prudential morality into attempting a burlesque of it. In Richardson's novel a housemaid, pursued by her unprincipled master, shows that honesty is the best policy and ends by marrying him. In *Joseph Andrews* Fielding gives Pamela an equally chaste 'brother,' a footman, on whom his employer, Lady Booby, has designs. Having begun the story as a burlesque, however, he gives his invention rein and ends by writing the first comic novel in English with the quixotic Parson Adams as a character that was to become immortal.

There are certainly, by Victorian standards, coarse touches in *Joseph Andrews*, but there is no laughing at the expense of genuine goodness. As in *Don Quixote*, we laugh at the ills that befall the virtuous, but that does not lessen our affection for them. It is the mean, false, and hypocritical characters who are held up not only to ridicule but to contempt. And what an easy and quick flow of narrative was Fielding's! How pleasant and refreshing the current of his prose! I have been dipping into *Joseph Andrews* again, and its humour and humanity seem to me to be as likely to captivate the right sort of reader to-day as two hundred years ago.

That Fielding outraged some of the standards of his own time as well as the Victorians is clear from the history of the reception of *Tom Jones*. In 1752, a year after it was published, when two earthquakes occurred in England, they were regarded by the strict as Heaven's condemnation of *Tom Jones* and similar lewd publications, and it was pointed out that Paris, where (it was said) the book had been refused publication, was not affected by the earthquakes. Richardson naturally regarded it as 'a dissolute book,' and some years afterwards Johnson was still censorious enough to dismiss Fielding as 'a blockhead,' explaining: 'What I mean by his being a blockhead is that he was a barren rascal,' and suggesting that Fielding took 'an ostler's low view of life.' I sometimes wonder whether, if Johnson had met Fielding, he might not have been charmed by him as he was by Wilkes, or even been converted to Gibbon's opinion that the romance of *Tom Jones*, that exquisite picture of human manners, 'will outlive the palace of the Escorial and the Imperial Eagle of the House of Austria.' Still, the whitewashing of *Tom Jones* has perhaps been overdone by its defenders, and there is one incident with Molly Seagrim which not only a novelist but a man of ordinary feeling for the decencies of ordinary life would think pretty low.

On the other hand, only a man of a twisted mind could regard Fielding as a corrupter of human nature. Expecting little sanctity from it, he was nevertheless a preacher of the more pedestrian and attainable virtues, and both as a writer and as a magistrate was a model of honesty. Refusing to enrich himself with the normal though not quite honest perquisites of office, he inaugurated a campaign against crime that had lasting effects on London life. Whether overwork or over-indulgence played the chief part in his early death at the age of forty-seven it is hard to say, but we know from his *Voyage to Lisbon*, written on his last journey in search of health, that even in his last moments he maintained his gallantry of spirit.

The *Voyage* contains one paragraph which seems to me a perfect revelation of the smiling truthfulness of the man. Fielding tells how he had a quarrel with the captain, who was a bully, and how by threatening him with the law he reduced the man to begging for mercy. 'I immediately forgave him,' he writes,

and here, that I may not be thought the silly trumpeter of my own praises, I do utterly disclaim all praise of the occasion. Neither did the greatness of my mind dictate, nor the grace of my Christianity exact this forgiveness. To speak truth I forgave him from a motive which would make men much more forgiving if they were much wiser than they are, because it was convenient for me to do so.

Who could help loving a man so unpretentious, so good-humouredly candid, so worldly-wise and at the same time so wise?

Oliver Goldsmith

(1928)

'To be the most beloved of English writers, what a title
that is for a man!' So wrote Thackeray of Oliver Goldsmith
nearly a century ago. I doubt if it could be truly said of
Goldsmith to-day. I fancy that Charles Lamb and Dickens, in
their different fashions, have now a stronger hold on the affections of English readers. At the same time it is impossible to
imagine that a time will ever come when Goldsmith will cease
to be loved.

He is the Ugly Duckling of literary history. He was in
person so ugly—partly as a result of an attack of smallpox in
his childhood—that two ladies once shook hands warmly over
his being the ugliest man they knew, and he was as unfortunate
as he was ugly. He lived for the most part in poverty and he
died in debt. 'Was ever poet so trusted before?' wrote Johnson
to Boswell, announcing that Goldsmith had left £2,000 worth
of debts behind him. Not even prosperity and fame could
rescue Goldsmith from misfortune.

It may be that the miseries of his childhood and youth have
been exaggerated. Born on 10th November 1728, the son of
a poor Irish parson with a large family, he was remembered by
his contemporaries mainly as 'a stupid heavy blockhead, little
better than a fool, whom every one made fun of.' I suspect,
however, that it was the blockheads among his schoolfellows
who regarded him as a blockhead. He must have shown some
signs of capacity since his Uncle Contarine rescued him from
apprenticeship to a trade and helped him to continue his
education at Trinity College, Dublin.

If he was miserable at college, that was partly owing to the
fact that, being a youth of ultra-sensitive temper, he hated the
menial offices imposed on him by the sizarship he had won, and
that, poor as he was, he was thriftless even with the few shillings
that came his way. We hear of his writing street ballads for
five shillings each as a means of saving himself from starvation,
and of his slipping out at night to hear them sung; and it is said

that, after earning his five shillings, he was as likely as not to give it away to a beggar. As an example of the reckless charity that has endeared him so much to readers of his biography, we are told that on one occasion he gave away the blankets off his bed to a starving woman with children.

He came still nearer starvation when he ran away from college, and set out from Dublin for Cork with a shilling in his pocket. He had won an exhibition and given a dance in his rooms to celebrate it; and a rough-natured tutor, hearing of the orgy, had come in and angrily knocked him down. Persuaded to return to college, he showed enough capacity to take a degree, but, when he had taken it, he was at a loss what to do with himself. He refused to enter the Church because, it is said, he loved coloured clothes. After a short experience of teaching he was given £50 by his uncle to go to London and study for the Bar, but, being a born gambler, he lost the money at play before he could catch the boat at Dublin, and had to return to his brother's house.

Life offered few bright prospects to a young man of twenty-four who did not seem particularly anxious to do anything and whose chief assets were the ability to play the flute and a 'knack of hoping.' A chance remark and another present of money from his uncle sent him to Edinburgh to study medicine; and, after studying there and at London, he set out on his travels through Europe, often paying for a night's lodging with an air or two on his flute, and leaving a small trail of debt behind him in one country after another. He was a man of twenty-eight when he arrived utterly friendless in London.

In London he drifted, rather than fought his way, into literature. The schoolmaster, in whose school at Peckham he was an usher, was a friend of Griffiths, the bookseller, and Griffiths, being struck by something that Goldsmith had said, one day took him aside and invited him to let him have 'a few specimens of criticism' with a view to writing for the *Monthly Review*. It was in this way that Goldsmith began his career as a hack-writer. He was a man of thirty, still threatened with starvation, when he wrote to a friend from the Temple coffee-house: 'Oh, Gods! Gods! here in a garret, writing for bread, and expecting to be dunned for a milk-score!'

It was in the following year that he began his career as an

essayist.   Wilkie, the bookseller, wished to publish a periodical on the lines of Johnson's *Rambler*, and Goldsmith was invited to write the necessary essays and criticisms.   *The Bee*, as the paper was called, did not last beyond eight numbers.   Already in the fourth number we find Goldsmith smiling wryly at his unsuccess. 'While the works of others,' he wrote, 'fly like unpinioned swans, I find my own move as heavily as an unplucked goose.' 'I am,' he added, in a tone of mock indignation at the indifference of the learned world, 'resolved to write on, if it were only to spite them.   If the present generation will not hear my voice, harken O posterity, to you I call, and from you I expect redress.' I doubt if a single reader of *The Bee* read this at the time as any-thing but a joke.   Possibly Goldsmith wrote half in jest and half in trembling earnest.   He had the 'knack of hoping.'

In a sense Goldsmith was a born essayist, and yet he seldom wrote the essays he seemed born to write.   Candid, humorous, a man with an eye on his own follies, one who had experience of all companies of men from scholars to beggars, a smatterer with a thousand interests, a moralist, he ought, we feel, to have written essays second only to the *Essays of Elia*.   Unfortunately, he was too seldom personal in his essays.   Too often, no doubt, he wrote as a hack-writer intent mainly on providing the printer with 'copy.'   And yet, both in *The Bee* and in his later essays, how charming the prose becomes under the influence of his sweet and charitable humour!

There are few better essays in English than *The Distresses of a Common Soldier*, which describes the cheerfulness of an old beggar with a wooden leg, who explains how lucky he has for the most part been, and who is full of patriotic fervour over the country that has left him to starve.   The essay at its greatest is often a kind of fiction; and we see in this essay the hand of one who was to bequeath an immortal short novel to English literature.

Excellent, too, is *Adventures of a Strolling Player*, which is, in effect, a short story, and the *Beau Tibbs* essays, describing the vanities of dress and conversation of an impoverished beau, are perhaps the most popular that Goldsmith ever wrote.

It is amusing, if not surprising, to find Goldsmith, the natural Bohemian, exalting in some of his essays the virtue of frugality and denouncing ale-houses.   'Ale-houses,' he writes with pro-hibitionist ardour, 'are ever an occasion of debauchery and excess, and, either in a religious or political light, it should be our highest interest to have the greatest part of them suppressed.'

It is only fair to say that, while Goldsmith in attacking the love of pleasure and wastefulness was like Satan rebuking sin, there was no inconsistency in his attack on the ale-houses. If Johnson found him drinking a bottle of Madeira on the day on which, having heard he had been arrested for debt, he hurried to his assistance and rescued him by taking *The Vicar of Wakefield* to the bookseller, this does not mean that Goldsmith was much given to drinking.

His life was still haphazard enough, however, when, at the age of thirty-six, with only ten years more to live, he was received as a member into Dr. Johnson's Club, though Hawkins declares that he was generally regarded as 'a mere literary drudge.' He had as yet written neither *The Traveller* nor *The Deserted Village*, neither *The Vicar of Wakefield* nor *She Stoops to Conquer*, yet Johnson was already convinced, as he told Boswell, that Goldsmith was 'one of the first men we now have as authors.'

This is surely evidence that Goldsmith, the penurious hack-writer, the slovenly beau, the awkward and ugly foreigner, strutting with his vanity, impressed his contemporaries with his genius by his personality and conversation even more than by his writings. I find it difficult to believe that Goldsmith was such a man in society as Garrick painted him—writing like an angel and talking like poor Poll. Some of the wittiest things in Boswell are said by Goldsmith, and the legend of his idiocy in conversation will not bear an hour's examination. He charmed nearly everybody he met as he charms us to-day—charmed the greatest of his contemporaries as he charmed the poor street children who danced to his flute. Easy-going and hard-working, a drudge and a man of genius, he won friends as triumphantly as Dr. Johnson himself.

He died at the age of forty-six, still struggling to earn as a hack-writer enough money to pay the debts that grew faster than his income. 'Is your mind at ease?' the doctor asked him as he lay dying. 'No, it is not,' replied Goldsmith, and these are the last words he is known to have spoken. It is one of the most melancholy death-bed utterances on record—all the more melancholy because it came from the lips of a man who was to afford enchantment and delight to the world for ever.

William Butler Yeats

(*1939*)

W. B. YEATS, before he died, had become one of the
most famous of poets, some of whose work at least was known
to every schoolboy and schoolgirl. Yet, until he was middle-
aged, he received only the most grudging reward from the world
to which he gave so ungrudgingly of his art. 'Until I was near
fifty,' he once said, 'my writing never brought me more than
two hundred a year, and most often less.' Such was his comparative poverty, indeed, that in 1910, when he was forty-five
years old, he was compelled to accept a Civil List pension
of £150.

He was a pure artist, above most of his literary contemporaries.
And he was not only a great artist himself but a great missionary
of art, devoting himself to the founding of a literary and dramatic
movement that was to make his country honoured among the
nations. Most people, looking at him in his early life, with his
long black hair, his loose tie, and his pale hands, would have
thought that here was an unpractical dreamer unfit for the
business of organization. But Yeats possessed boundless spiritual
energy and enthusiasm and was at the same time as hard-headed
as any business man in committee work. He once said: 'I
would rather see a young writer a drunkard than serving on a
committee'; but he was thinking at the time of young writers
who join political societies. He himself created through
committees no less effectively than as a poet.

I have dwelt on this side of Yeats's character because he was
one of the few men of the first genius who have set out deliberately
to create a national literature. And, if the Irish literary
revival is one of the most famous events of our time, it is to
the passion and propaganda of W. B. Yeats that most of the
praise must be given. From a superficial glance at his earlier
poems, one might have thought that he was one of the unlikeliest

of men to create a new and distinctive Irish literature. There were Pre-Raphaelite influences in his work which, one would have said, reflected the taste of sophisticated London rather than of the Irish people, and the 'pale brows, still hands, and dim hair' that appear in his verse suggested an imagination grown weary rather than rejuvenescent. Yeats, however, drew imaginative vigour from the face of the Irish countryside, from Irish legends and the stories handed down in the houses of the poor, and—it should never be forgotten—from Irish politics. Had it not been for his friendship with the old Fenian, John O'Leary, and his interest in revolutionary politics, Yeats might well have been a poet of smaller stature than he ultimately became.

He himself rebelled repeatedly against this absorption in politics. There was a time when he maintained that for an artist politics are impure, and when some of his old associates thought of him as a renegade. In one of his poems he speaks bitterly of the patriotism on which he had spent so much of his life:

> All things can tempt me from this craft of verse:
> One time it was a woman's face, or worse—
> The seeming needs of my fool-driven land;
> Now nothing but comes readier to the hand
> Than this accustomed toil. When I was young
> I had not given a penny for a song
> Did not the poet sing it with such airs
> That one believed he had a sword upstairs;
> Yet would be now, could I but have my wish,
> Colder and dumber and deafer than a fish.

It was probably the divided, tumultuous nature expressed in these lines that converted Yeats from a minor into a major poet, and, indeed, there are traces of the minor poet in his early work that only fiery passion could have burnt away. If he had lived in an atmosphere free from political turmoil, he might easily have made an aesthetic cult of Beauty with a capital B; and for the making of great poetry Beauty with a capital B is not enough.

If you compare a fairly early poem of Yeats's, 'He Gives his Beloved Certain Rhymes,' with 'No Second Troy,' a poem written later, you will see how he succeeded in ridding his work of its aesthetic embroideries. The first poem runs:

Fasten your hair with a golden pin,
And bind up every wandering tress;
I bade my heart build these poor rhymes:
It worked at them, day out, day in,
Building a sorrowful loveliness
Out of the battles of old times.

You need but lift a pearl-pale hand,
And bind up your long hair and sigh;
And all men's hearts must burn and beat;
And candle-like foam on the dim sand,
And stars climbing the dew-dropping sky,
Live but to light your passing feet.

The second—containing once more a protest against political passion—runs:

Why should I blame her that she filled my days
With misery, or that she would of late
Have taught to ignorant men most violent ways,
Or hurled the little streets upon the great,
Had they but courage equal to desire?
What could have made her peaceful with a mind
That nobleness made simple as a fire,
With beauty like a tightened bow, a kind
That is not natural in an age like this,
Being high and solitary and most stern?
Why, what could she have done being what she is?
Was there another Troy for her to burn?

There is a vast difference, it will be seen, between the styles in which these poems are written. In the first, we have the beautiful rhetoric of a young aesthete of the nineties; in the second, decoration is no longer sought after for its own sake, and the passion expresses itself in more natural images. Some people would say there has been a gain in sincerity, but Yeats's early work, too, was sincere. Its fault was rather that it was at times too deliberately beauteous.

In whatever manner he wrote, however, Yeats was always a stylist. He once spoke of 'the fascination of what's difficult,' and the very difficulty he met with in putting his thoughts and visions into verse seems to have compelled him to take especial pains in the search for perfect speech. He says somewhere that he found writing blank verse too easy—almost as easy as writing prose—and that he needed difficulty to stir the fire in his imagination.

He was not a natural singer: he could never have said of himself: 'I sing but as the linnets sing.' He says of his early attempts at poetry: 'My lines but seldom scanned, for I could not understand the prosody in the books, although there were many lines that taken by themselves had music.' In later life he said that he could now write more easily—six or seven lines of poetry a day instead of the six or seven lines a week that were his usual output when he was young.

All this may seem to suggest a lack of spontaneity in his genius; but I should prefer to put the matter in this way—that his genius was spontaneous in its activity but that a genius so original had to create laboriously a new and fitting instrument for its expression.

As a man, Yeats—especially in his younger days—looked the part of the poet he was. George Moore has described him sitting in the dress circle of the present Playhouse, 'a long black cloak drooping from his shoulders, a soft black sombrero on his head, a voluminous black silk tie flowing from his collar, long black trousers dragging untidily over his long, heavy feet,' and he admits that he conceived such an antipathy to Yeats that he refused to be introduced. Yeats, however, thought of the artist as a man apart—one who was as separate from the common herd as the member of a priesthood—and he dressed accordingly. No student in the Latin Quarter was ever more scornful of the respectable bourgeois world whose very morality he despised.

He sometimes spoke of morality almost as though it were a form of bourgeois cowardice and an enemy of the soul, and his heresy led him into such extravagances of opinion as we find in his comment on the self-absorption of Synge. 'I have often,' he wrote, 'envied him his absorption as I have envied Verlaine his vice. Can a man of genius make that complete renunciation of the world necessary to the full expression of himself without some vice or some deficiency?' It is interesting to contrast this attitude of mind with that which he records of an earlier stage in his life when he wanted to go and live in a cabin on Innisfree. 'I thought,' he writes, 'that, having conquered bodily desire and the inclination of my mind towards women and love, I should live, as Thoreau lived, seeking wisdom.'

Luckily, or unluckily, it was not in Yeats's destiny to become a solitary. He was a man of action, a fighter, and even the theatre he did most to build became a battleground. His early play, *The Countess Cathleen*, was assailed by the orthodox as heretical, and, later on, with the aid of the police, he was throwing men and boys out of the Abbey Theatre for attempts to create a riot over the production of *The Playboy of the Western World*. I think Yeats looked forward to that uproar. Even before *The Playboy* was produced he was relishing the thought that here was something to provoke those who deserved to be provoked. He was a campaigner for art and out for conquests.

The extent of his conquests is obvious to any one who compares the position of Irish literature in the English tongue as it was before Yeats began to write and its position at the time of his death. Ireland before Yeats scarcely existed on the literary map of the world. Under his leadership it became a house of genius. No writer of our time can boast of a more remarkable achievement than this.

Yeats was a man who compelled fascination rather than affection. He had great and noble qualities: he fought for freedom of the arts with the courage of a tigress defending her cubs and he sacrificed every worldly ambition to his zeal for doing the best work of which he was capable. He more than any other man transformed Ireland from a province into a nation in the sphere of modern literature. He founded a national theatre and made one woman an immortal. And he was a faithful friend.

Yet, with all this, he seemed a little inhuman. One thought of him at times as a priest performing magic rites in a temple and the God in whose honour the temple was built did not appear to be the God of the common man. He dabbled in psychical research and theosophy, and in an earlier century might well have been shuddered at as a heretic. His remoteness from common people was increased by his over-endowment with the gift of scorn. His scorn for the middle classes and their morality surpassed that of any Marxian. His scorn for the modern English and their love of compromise—he liked to think that the typical Englishman of Shakespeare's day had been 'witty, boastful, and profane'—was extreme. 'You know,' he said to

me one evening, 'what the Englishman's idea of compromise is.
He says: "Some people say there is a God.   Some say there is
no God.   The truth probably lies somewhere between these
two statements."'

It is easy to see why a poet of such temper admired Nietzsche
and was drawn towards Fascism: he even went so far as to
compose songs for the Irish Blueshirts.   Yet he was not at his
ease among the extremists of his own country.   For a time he
was a member of the Irish Republican Brotherhood; but, when
some of the members decided that Frank Hugh O'Donnell
should be murdered, he resigned along with Maud Gonne.
More and more he drifted away from politics, realizing that
what most politicians, including the extremists, wanted from
writers was good propaganda rather than great literature.   He
began to hate Arthur Griffith, the founder of the Sinn Fein
movement, even more bitterly than Griffith hated him.

Yet, when the Irish Insurrection of 1916 failed and the leaders
were executed, he was so moved by their courage and self-
sacrifice, though he did not agree with them, that he came
nearer being a popular national poet than he had ever been
before.   After that, however, he seems to have become more
interested in the Anglo-Irish civilization into which he was born
than in the Gaelic civilization that is reflected in his earlier
work.   He glorified Bishop Berkeley and the other great Irish
writers of the eighteenth century as enemies of the Whiggery
and compromise that he hated, and wrote:

> Whether they knew it or not
> Goldsmith and Burke, Swift and the Bishop of Cloyne
> All hated Whiggery; but what is Whiggery?
> A levelling, rancorous, rational sort of mind
> That never looked out of the eye of a saint
> Or out of a drunkard's eye. . . .

It is not here, or in other verse expressive merely of opinions,
it seems to me, that we find the inspired Yeats.   Yeats is to my
mind greatest in the remote solitariness of his art, not in his
life and opinions of which we learn so much in his later verse.
The enchanted lover who speaks in *The Wind Among the Reeds*
enraptures us where Yeats minus his singing robes often puzzles
us.   Consider, for example, his story of how, crossed in love,
he thought of consoling himself with another woman who had

D

been unhappily married. 'I took a fortnight,' he wrote after-wards, 'to decide what I should do. I was poor and it would be a hard struggle if I asked her to come away and perhaps after all I would be adding my tragedy to hers, for she might be returning to the evil life, but after all, if I could not get the woman I loved, it would be a comfort, even but for a little while, to devote myself to another.'

Unlike the poet of the great love-poems, again, is the Yeats who, when he thought another woman was trying to blackmail him into marrying her, wrote verses about her that Dr. Jeffares describes as 'disgusted and disgusting.'

Finally, how strange is the story of his marriage as Dr. Jeffares relates it! Maud Gonne having refused to marry him, he fell in love with her daughter, Iseult.

He was told by Maud that she had no objection to his proposing to Iseult but that the young girl would probably not take him very seriously. In fact, it was Iseult who had made the first proposal to him when she was fifteen and had been refused because there was too much Mars in her horoscope.

In 1917 he visited the Gonnes in France, and brought them back to London. He had meanwhile asked Iseult again and again to marry him.

On the boat Yeats had delivered an ultimatum to Iseult: that she must make up her mind one way or the other, that he found the whole business an immense strain, and that if she would not marry him, he had a friend who would be very suitable, a girl strikingly beautiful in a barbaric manner. He must receive her answer within a week at a certain A.B.C. in London. Iseult refused him, and he married Miss Hyde-Lees on 21st October.

What a picture this conjures up of the author of the most beautiful and passionate love-poetry of our time sitting in a tea-shop, waiting for a girl to decide whom he was to marry! It is as though the man and the poet were two different persons.

There are probably, however, in biographies of most poets details that seem at variance with the splendour of their finest hours. And, after all, it is by the splendour of their finest hours that they must be judged. The Yeats who wrote that great line about the ageing beloved:

Time can but make her beauty over again,

is the Yeats who is secure against mortality. Year after year from his twenties till his later life he had one ever recurrent theme in his verse—that lovely lady to whom he addressed the poem beginning, 'When you are old and grey and full of sleep,' to whom he wrote, 'Had I the Heavens' embroidered cloths,' and whom he celebrated in 'No Second Troy.'

Even his railings contribute to her glory. He judges her, he censures her, but always in the end the fire of adoration revives in such a line as

> Was there another Troy for her to burn?

One of the younger writers, writing of Yeats after his death, said that, if Yeats had died at the age of fifty, he would have been remembered only as a minor poet, and that he had become a great poet only in later life. To me it seems, on the contrary, that Yeats's greatest verse was written before he was fifty. Dr. Jeffares appears to prefer the later verses and the last sentence of his book runs: 'He had made himself a great poet.' Yet though he quotes freely from the later poems he seems to me to quote little that is on a level with the verse of Yeats's early and middle periods. Yeats himself wrote of his latest period:

> You think it horrible that lust and rage
> Should dance attendance upon my old age;
> They were not such a plague when I was young;
> What else have I to spur me into song?

It may be the very harshness of some of the later verse that commends it to the taste of many readers.

Perhaps one of the things that alienates some readers in Yeats's earlier work is his excess of decoration in the Pre-Raphaelite tradition. The people of his dreams lead a decorative existence, and the perfect life seems to express itself in beautiful gestures. It was in his thirties that he wrote:

> The fine life is always a part played finely before fine spectators. . . .
> When the fine spectators have ended, surely the fine players grow weary, and the aristocratic life has ended. When O'Connell covered with a dark glove the hand that had killed a man in the duelling field, he played his part; and when Alexander stayed his army marching to the conquest of the world that he might contemplate the beauty of a plane-tree, he played his part.

That aesthetic attitude to life is no longer fashionable, and, indeed, in a man of smaller genius than Yeats, would have been the mark of a minor poet.   Aestheticism, however, may have provided Yeats with a mask behind which he could express himself more passionately and sincerely than in plainer verse. We must judge by results, and in the result is not Yeats's love-poetry as sincere, as passionate, and as moving as Donne's?

G. B. S. as Idol

(1946)

I AM sure no one would have been more sceptical than
Bernard Shaw himself if, at the beginning of the century, a gipsy
fortune-teller had told him that he would live to be one of the
most popular writers in England. Then and for many years
afterwards he had an unrivalled capacity for infuriating the
ordinary Englishman into searching in his vocabulary for epithets
violent enough to be flung at the most conceited imposter and
mountebank of all time.

The ordinary Englishman, it is true, knew little about him;
but some of the audacious sayings of G. B. S. had begun to
creep into the newspapers, and people found it hard to be patient
with a man who seemed not only to be a Socialist, an atheist,
and an all-round crank, but to take a particular pleasure in
abusing Shakespeare and suggesting that he could write better
himself. One night, I remember, when I was crossing in the
boat from Liverpool to Belfast, I introduced two men to each
other, one of whom foamed at the mouth, as the saying is,
about some remark of Shaw's that had recently been quoted in
the press. 'Do you hate Shaw?' the other asked, his eyes
brightening. 'I loathe and detest him,' replied the first.
'Shake hands,' said the other warmly, and they wrung each
other's hands like men swearing blood-brotherhood.

I myself never shared the common antipathy to Shaw. When
I heard of him first, I was a devoted and, indeed, a devotional
reader of the *Clarion*, in which A. M. Thompson, writing on
the theatre over the pseudonym 'Dangle,' made frequent laudatory references to him; and I was not so badly shocked as I
might otherwise have been when I came on the famous dramatic
criticisms signed 'G. B. S.' in the *Saturday Review*. It was
certainly startling to find a journalist 'giving cheek,' as it were,
to Shakespeare; but this was the most amusing 'cheek' of the
kind I had ever read. One enjoyed it as one would have enjoyed
a sparkling heretical speech by a youth of enormous talent at

a college debating society. In such circumstances it scarcely matters what side the speaker takes or whether he is entirely serious. One is carried away by the brilliance of the performance.

As a regular galleryite in the local theatre, hungering for news of the great plays and players of London, I was, of course, immensely interested in Shaw's criticisms; but I delighted in them chiefly because of the character G. B. S., who appeared in them, as at an earlier age I had delighted in the very different character R. L. S., who appeared in the writing of Stevenson.

When I first came to London in 1901, or whenever it was, it was Shaw, of all the great inhabitants of the place, whom I most wished to see. As a boy I had worshipped Joseph Chamberlain, but now I would have walked miles farther to see Shaw than to see Chamberlain. The first time I saw him, I think, was when he gave a Sunday afternoon lecture on Shakespeare in the smaller St. James's Hall. The subject he discussed was *All's Well That Ends Well*, which most of the audience, I am sure, like myself, had always found one of the least enjoyable of Shakespeare's plays. Shaw, however, proved to his own satisfaction and to the great entertainment of the rest of us, that it was one of Shakespeare's most remarkable achievements, infinitely to be preferred to such potboilers as *Twelfth Night* and *As You Like It*, and that in his heroine of the play Shakespeare had anticipated the New Woman of our own time—an emancipated woman doctor. He also portrayed her as the eternal feminine who, like the later-born Ann Whitfield in *Man and Superman*, pursues her mate without ruth and without rest. The notion that it is the woman who pursues the man, not the man the woman, was then a novelty that, played with by Shaw, kept his audience in a long succession of ripples of laughter.

The next time I saw him, he was speaking in Queen's Hall at a meeting held to protest against Tsarist Russia's barbarous treatment of its revolutionaries. The previous speakers had been ablaze with passion and rhetoric, when Shaw, stepping towards the edge of the platform and standing with one arm akimbo, set out to prove that they had all been denouncing the tsar and his government for the wrong reasons, and suggesting quite a number of different reasons for condemning them. And with such skill did he press his arguments that the same people

BERNARD SHAW

who had been applauding the rhetorical earnestness of the earlier speakers were even more delighted as with characteristic comic seriousness Shaw turned them inside out.

Later came the great Vedrenne-Barker season of matinées at the Court Theatre at which play after play of Shaw's was produced. I was lucky at the time, for I was writing for a paper everybody on the staff of which, except myself, detested the theatre, so that I slipped into the job of dramatic critic. I was still young enough to think and feel in superlatives; and I have never come out of the theatre with more superlatives ringing in my brain than after the first performance of *John Bull's Other Island*. I remember declaring in my criticism of the play that not since Aristophanes had anything to equal it been written for the comic stage. I had not even a nodding acquaintance with most of the plays that had been written for the comic stage since Aristophanes, but that did not matter. I was convinced that Shaw was the greatest of living writers, and that he could hold his own in comparison even with the mighty dead.

It was a few years after this that I first met him. He had come to a week-end party, organized by the Webbs, at the Beacon Hotel at Hindhead, and I, too, was a member of the party. After dinner on Saturday evening, Sylvia came up to me and said: 'Come and be introduced to Bernard Shaw.' As I went into the lounge and approached the tall figure standing by the fireplace, I trembled with excitement—the excitement of joy—as never on any other occasion in my life have I trembled before mortal man. My heart was like a singing-bird; and fortunately Shaw did nearly all the talking, for I doubt whether I could have articulated more than a very short sentence, so great was my ecstasy. Then, when, after a few minutes, he said: 'Do you feel disposed for a walk?' it was as if I had been shot upwards from the sixth heaven into the seventh. As I hurried to get my hat, I remember hoping passionately that he would not, before I returned, have asked someone else to join us. To go for a walk with Bernard Shaw, and to be the only person going for a walk with him—outside the realm of love, what could life offer better than that?

As we walked, I soon found that Shaw wore seven-league boots, and that he could apparently see in the dark. We reached the common, and he took me by invisible ways through the deep night at a pace that I could not have kept up with if my strength had not been made as the strength of ten by walking beside a god. And all the time he talked—delightful natural talk about people, especially the Webbs, and his wife (whom he always spoke of simply as 'Charlotte'), and his plays, and all sorts of things. I use the word 'natural' because no man commonly accused of being a *poseur* ever talked with less affectation than Shaw. He may have claimed in print to be in some aspects superior to Shakespeare, but in conversation he is the least 'superior person' who ever breathed.

The explanation of this is that he is one of the most good-natured men alive. He gives himself generously in his conversation to his listeners, and, though he enjoys charming them, you would never suspect him of setting out deliberately to charm them. His charm is of the essence of his nature. Otherwise how could he have achieved his enormous popularity in spite of the fact that he repeatedly outrages the finer feelings and the deep-seated beliefs even of many of his idolaters?

Some people attribute his readiness to be interviewed by the press on every conceivable subject from 'What do you think of Buddhism?' to 'What is your favourite pudding?' to his love of advertisement, and he certainly began his career with the determination to advertise himself, his beliefs, and his wares. At the same time, the journalist who goes to see him soon becomes aware of the exceptional courtesy and kindness of the man. I remember being sent to interview him at Torquay after the outbreak of war in the summer of 1914. He asked me to go up to his suite in the hydro, where Mrs. Shaw was sitting, and said: 'Why should you bother with this interview? Sit down there and talk to Charlotte, and I'll write something myself.' And while Mrs. Shaw and I talked he sat with a pad on his knee, writing at full speed, and joining in the conversation when he felt inclined, for apparently he can write and listen and talk at the same time. When he had finished he handed me a wonderful article with not a word said about the price to be paid. Next morning we had another seven-league-boot walk along the uneven coast path, in the course of which I gathered that Napoleon had won the battle of Waterloo.

Do I still idolize him? I certainly think that, of all prose-writers whose work I know, he is the most secure of immortality.

I occasionally wobble in regard to this, but when I see one of his plays again, I am astonished to find how fresh it remains, how much less dated than I expected. His opinions on religion and politics often goad me into contradiction; but his genius, to my mind, is that of an artist, not of a sage. As a man— well, how can I ever forget my ecstatic experience at Hindhead? I remember it as Wordsworth remembered the daffodils, and, as I remember it, I wouldn't change places with Wordsworth.

Rudyard Kipling To-day

(1948)

IN 1893, when I was a boy of fourteen, I bought a newly published book, *Many Inventions*, written by a young man of twenty-eight, Rudyard Kipling. He was already famous; he had been the youngest English writer of genius ever to become so famous since Dickens. 'Everybody' read him—intellectuals and lovers of magazine stories, clergymen and the black sheep of their flocks. He was acclaimed by his fellow writers along with Stevenson as one of the new gods in the pantheon of prose fiction. My father, who was a Presbyterian minister, had his *Barrackroom Ballads* and the grey-paper-backed editions of some of the early stories in his study. Schoolmasters as well as schoolboys came under his spell, and there was scarcely a dissentient voice as he was welcomed into the company of the immortals.

This seems all the more surprising, as one looks back at it, because the Victorian era was supposed to be an era of Mrs. Grundyism, and Kipling was not conspicuously a disciple of Mrs. Grundy. His most popular characters were three soldiers, one of whom, though not a sot, had on occasion one of the most unquenchable thirsts ever known even east of Suez, and another of whom was a dog thief and a most artistic liar. His poetry was largely about soldiers, most of whom seemed to look forward to spending their after-life in hell. I do not think the Methodist minister who was Kipling's grandfather would have thought the prose annals of Simla edifying reading.

How is it then that Kipling with his delight in the disreputable himself became the delight of the respectable? I think that there are two principal reasons. One is that he was an imperialist in an age of imperialism. Mr. Rupert Croft-Cooke, in his enjoyable book, *Rudyard Kipling*, in the English Novelists Series, denies that in his work Kipling was 'an Imperialist, a jingoist, a Tory diehard,' and certainly he was no jingo of the common sort. But you have only to read his verse to see that he was the most powerful evangelist of imperialism in the history of English literature.

He gave imperialism a religious and moral authority so that good men were enabled to blind themselves to the injustice of the war against the Boers. He incited them to imperialism as an assertion not of their rights so much as of their duties. Empire was in his eyes something that had been won, not by sin, but by sacrifice. The pioneers who built it were dreamers and sufferers:

As the deer breaks—as the steer breaks—from the herd where they
    graze,
In the faith of little children we went on our ways.
Then the wood failed—then the food failed—then the last water
    dried—
In the faith of little children we lay down and died.
On the sand drift—on the veldt-side—in the fern-scrub we lay,
That our sons might follow after by the bones on the way.

Then, the Empire having been won, there remained the duty of imposing on it law, justice, and peace:

Keep ye the Law—be swift in all obedience—
Clear the land of evil, drive the road and bridge the ford.
    Make ye sure to each his own
    That he reap where he hath sown;
By the peace among Our peoples let men know we serve the Lord!

We who were boys in the nineties and drunk with this vision, communicated with the red-hot sincerity of a prophet, did not regard 'Imperialist' as an epithet of belittlement, but would have affixed it to Kipling as a badge of honour.

Ultimately, it was another aspect of his imperialism—his rancorous attacks on Irish nationalism—that changed my point of view and led me to turn against the idol of my boyhood. But I am sure that in the early days, when Kipling lay desperately ill of pneumonia in America, it was for the beloved evangelist no less than for the beloved artist that we felt an anguish of anxiety as we waited for each day's bulletin from the sick-room.

Mr. Croft-Cooke makes the point that 'whatever his point of view may have been, Kipling was too great an artist to let it give him a squint as he examined the world about which he wrote,' and it is true that his imperialism is not as obtrusive in his prose as in his verse. But even in his prose I think it is implicit. Though he could laugh like a little Englander at flag-wagging patriotism, his tales as a whole were written in imperial ink.

Another reason why he appealed so strongly to respectable Victorians was that, however disreputable or disorderly some of his best-loved characters might be, they were faithful in the last resort to the same ideals of duty as their better-behaved superiors. Kipling's three soldiers and his three schoolboys were anarchists, but they were not subversive anarchists. The soldiers, when not nefariously occupied, were models of law and order and their code did not differ from that of their officers. The schoolboys were rebels, but rebels whose ideals were oddly in accord with those of their headmaster. I fancy it was the mixture of the moralist and the anarchist in Kipling himself that gave him a hold over so vast and varied a public. In this respect at least he might be compared with Robert Burns.

That he conquered the critics as well as the general public was due to the religious zeal with which he applied himself to the art of writing. He was a writer who never betrayed his art through slackness or self-repetition. He passed from territory to territory in his triumphs—from soldiers and Anglo-Indians to the stuff of the *Jungle Books*, on to *Kim*, and thence to *Puck of Pook's Hill*, searching the world of men and animals, of time present and time past, with that intense vision of his that never grew dim. He was fond of psychic themes, and one feels at times that there is an element of the mediumistic in his vision, as though he were seeing wonderful things in a trance.

As for his style, I doubt whether Stevenson himself took the art of writing more seriously than Kipling. There are graces in Stevenson that were beyond Kipling's range, but with what mastery Kipling handles his own more workaday vocabulary. He may go wildly astray at times, as he does with Mulvaney's picturesque brogue; but this does not prevent him from being a prince of narrators even here.

As regards Kipling's scrupulous artistry, Mr. Croft-Cooke gives us an illuminating quotation in the form of a recipe for young writers aiming at the same end as himself—advice com-

parable to the advice offered to young poets nearly two thousand
years ago:

> This leads me to the Higher Editing.   Take of well-ground Indian
> Ink as much as suffices and a camel-hair brush proportionate to the
> interspaces of your lines.   In an auspicious hour, read your final draft
> and consider faithfully every paragraph, sentence and word, blacking
> out where requisite.   Let it lie by to drain as long as possible.   At
> the end of that time, re-read and you should find that it will bear a
> second shortening.   Finally, read it aloud alone and at leisure.   Maybe
> a shade more brushwork will then indicate or impose itself.   If not,
> praise Allah and let it go, and 'when thou hast done, repent not.'
> The shorter the tale, the longer the brushwork and, normally, the
> shorter the lie-by, and vice versa.   The longer the tale, the less brush
> but the longer lie-by.   I have had tales by me for three or five years
> which shortened themselves almost yearly.

This is obviously not advice to be given to the giants of fiction
—exuberant novelists such as Dickens or Dostoevski—but it
would be well if it were followed more often by those practising
the more economical art of the short story.   It is certainly
worth remembering that it was by such pains and patience that
the greatest body of short stories ever written by an Englishman
was produced.

On Kipling's stature in comparison with that of the other
great writers of short stories, such as Chekhov and Maupassant,
it is hard—perhaps foolish—to dogmatize.   Chekhov, I think,
had a profounder sympathy with common life, its griefs and
tendernesses.   In his knowledge of life Chekhov had the intimacy
of a family doctor in contrast with Kipling who was so much
more the gadabout and casual visitor.   Few of Kipling's best
stories are about people in their homes.   I doubt again whether
Kipling ever wrote as great a short story as Maupassant's *Boule
de Suif* or as Conrad's *Typhoon*.   These, however, are stories of a
length half-way between that of a short story and a short novel.

Mr. Croft-Cooke is content to praise Kipling as a writer who
did magnificently 'the job for which he was fitted, the only job
which interested him, the noble and eternal job of telling a
good story'; and that was unquestionably a great achievement.
But I think he blinds himself to a certain narrowness of spirit
which appears in some of the stories such as *Mary Postgate* and
A Walking Delegate—a narrowness of spirit shown in the way in

which, on being introduced to Bernard Shaw at Hardy's funeral, he shook hands hurriedly and at once turned away as if from the Evil One.

True, we forget all about his antipathies and prejudices as we read his glorious tribute to Jane Austen in *The Janeites* or laugh for the twentieth time over *Brugglesmith* or *The Village that Voted the Earth was Flat*.

To-day, when I read Kipling, it is more often than not to one of the comic stories that I turn; and I am sure that a collection of his comic stories would make one of the richest humorous books in the English language. Here his prejudices give no offence—to most of us, at least—and he becomes the perfect host, sharing his box with us in the vast variety theatre of life.

Even so, we must recognize the fact that his very drolleries would not have been so re-readable if it had not been for his zealous self-dedication to the difficulties of his art—in other words, to his intensely religious conception of his task as an imaginative writer.

Tolstoy's Double Life

(1949)

MANY people, if they were asked to name the greatest novelist of the nineteenth century, would say 'Tolstoy.' Tolstoy himself said 'Dickens.' 'I think,' he wrote as late as 1904, 'that Charles Dickens is the greatest novel writer of the nineteenth century, and that his works, impressed with the true Christian spirit, have done, and will continue to do, a great deal of good to mankind.'

The truth is, of course, that they were both supremely great, each in his own sphere. At the same time I often feel that Tolstoy was a giant in comparison with Dickens. He was a giant not only as a novelist, but in his passions, in his spiritual wrestlings, in his sacrificial search after the good life, in his courage to stand alone.

Professor Ernest J. Simmons has written a biography, *Leo Tolstoy*, which presents faithfully the good and evil in Tolstoy's nature—good and evil in unending battle until the last days of his life. Cynics used to depict Tolstoy as a man who in youth enjoyed all the pleasures of sin and who, having grown compulsorily virtuous through age and loss of appetite, began to preach the necessity of virtue for everybody. Professor Simmons's book, however, makes it clear that Tolstoy was never a sanctimonious humbug of this kind. Even as a youth he was a quarry for the Hound of Heaven: as Professor Simmons puts it: 'He heard the divine voice in him urging him to perfection.' When he was soldiering in the Caucasus 'contemplation of his life . . . up to this point filled Tolstoy with regret. Gambling, sensuality, and vanity, he asserted, were the three evil passions he had to contend with.'

Debauchery gave him no lasting happiness. 'So strong was his desire to reform,' we are told, 'that he tried to do a good deed every day, once giving away his horse to a passing Cossack for lack of a less expensive opportunity to appease his conscience.' His diary, indeed, becomes almost tedious in its record of his sins and of his resolve to do better. 'I am firmly resolved,' he wrote in a fit of remorse, 'to dedicate my life to the service of my neighbours. For the last time I tell myself: "If three days pass without my having done anything of service to people I will kill myself."' One of his Sevastopol comrades has left an interesting description of him as a repentant sinner. Telling how Tolstoy would vanish for three days at a time on his sprees, he goes on: 'At last he would return, like the prodigal son, gloomy, worn out, and disgusted with himself. . . . He would take me aside, quite spent, and begin his confession. He would tell all, how he had caroused, gambled, where he had spent his days and nights, and he would condemn himself and suffer as though he were a real criminal. He was so distressed that it was pitiful to see him.' It was as though he found it equally impossible to resist the lure of goodness and the lure of evil.

Most prodigals, no doubt, have something good in them: but few have longed so passionately to devote their lives to the good of others and have dreamed so ardently of family happiness as the ideal to be sought after. Tolstoy, unfortunately, was not born for family happiness. Not one woman in a thousand could have been content for long in the company of a husband whose ideals robbed her of the social life she loved, endangered the future of her numerous children, exposed him to excommunication by the Church and to Government hostility and censorship, a husband who preferred living the life of a peasant to enjoying the fruits of fame in the most brilliant society of the capital. Countess Tolstoy, who was married at eighteen and kept perpetually nursing yet another baby, became less reconciled to life with the greatest Russian of his time the longer she lived.

Nor could Tolstoy himself be happy. Believing that property-owning was wrong, he nevertheless could not give his property away because he had married and begotten children and had thereby accepted responsibility for their welfare. Professor Simmons suggests on one page that the reason why he did not give his property away was that, 'had he attempted such a solution . . . he knew that his wife would appeal to the Government, which would have been only too eager to declare him incapable of managing his affairs.' He then offered to give everything to his wife, who told him: 'So you wish to hand over that evil to me, the creature nearest to you. I do not want

it and shall take nothing.' Finally, he got rid of his property
by dividing it between his wife and his children, 'just as if he
were dead.'

He had already been called a Pharisee for holding on to his
estate while asserting that it was wrong to have property: and
his critics were equally venomous when, having parted with his
property, he continued to live on the estate with a wife who
saw that his clothes were comfortable and his meals good. His
fellow novelist, Merejkowski, wrote an able book, portraying
him as a humbug whose sacrifices to principle were merely
nominal. It was a false portrait. Tolstoy, as far as he could,
lived the life of a peasant, denying himself wine, tobacco, and
even white bread, working in the fields and doing his share of
the household chores. If, in addition to this, he had given his
property away without considering the future of his family
what a monster of doctrinaire inhumanity we should all have
thought him!

Having provided the family with his estate, he hoped at least
to persuade his wife to let him renounce property rights in his
books. 'Would it not be better,' he wrote in his diary, 'if she
should reject at least the income from literature? How it would
leave her in peace, her sons morally healthful, more joyous, and
how useful to people and pleasing to God!' Later he decided
to ignore her opposition and wrote a letter to the press,
renouncing the copyright in all his works published after 1881.

Tolstoy's attempts to put into practice a creed that might be
described as Christian Anarchistic Communism was, perhaps, the
chief cause of the hysteria that nearly drove his wife to suicide.
If her diary is to be believed, however—and some of it is
obviously the product of hysteria—she was in revolt, not only
against his idealism but against his sensuality. Her 'whole moral
being protested against it,' she said. Yet she dreaded the day
'when he will no longer be *amorous*, and then he will cast me
out of his life—cynically, cruelly, and coldly.' As one reads
some passages in her diary one wonders how she went on living
with a man whom she obviously often loathed. 'Last night,'
runs one entry, 'I became so angry that I would not talk to him.
He kept me awake until two in the morning. To begin with,
he was downstairs washing himself for so long that I thought he
was ill. For him, washing is an event. He told me that his

feet were so calloused with dirt that they had become sore.   It quite revolted me. . . .   I can never get used to the dirt, the smell.'   Yet she added pathetically: 'I try with all my strength to see only his spiritual side, and I succeed when he is kind to me.'   The surprising thing is that this ill-assorted couple went on living together, despite frequent 'scenes,' till the last year of Tolstoy's life.

There was clearly some bond of love between them, incompatible in some respects though they were.   When, near the end of his life, he comes in to tea in a gloomy mood, complaining that life is a burden, the countess tries to comfort him by saying: 'Why is it a burden to you?   Every one loves you.'   We read of them about this time: 'After another unpleasant scene . . . husband and wife parted in loving fashion, kissing and weeping, and begging each other's forgiveness for all that had passed.' It is hard to believe that, if Tolstoy had entirely ceased to love his wife, he would have taken the trouble to write her that letter containing the beautiful passage:

I rode back through the woods of Turgenev and Spasskoye; it was twilight; the fresh green of the forest under my feet, the stars in the heavens, the smell of the flowering osier, of the drooping birch leaves, the sounds of nightingales, the noise of cockchafers, cuckoos—the cuckoo—solitude and the pleasant, cheerful motion of the horse under me, and physical and spiritual health.   And I thought, as I think constantly, about death.   It became clear to me that it will be as fine on the other side where death is as it is on this side, but only different, and I then understood why the Hebrews have described paradise as a garden.   The most pure joy is the joy of nature.   It became clear to me that there it will be just as fine—even better.

Professor Simmons's book is concerned with Tolstoy's life rather than with his writings, and it was only to be expected that the story of a tragic—certainly a tragically ending—marriage would occupy a large part of it.   At the same time, we are given many enlightening pages on Tolstoy's beliefs, religious and political.   With what insight he wrote on the prospect of a Marxian revolution!   'Even if that should happen which Marx predicted,' he foretold, 'then the only thing that will happen is that despotism will be passed on.   Now the capitalists are ruling, but then the directors of the working class will rule.'

I should like to have more records of the happy scenes in

LEO TOLSTOY

Tolstoy's life, like that in which he and Turgenev enjoy themselves, sitting opposite each other on a see-saw, for the very frequency of his moods of gloom tends to deaden our sympathy. Sympathy revives, however, when Tolstoy, at the age of eighty-two, tormented beyond endurance by his wife's hysterical behaviour—she pretended to have taken poison in order to frighten him into giving her his diaries which she feared would one day expose her faults to the world and, at other times, she threatened to murder his chief disciple, Chertkov—rose in the darkness of a winter morning and, trembling for fear that he might be pursued, drove to the nearest railway station, bent upon escape. Even then pity for the wife he was deserting disturbed him. 'My fear passed,' he wrote, 'and pity for her arose in my heart.' He was dying of pneumonia and unconscious of her presence when she found him at last at about two in the morning in the monastery in which he had taken refuge:

She entered (the sick-room), her face frozen in grief, and for a few moments stared at the bed from a distance, as though afraid to approach. Then she swiftly went to her husband, kissed his forehead, sank on her knees and murmured, 'Forgive me!' Fearful he might not recognize her, a doctor led her into the next room.

Thus ends what is surely one of the most tragic stories in the history of men of genius.

A Passion for Style
(1947)

I WONDER whether the young would-be writers of to-day revere the name of Gustave Flaubert as young would-be writers did when I was in my teens. Style was an object almost of worship in those days, and Flaubert was the hero as stylist, worthy of a place in Carlyle's gallery of heroes. Not that the French we had learnt at school enabled us to appreciate the excellence of the prose in *Madame Bovary*. It was not Flaubert's writing that excited us, but what we had heard about his manner of writing—how he would spend hours at a time in pursuit of the right word—how he became a monk of prose, a martyr to perfection. This, even when we did not do more than aspire to imitate it, seemed the true literary sanctity.

Henry James, in his *Notes on Novelists*, showed that even in his maturity he never lost his feeling of reverence for Flaubert as a literary martyr. 'He may stand,' he wrote, speaking of novelists in general, 'for our operative conscience or our vicarious sacrifice; animated by a sense of literary honour, attached to an ideal of perfection, incapable of lapsing in fine from a self-respect, that enable us to sit at ease, to surrender to the age, to indulge in whatever comparative meannesses (and no meanness in art is so mean as the sneaking economic) we may find most comfortable or profitable. May it not in truth be said that we practise our industry, so many of us, at relatively little cost just *because* poor Flaubert, producing the most expensive fictions ever written, so handsomely paid for it?'

This seems to suggest that Flaubert's sufferings in pursuit of style were an atonement for the shortcomings of his fellow novelists rather than an inspiration to them to do better: but how beautiful a tribute it is to one who never yielded to 'the infection of bad writing'—one of whose methods James could say: 'The production of a book was, of course, made inordinately slow by the fatigue of these measures; in illustration of which his letters often record that it has taken him three days to arrive at one right sentence, tested by the pitch of his ideal of the right for the suggestion aimed at.'

In the nineties of last century many of us believed that all writers should toil as Flaubert and Stevenson toiled after perfect expression, and I am sure such toil is as a rule a good education for the young writer. At the same time, it is obvious that few of the great novels have been written according to Flaubertian principles. Scott, Dickens, Thackeray, and Trollope in England, Balzac in France, and Dostoevsky in Russia, simply had not the means to indulge in the pursuit of style at all costs. And it may even be that if they had laboured harder at their sentences, their genius as story-tellers would have suffered and their narration would have lost something of its easy and vigorous flow. All good novelists, it seems to me, are in their own fashion stylists; but few of them pursue form as an end in itself. Style is a workaday matter with most, not a temple ritual.

To say this, however, is not to detract from the praise due to Flaubert. He, too, achieved great things in fiction even if not the greatest; and it was only as a stylist with an infinite capacity for taking pains that he could have done so. He believed, as Henry James says, in 'the fertilization of the subject by form, penetration of the sense, ever, by the expression—the latter reacting creatively on the former,' and it was only his unsparing servitude to this theory that enabled him to make the story of Emma Bovary a masterpiece. 'This work is a classic,' as James says, 'because the thing, such as it is, is ideally *done*, and because it shows that in such doing eternal beauty may dwell.'

In *Flaubert and Madame Bovary* Mr. Francis Steegmuller tells us in a very interesting fashion how *Madame Bovary* came to be written. That is the vitally important part of his book. He writes too many pages, to my mind, on Flaubert's relations with his mistress, Louise Colet, an egotistic poetaster with whom Flaubert can hardly be said ever to have been in love.

Flaubert, so far as one can gather, was incapable of a grand passion. He was incapable of heartbreak or tragic suffering in love, and he never experienced the lover's longing to be for ever in the company of the beloved, or felt that absence from her was to be shut out of Paradise. Love for him was mainly a physical indulgence and he was able to write to Louise:

If you consider love as the principal dish of existence, my answer is no. If as accessory, yes. If you mean by 'loving' to be exclusively preoccupied with the loved one, to live only in her, to see, of everything there is to see in the world, only her, to be full of the idea of her—to feel, finally, that your life is bound up in her life and that she has become an organ of your soul, then no. I have never felt the necessity of the company of any one. The desire, yes. The need, no.

It is only fair to say that, when he wrote this, he was getting tired of Louise.

But such a letter was never written by one of the world's great lovers. And what an end the story of his association with Louise had! 'One evening in April, when she began to scream abuse at him and to kick him and scratch him, he was suddenly filled with so overpowering a desire to assassinate her with a log that was burning in the fireplace that he fled the house, his mind full of visions of arrest, trial, and prison. After that he dared not see her again.'

As I read some of the passages describing Flaubert's relations with persons of the opposite sex, I felt how wise old George Saintsbury was who wrote in *A History of the French Novel*: 'There is some scandal and infinite gossip about Flaubert with all of which I was once obliged to be acquainted, but which I have done my best that a rather strong memory will allow me to forget.' Biography, I agree, can provide useful material to a critic, but the biographer should keep a sense of proportion, and I do not think Mr. Steegmuller has always done this.

He is an able writer, however, and he gives us an exceptionally interesting picture of a man of genius at work. How astonishing a phenomenon is a great writer—a man who lived for writing— who did not produce his first complete book till he was thirty-eight years old! Before this Flaubert had written, among other things, a draft of *The Temptation of Saint Anthony*, which he had read aloud to his friends, Bouilhet and Du Camp, telling them in advance: 'If you don't howl with pleasure at this, you're incapable of being moved by anything.' He read his manuscript to them for periods of four hours—'from noon until four and from eight until midnight'—and his friends listened in misery through four eight-hour days.

Near midnight on the fourth day Flaubert called for their verdict, and when Bouilhet reluctantly told him: 'We think you ought to throw it in the fire and never speak of it again,' he jumped from his chair, we are told, with a cry of horror. It was during the talk that followed that Bouilhet suggested that Flaubert should write a realistic novel, for 'it was in the novel concerned with living human beings and their daily life that the future of prose almost certainly lay.' He made his advice all the more unpalatable by proposing Balzac as a model—Balzac of whom Flaubert the stylist exclaimed to Louise: 'What a man Balzac would have been if he had known how to write!'

The seed had been sown, however, and in time, taking a hint from a local scandal, he began work on *Madame Bovary*. 'What I should like to write,' he told Louise, 'is a book about nothing at all, a book which would exist by virtue of the mere internal strength of its style, as the earth holds itself unsupported in the air—a book which would have almost no subject, or in which, at least, the subject would be almost imperceptible, if such a thing is possible. The finest books are those which have the least subject-matter: the more closely the expression approximates the thought, the more beautiful the book is. I believe that the future of art lies in that direction.' It was a heresy that would have gone far towards ruining a writer of less monumental patience than Flaubert. 'Only twenty pages a month,' he lamented on one occasion, 'working at least seven hours a day!'

And all these pains were endured not from a desire of fame or money or under any compulsion of love of the world's loveliness or of a woman or from a need of confession. 'I care nothing for the world,' he declared, 'for the future, for what people will say, for any kind of established position, or even for literary fame, which in my early days I used to stay awake so many nights dreaming about.' It is, however, a dangerous thing to take the passing moods of an artist too literally. Other quotations might be made, showing that, though Flaubert could afford to do without temporary celebrity, he was not immune from the hope of fame after death. Unhappily, he was so incapable of normal happiness that the temporary fame of *Madame Bovary* seems to have deprived him of the belief that the book deserved to endure, and he came to hate it. 'I should like,' he wrote to Du Camp, 'to find some way of making a lot of money so that I could buy up every copy of *Madame Bovary* in existence —throw them all into the fire, and never hear of the book again.'

Such moods were probably the result of an incurable misanthropy. 'Though I have never suffered, thank God,' he once wrote, 'at the hands of man, and though my life has never been lacking in cushions on which I could curl up in corners and forget every one else, still I detest my fellow beings and do not feel that I am their fellow at all.' Life bored and tortured him. 'The opiate of boredom in which I was steeped in my youth,' he told Du Camp, 'will affect me to the end of my days. I hate life. Yes, life, and everything that reminds me that life must be borne. It tortures me to eat, to dress, to stand on my feet. I have dragged this misery about with me everywhere.'

It may have been this very hatred of life, however, that so burned in him as to compel him to give it lasting expression in *Madame Bovary*. 'Madame Bovary, c'est moi,' he used to say; and it is in the light thrown by that sentence that Mr. Steegmuller interprets the book.

Flaubert and Madame Bovary is a fascinating account of a neurotic as a great artist, and perhaps I have been unjust to what seems to me Mr. Steegmuller's over-emphasis of some of the uglier features of Flaubert's biography. Flaubert was certainly a man oddly compounded—the romantic lover of the exotic and the pitiless realist—the man who 'always declared that the discovery of a human turpitude gave him more pleasure than any other gift,' and the lover of Louise Colet who gave as a rule for young artists: 'Be regular and ordinary in your life, like a bourgeois, so that you can be violent and original in your works.'

The Beloved Novelist

(1947)

I CAN remember a time when Turgenev was the best-loved of the Russian novelists among English men and women who read foreign literature. Tenderness and compassion seemed to flow in a more equable stream through his writings than through the Himalayan masterpieces of Tolstoy and Dostoevsky. Dostoevsky, however, was then scarcely known to English readers, who, if I remember right, possessed none of his works in translation except *Crime and Punishment* and *Poor Folk*.

Turgenev was a particular favourite among men of letters. In France Flaubert loved him like a brother, and Maupassant spoke enthusiastically of him both as a writer and as a man, regarding him as 'a still greater man than Flaubert.' Renan, George Moore tells us in *Avowals*, said that 'a tale told by Turgenev is the most beautiful thing that art has given since antiquity'; and in the same book Moore himself writes: 'There have been no other tale-tellers but Balzac and Turgenev, only two out of the myriad have been able to write tales that are read by succeeding generations'—a rather foolish sentence to write even in a mood of idolatry.

I first read Turgenev in the late nineties after my noble Viking of an English professor, S. J. Macmullen, had spent an hour at the lecture stand telling us what a great book *Fathers and Children* was, and convincing us with his flush of enthusiasm that what he said was true.

Fathers and Children seemed to me to deserve all the praise he had lavished on it, and the more I read of Turgenev the more enchanted I became by him. I should have found it hard to forgive Tolstoy if I had been told at the time how contemptuously he had treated *Fathers and Children* when Turgenev, who had just finished it, gave it to him to read. He was staying with Turgenev, who naturally wanted his opinion on it and left him alone in the drawing-room to read it. 'To do this more comfortably,' says Aylmer Maude, 'Tolstoy . . . lay down on a large sofa. He began to read, but the story seemed to him so artificially constructed and so unimportant in its subject-matter that he fell asleep. "I awoke," he narrates, "with a strange sensation, and, when I opened my eyes, I saw Turgenev's back just disappearing.'''

Turgenev, the older man by ten years, had been one of the first of his fellow writers to hail Tolstoy's success. But by an irascible man the enthusiasm, and even the help, of an elder can easily be misinterpreted and resented as patronage; and neither Tolstoy nor Dostoevsky could endure the thought of this. Dostoevsky began by almost worshipping Turgenev, but after a time turned on him, talked of treading him 'into the mud,' and denounced his 'monstrous airs' and the 'aristocratic and patronizing sort of way he embraces one and offers his face to be kissed.' If we knew of Turgenev only from his Russian rivals, indeed, what a different impression we should get of him from the impression left by his novels and by the testimony of his French friends, who portray him as a giant of inexhaustible amiability.

The second impression, I think, is the truer. I cannot believe in Tolstoy's description of Turgenev as 'our splenetic and dyspeptic Turgenev' any more than I can accept his criticism that the girl in On the Eve is 'hopelessly bad,' and that in Turgenev 'there is no humanity or sympathy for the characters, but the author exhibits monsters whom he scolds but does not pity.' Tolstoy, however, was in no mood for reading fiction just then, if we may judge from his remark: 'This is my opinion: to write novels is undesirable, especially for people who are depressed and do not well know what they want from life.'

Even while condemning On the Eve, however, he declared that it was much better than A House of Gentlefolk, which has been retranslated into English under the title A Nobleman's Nest. It would be easy, I admit, to argue that the plot of A Nobleman's Nest is thin and commonplace. A young landowner, brought up in seclusion from the great world, goes to Moscow and falls in love with a beautiful creature he sees in the theatre. He marries her, and she proves to be self-indulgent and unfaithful.

He allows her an income which she spends on a separate existence abroad, and after many years, when he is living at

IVAN TURGENEV

home, he reads in a society paper the news that she is dead. He now realizes that he has found the love of his life in Lisa, a girl in her teens, and Lisa returns his love. Suddenly the 'dead' wife turns up. Lisa, who is a saint both in her goodness and in her strictness, bids him go back to her, and she herself becomes a nun.

That is the end, except for a visit that the lover afterwards pays to the convent. 'As she walked down the aisle she passed close by him, passed on steadily with the gentle and humble step of a nun, and never looked at him. Only a scarcely perceptible tremor moved her eyelashes as her eyes turned in his direction, only she bent still lower her emaciated face, and the fingers of her clasped hands, enlaced in her rosary, tightened their grasp still more firmly.'

One could imagine all this as a plot for a Hollywood film but for the fact that Lisa is never for a moment torn in opposite directions by her love and her sacred duty. Perhaps that is what Tolstoy meant when he accused Turgenev of banality.

A Nobleman's Nest, however, happens to be a novel in which however ordinary the plot may be the characters are extraordinarily alive—not only the landowner and his selfish wife and Lisa, but her worldly-minded mother, her exquisitely wise and good-hearted great-aunt, the clumsy old German music-master, and the rest.

It is a story of the triumph of evil—at least of the success of the worldly in wrecking the happiness of the innocent and the kind—yet there is such a revelation of the human heart in its tenderness and in its finest exaltations that it has all the charm of an idyll written by a poet of genius.

Turgenev was aware of the ugliness, physical and spiritual, of many men and women, and of much of the earthly landscape: and in his description of these things he is a realist. But in spite of this he leaves one with the impression that he is chiefly a poet of the goodness of human nature and of a landscape of lovely woods and singing birds.

I do not know whether Turgenev was the first person to suggest that a novel should be 'a slice of life'—a once popular phrase that always seemed ugly to me—but that, I think, was what he himself aimed at in his fiction. Poet though he essentially was, he was more real than the realists in portraying human beings, old and young, as they live and feel and think and talk. *Rudin*, for example, which has been published in a new translation in a volume entitled *Fathers and Children: Rudin* is a slight enough story, judged by its plot alone, but Rudin himself—idealist, master of beautiful words, sponger, and weak of will—is a living man surrounded by living human beings.

Settling down for a long stay with his country hostess, he entrances everybody by his noble and wonderful talk, triumphing to our delight over a bitter-tongued sceptic and egotist who frequents the house. Then from the lips of a man we can trust who had known him as a student we learn what a man of words and how worthless Rudin really is, and are disillusioned. All Rudin's incapacity for acting finely is revealed when he realizes that his hostess's young daughter loves him, and that he loves her.

His ardour turns to alarm when he learns that his hostess has got to know this and is very angry; and at his next meeting with the girl, who is willing to follow him to the ends of the earth, he tells her nervously that she must obey her mother. Having humiliated her by his lack of courage he makes a hurried departure from the house, weeping from wounded vanity. No sooner, however, is our opinion of Rudin at its lowest and he appears as a man who inevitably fails those who love and trust him, than the very man who had first exposed his weakness recalls with gratitude what an inspiration Rudin has been to him in their student days. 'He himself achieves nothing,' says the apologist, 'precisely because he has no character, no fire in his blood, but who has the right to say that he has not been of use?—that his words have not scattered many good seeds in young hearts, to whom nature has not denied, as she has to him, the power of action, the ability to carry out their intentions? Yes, I myself was the first to experience all this through him.' Hence we remember Rudin as one of nature's ineffectual angels. We learn on the last page that he has died fighting on the Paris barricades in 1848. It is the only thing related of him that I do not quite believe.

Fathers and Children is richer in plot, but not in life-likeness. At my present age, I rather dislike the chief character Bazarov —the young nihilist who is so rudely impatient of the ideals of the older generation, and whom as a youth I regarded as a man of heroic stature. He is true to life, however, as a certain type of unidealistic idealist. One of the most memorable figures in Russian literature, he towers above the other characters in the story like an intellectual despot; yet it is the older people—mere pygmies compared with him—who with their goodness of heart make the book a thing of beauty.

How characteristic of Turgenev's compassionate spirit are the closing sentences of the book where he speaks of the father and mother visiting their son's grave:

Can it be that their tears and prayers are fruitless? Can it be that love, sacred devoted love, is not all-powerful? Oh, no! However passionate, sinful or rebellious the heart hidden in the tomb, the flowers growing over it peep at us serenely with their innocent eyes; they tell us not only of eternal peace, of that great peace of 'indifferent nature'; they tell us also of eternal reconciliation and of life without end.

You may think this sentimental and within the compass of a commonplace writer; but the feeling is too sincere to be called sentimental. Turgenev's tenderness is always profound. That is why he will probably become one of the beloved novelists to the new generation that reads him in Mr. Richard Hare's translation, as he was to those who read him in Constance Garnett's beautiful translation half a century ago.

II

Odd Books, People, and Themes

The Literary Life

(1948)

I HAVE sometimes wondered why it is that authors so often provide the biographer with his ideal subjects and yet are so seldom made the leading characters in works of fiction. There is no literary hero in fiction to be compared with Boswell's Johnson or Lockhart's Scott. Perhaps the man of genius in any sphere is always more interesting in fact than in fiction— Napoleon and Nelson, for example. But it seems strange that the great novelists should so generally have refrained from looking for their characters in the profession of which they know most.

Henry James was unusual in this respect, as a new generation of readers has probably noticed; and in some of his most famous short stories an author is the principal character. I have been re-reading these stories lately in the volume called *The Lesson of the Master and Other Stories*, and feeling a little astonished that they should once have seemed such masterpieces. Henry James's art—his conscious art in shaping his sentences—is so fascinating that, when once you become his victim, you keep on reading him, greedy for more and more even when you begin to suspect that his manner is profounder than his matter. It was in this double-mindedness that I re-read the stories in *The Lesson of the Master*, thinking at one moment, 'How good!' and at another, 'What nonsense!'

No story in the book has been more enthusiastically praised than 'The Figure in the Carpet,' in which Hugh Vereker, the novelist, is the principal character. Like Henry James himself, Vereker 'wasn't, of course, popular. . . . He had none the less become in a manner the fashion; the critics at least had put a spurt on and caught up with him.' We find him, just after the appearance of a new novel, a guest at a dinner party at which a fellow guest—'the vicar's sister, a robust, unmodulated person' —asks him whether he had read a certain laudatory review of the book. Ignorant of the fact that the writer of the review is present, he 'calls back gaily, his mouth full of bread: "Oh it's all right—the usual twaddle!"'   This naturally leads to an apology later on when Vereker answers the young reviewer that all the critics have always missed the point of his novels.   'It always struck me,' he declares, 'they missed my little point with a perfection exactly as admirable when they patted me on the back as when they kicked me in the shins.'   And he goes on to explain:

By my little point I mean—what shall I call it?—the particular thing I have written my book most *for*.   Isn't there for every writer a particular thing of that sort, the thing that most makes him apply himself, the thing without which he wouldn't write at all, the very passion of his passion, the part of the business in which, for him, the flame of art burns most intensely?   Well, it's *that*!

No wonder the reviewer, who relates the story, tells us at this point: 'I followed at a respectable distance, rather gasping.'
    Vereker continues, however, as mystifyingly as ever: 'At any rate,' he went on,

'I can speak for myself; there's an idea in my work without which I wouldn't have given a straw for the whole job.   It's the finest fullest intention of the lot, and the application of it has been, I think, a triumph of patience, of ingenuity.   I ought to leave that to somebody else to say; but that nobody does say it is precisely what we're talking about. It stretches, this little trick of mine, from book to book, and everything else, comparatively, plays over the surface of it.   The order, the form, the texture of my books will perhaps some day constitute for the initiated a complete representation of it.   So it's naturally the thing for the critic to look for.   It strikes me,' my visitor added, smiling, 'even as the thing for the critic to find.'
    This seemed a responsibility indeed.   'You call it a little trick?'
    'That's only my little modesty.   It's really an exquisite scheme.'
    'And you hold that you've carried the scheme out?'
    'The way I've carried it out is the thing in life I think a bit well of myself for.'
    I had a pause.   'Don't you think you ought—just a trifle—to assist the critic?'
    'Assist him?   What else have I done with every stroke of my pen? I've shouted my intention in his great blank face!'

I don't know whether other people find it as difficult as I do to believe in the existence of a brilliant novelist who is a favourite of the critics, not one of whom can see the point of what he writes, however, though he has done all in his power to assist them. After all, the critics include in their circle a good many brilliant novelists—Henry James himself, for example—and one of them was surely bound to spot Vereker's secret.

If this had happened early, however, there would have been no story; for 'The Figure in the Carpet' is simply the story of the hunt for Vereker's secret. The reviewer asks him frankly: 'Should you be able, pen in hand, to state it clearly yourself— to name it, phrase it, formulate it?' 'Oh,' sighs Vereker, 'if I were only, pen in hand, one of *you* chaps!' But he is as mum about his secret as if his life depended on his keeping it.

The reviewer soon retires from the quest, exasperated by an apparently insoluble puzzle. His editor, a Vereker enthusiast, is more dogged, and is at length able to announce his success in a telegram to his fiancée: 'Just seen Vereker—not a note wrong. Pressed me to his bosom.' He did not reveal the secret, how- ever, believing that he had now the materials for producing 'the greatest literary portrait ever painted.' He marries, and on his honeymoon is killed in a driving accident, having written merely a scrap of his great article. Some time afterwards the reviewer asks the widow in an extraordinarily phrased sentence: 'Did you hear in those few days of your plighted bliss what we desired so to hear?' 'I heard everything,' she replies, 'and I mean to keep it to myself!' Was there ever such a succession of sphinxes outside a fairy tale?

For a time the reviewer thinks of proposing marriage to the widow in order to be allowed to share the secret, but she marries another reviewer of a more commonplace type and dies when her second child is born. Vereker himself is by this time dead, and the reviewer's only chance of learning the secret now is to approach the widow's widower and discover whether she had imparted it to him before her death. The widower was appalled to learn that his wife had not trusted him even to the point of letting him know that the Vereker secret existed:

I drew him to a sofa, I lighted another cigar and, beginning with the anecdote of Vereker's one descent from the clouds, I recited to him the extraordinary chain of accidents that had, in spite of the original gleam, kept me till that hour in the dark. I told him in a word just what I've written out here. He listened with deepening attention, and I became aware, to my surprise, by his ejaculations, by his questions, that he would have been after all not unworthy to be trusted by his wife. So abrupt an experience of her want of trust had now a disturbing effect on him; but I saw the immediate shock throb away little by little and then gather again into waves of wonder and curiosity —waves that promised, I could perfectly judge, to break in the end with the fury of my own highest tides. I may say that to-day as victims of unappeased desire there isn't a pin to choose between us. The poor man's state is almost my consolation; there are really moments when I feel it to be quite my revenge.

And so the secret remains a secret for ever.

Henry James suggests in a preface that the starting-point of his story may have been the 'acute impression . . . that no truce, in English-speaking air, had ever seemed to me really struck, or even approximately strikable, with our so marked collective mistrust of anything like close or analytic appreciation'; and 'The Figure in the Carpet' may be read as the defence offered by a too subtle and increasingly unpopular author both to an indifferent public and to an equally depressing claque of yes-men and yes-women. The assumption that a novelist with an undiscoverable secret of this kind would be worth reading, however, seems to me absurd; hence I should agree with any one who described 'The Figure in the Carpet' not as a literary masterpiece but as a first-rate magazine story for the intellectuals.

'The Lesson of the Master,' which is the story of a writer of great gifts who under the influence of his ambitious wife becomes second rate and a best seller, also fails to convince me of the reality of the chief character. I distrust most stories about potboiling writers who but for their wives might have been great geniuses. The successful pot-boiler is, as a rule, a born pot-boiler, and the man of genius cannot hope to compete with him in his particular market. Perhaps, however, I am in a captious mood at the moment. I should not like anything I say to deter potential readers from enjoying 'The Lesson of the Master,' with its exquisitely ironical ending.

I feel, however, as I read these stories, that Henry James fails to persuade us—or, at least, to persuade me—that literary figures are such as he depicts them. He does not convince me that the manuscript the wife made the author burn in 'The Lesson of the Master' was anything to grieve about. He does not convince me that the manuscript lost by bogus admirers in 'The Death of the Lion' was any great loss. And as for the writer of genius in 'The Coxon Fund,' he has all the weakness and flabbiness of Coleridge at his weakest and flabbiest, but there is no evidence of his having a spark of Coleridge's genius. The truth is that, to enjoy the story, we have to forget that it is founded on the Coleridge legend, and to read it as an anecdote about a glorious sponger who spellbinds his victims with high-flown humbug—being able, for example, after making a mess of his own marriage, to entrance his hearers by discoursing on the sublimity of the married state.

In the early part of the century there were critics who maintained that Henry James was the first writer to introduce psychology into English fiction. It was an absurd statement, of course, for psychology of one kind or another is as old as imaginative literature. Still, here is a book in which James did at least attempt one or two investigations into the psychology of genius, though, as it seems to me, with no great success.

His wonderful writers are mere minnows in comparison with the wonderful writers we know, from Scott to Balzac, from Dickens to Tolstoy, from Turgenev to Henry James himself. It is almost a relief to know that they never lived and that, if their books had ever been written, the manuscripts would have been either burnt or lost beyond recovery, so that we should not have had to read them.

Read the stories as magazine stories, however—some of them were originally written for *The Yellow Book*—and you will find them magazine stories shaped by the mind of an artist and among the most entrancing that have been written in English.

That, at least, is my view at the moment.

Books and their Authors

(1945)

WHEN I was a good deal younger, there was a prejudice against books about books in some literary circles, the assumption being, I suppose, that the only literature worth reading was imaginative literature—poetry, fiction and, perhaps, history. Nonsense of this kind is talked in most generations. People used to discuss the question whether Pope was a poet instead of asking themselves what were the qualities that made him the wittiest poet in the English language. Others kept telling us that criticism was not creative, as though the phrase made criticism not worth reading. Most generalizations of this kind seem to me to be as silly as most generalizations about men and women, about the rich and the poor, about modern youth and nearly everything else.

I see that Mr. Holbrook Jackson quotes Charles Lamb's confession, 'I like books about books,' at the beginning of his new anthology of quotations, *Bookman's Holiday*; and I am sure that about nine out of ten people who like good books also like good books about books. Good books about books are unpopular only among those whose ordinary reading is mainly and by preference rubbish.

After all, if you enjoy a good book you enjoy learning the opinion of some clever person who has read it. You like to know what Dr. Johnson thought of Fielding's novels, what Hazlitt thought of Coleridge, what Matthew Arnold thought of Tolstoy, what Ruskin thought of Scott. The opinions of such judges are interesting even when we disagree with them. It is amusing to find Byron calling Shakespeare 'a damned humbug,' or Carlyle speaking of *The Beggar's Opera* as 'a mere pouring out of bilge-water and oil of vitriol on the deepest wounds of humanity.' It tickles one to learn that Samuel Butler curtly dismissed Richard Jefferies as 'an ass,' that Emerson declared that 'Shelley is never a poet,' and that George Moore described Conrad as 'a completely worthless writer.'

Such aberrations of judgment, however, amusing though they are, are only one of the minor attractions of bookish literature. They are the Billingsgate of men of letters, and Billingsgate is comic only in small doses. Praise has deeper pleasures. Praise is often not only enjoyable in itself, but an introduction to the enjoyment of a writer of genius. If you had never read Sir Thomas Browne, would you not be tempted to do so by Mr. Somerset Maugham's description of the last chapter of *Hydriotaphia* as 'a piece of prose that has never been surpassed in our literature'? Such praise is an invitation to a banquet; and Mr. Jackson quotes scores of examples of it. Thackeray is at the moment a less popular writer than Anthony Trollope; but Trollope's praise of *Esmond* as 'the greatest novel in the English language' should whet the appetite of some young readers for the work of a neglected Victorian. I have been told that the new generation finds *Esmond* artificial and mannered, but how exquisite the artifice is, and Beatrice surely is still a heroine for schoolboys to fall in love with!

Tennyson is another author who has not yet returned to fashion; otherwise many people who 'cannot read' Scott might be tempted to try again by Tennyson's tribute to him as 'the author with the widest range since Shakespeare.' Gladstone, too, was nobly over-enthusiastic. 'No man since Aeschylus,' he declared, 'could have written *The Bride of Lammermoor*.'

Some of the praise quoted by Mr. Jackson, however, is so excessive as to make the reader dubious. We suspect exaggeration in a gross degree when we read Emerson's eulogy of Carlyle —'an imagination such as never rejoiced before the face of God since Shakespeare.' Carlyle was a great man, but he had a gospel for his time that made him greater in the eyes of his contemporaries than he can ever be in the eyes of posterity. Wild exaggeration, again, nullifies the effect of Ruskin's eulogy of Mrs. Browning's *Aurora Leigh*—'the greatest poem in the English language, unsurpassed by anything but Shakespeare—*not* surpassed by Shakespeare's sonnets, and therefore the greatest poem in the language.' Even if one is only slightly acquainted with Mrs. Browning's work, one knows enough to be sure that this sentence is simply generous balderdash.

Mr. Jackson's anthology, however, is not merely a collection of the sayings of authors about the books of other authors. Its

interest is even more biographical than critical. Here we have
hundreds of titbits about the lives of writers of genius—a most
delightful selection, full of surprises. Many people, for example,
will be astonished to see Wordsworth at the age of almost sixty
described by Charles Greville as 'very cheerful, merry, courteous,
and talkative.' In another quotation we find Wordsworth
reading *The Leech Gatherer* to his hairdresser—a subject worthy
of Sir Max Beerbohm. On another page Haydon tells us that,
walking with him across Hyde Park one day, Wordsworth
quoted his 'beautiful address to the stock dove.'

He said once in a wood Mrs. Wordsworth and a lady were walking,
when the stock dove was cooing. A farmer's wife coming by said to
herself, 'Oh, I do like stock doves!' Mrs. Wordsworth, in all her
enthusiasm for Wordsworth's poetry, took the old woman to her
heart; 'but,' continued the old woman, 'some like them in a pie; for
my part there's nothing like 'em stewed in onions.'

In his preface to *Bookman's Holiday*, Mr. Jackson writes: 'The
glimpses I have given of many authors—what they looked like,
where and how they lived, how they worked, played, talked,
dined, loved, quarrelled, and died—are intended to make a
composite portrait of a writer of books.' As to that, I doubt
whether such a thing is possible. Authors are as dissimilar as
human beings in general, and a composite portrait would be no
more than a blur. How can we merge the features of Sterne
into those of George Herbert, the deformity of Pope into the
physical beauty of Southey, Burns in love into Browning in love,
Bunyan's religion into the cynicism of Samuel Butler, Lord
Tennyson into Bernard Shaw? The psychology of genius is an
interesting study, but authors interest us most as individuals,
not as subjects for the students of a necessarily inexact science.

Originality involves unlikeness, and it is the very unlikeness
of authors that attracts us. Even their eccentricities fascinate
us. How delightful is Medwin's account of Byron's caravan
in Italy:

His (Byron's) travelling equipage was rather a singular one, and
afforded a strange catalogue for the *Dogana*: seven servants, five
carriages, nine horses, a monkey, a bulldog and a mastiff, two cats,
three pea-fowls and some hens . . . formed part of his livestock; these
and all his books, consisting of a very large library of modern works

(for he bought all the best that came out), together with a vast quantity of furniture.

Enjoyable, too, is Rogers's reference to Gibbon's exceptional physical indolence: Gibbon took very little exercise. He had been staying some time with Lord Sheffield in the country; and when he was about to go away, the servants could not find his hat. 'Bless me,' said Gibbon, 'I certainly left it in the hall on my arrival here.' He had not stirred out of doors during the whole of the visit.

If you are in quest of originality, again, you will find it in Wordsworth's attitude to letter-writing as it is reported by Tom Moore:

In talking of letter-writing this evening, and referring to what Tucker has told of Jefferson's sacrifice of his time to correspondence, Taylor again mentioned the habits of Southey in this respect, and Wordsworth said that, for his own part, such was his horror of having his letters *preserved*, that in order to guard against it, he always took pains to make them as bad and dull as possible.

I am afraid Wordsworth was rather successful in his aim.

Of the miseries of authorship Mr. Jackson has been sparing. 'I think,' he writes—and I for one agree with him—'there is justification for preferring the oblique ray of comedy to the more insistent bludgeonings of chance so beloved of our fashionable debunkers. My drinkers have stopped this side of dipsomania, and my lovers have loved, so far as they have revealed themselves in these pages, without undue self-pity.' Certainly, in a book bearing this title and described in the subtitle as 'a recreation for booklovers,' we look for the refreshment of comedy rather than for a panorama of misfortunes and broken lives.

And comedy is here in no small measure. What could be wittier than Sydney Smith's remark on Macaulay:

Yes, he is certainly more agreeable since his return from India. His enemies might perhaps have said before (though I never did so) that he talked rather too much; but now he has occasional flashes of silence, that make his conversation perfectly delightful.

And how much this tells us of Macaulay as a companion! It is all the more interesting to come elsewhere on a letter in

*E

which Macaulay tells how he has enjoyed a quiet holiday at Ventnor. 'I am perfectly solitary,' he writes to a friend. 'I have not opened my lips, that I remember, these six weeks, except to say "Bread if you please" or "Bring a bottle of soda water," yet I have not had a moment of ennui.' Obviously, of course, so voracious a reader and so voluminous a writer as Macaulay must have spent a vast amount of his time in solitude. The talkativeness of authors is probably often a reaction from a too exacting solitude.

Authors, whether silent or loquacious, are, it must be admitted, exceptionally good company—at least, when they are dead. Not many of us share Horace Walpole's dislike even of authors who are alive. 'I have always,' wrote Walpole, 'rather tried to escape the acquaintance and conversation of authors. An author talking of his works, or censuring those of others, is to me a dose of ipecacuanha.'

As for the last sentence, I should say that it all depends on who is the author. The egotism of a mediocre author can be fairly boring, but in a writer of genius even egotism has at times its charms. Mr. Jackson keeps us for the most part in the company of the geniuses—a first-rate host at a first-rate party.

A Very Gruesome Novel

(1947)

FEW English readers, nowadays, have read anything by James Hogg, the 'Ettrick Shepherd,' except what is to be found in the anthologies. Occasionally one sees a reference to him in some journal, as when a correspondent pointed out the other day the similarity of the story in his ballad 'Kilmeny' to the plot of Barrie's *Mary Rose*. But I doubt whether a reprint of his *Poetical Works* would be much in demand to-day even in Scotland, and it would need unusual courage on the part of a publisher to put out a new edition of Hogg's *Tales*, which were collected in six volumes after his death.

Hogg, indeed, is chiefly known to us as one of the most remarkable of the uneducated—or, to be more accurate, self-educated—poets, a literary curiosity who was taken up by Sir Walter Scott and became a contributor to *Blackwood's* in the great days of Christopher North. Born into a shepherd's family in Selkirkshire, he had less than a year's schooling, but this did not prevent him from becoming a great reader, and by good fortune he worked as a shepherd for a bookish employer, who put a library at his disposal. By the time he was thirty-two he had become acquainted with Scott, who made use of his help in his collection of Border ballads, and who persuaded Constable to publish a volume of his poems which—lucky poet!—earned him £300.

Readers of Lockhart's *Life of Scott* will remember an entertaining account of Hogg's appearance at dinner as Scott's guest during a visit to Edinburgh:

When Hogg entered the drawing-room, Mrs. Scott, being at the time in a delicate state of health, was reclining on a sofa. The Shepherd, after being presented, and making his best bow, took possession of another sofa, placed opposite to hers, and stretched himself thereupon at all his length, for, as he said afterwards, 'I thought I could never do wrong to copy the lady of the house.' As his dress at this period was precisely that in which any ordinary herdsman attends cattle to the market, and his hands, moreover, bore most legible marks of a recent sheep-shearing, the lady of the house did not observe with perfect equanimity the novel usage to which her chintz was exposed. The Shepherd, however, remarked nothing of all this—dined heartily and drank freely, and by jest, anecdote, and song, afforded plentiful merriment.   As the liquor operated, his familiarity increased.   From 'Mr. Scott' he advanced to 'Sherra,' and thence to 'Scott,' 'Walter,' and 'Wattie'—until, at supper, he fairly scandalized the whole party by addressing Mrs. Scott as 'Charlotte.'

It is clear, however, that the unconventional Shepherd was the best of good company, and that he never suffered from what is nowadays called an inferiority complex. In later life, as president of the club of Bowmen of the Border, he was the most popular of chairmen at the annual dinner after the celebration of the St. Ronan's Border Games at which, though over sixty, he carried off many of the prizes; and, dressed in a doublet of Lincoln green, he played the perfect host to Scott, the *bons vivants* of Edinburgh, and the local gentry.

I wonder how many of Hogg's acquaintances knew that the merry and muscular Shepherd was the author of one of the most gruesome novels in the English language. The nineteenth-century critics and biographers of Hogg make, so far as I know, no mention of *The Private Memoirs and Confessions of a Justified Sinner* in their lists of his works. I confess I had never heard of the book till that fine critic, never sufficiently praised during his lifetime, T. Earle Welby, brought out an edition of the book in the nineteen-twenties. Even then, though I had the book, I did not read it in spite of Welby's affirmation that 'Poe never invented anything more horrible or with so much spiritual significance; Defoe never did anything with more convincing particularity.' I have been looking for Welby's edition of the book during the past fortnight in the hope that his preface would throw some light on the causes of the book's neglect and produce the evidence of Hogg's authorship; but I could not find it. Unfortunately, in the new edition of the book, M. André Gide does not deal with such matters.

First published anonymously by Longmans in 1824, *The Confessions of a Justified Sinner* takes as its theme the effects of a belief in that perversion of the Christian religion according to which God predestines a certain number of the elect to eternal salvation, however evil their lives, and dooms others to eternal damnation, even though they live the lives of saints. It is a devilish creed, satirized by Burns in *Holy Willie's Prayer* and by Browning in *Johannes Agricola in Meditation*. You probably remember the opening of Holy Willie's outburst of blasphemy:

> O Thou, that in the heavens does dwell,
> Wha, as it pleases best Thysel',
> Sends ane to heaven an' ten to hell,
>   A' for thy glory,
> And no for onie guid or ill
>   They've done afore Thee!

It is hard to believe that any one, having read of the loving-kindness and tender mercies of God in the Old and New Testaments could persuade themselves that He was nevertheless a monster, but this form of religious fatalism probably is not quite dead even to-day. I remember how, when I was a boy, a lay evangelist who used to hold mission services in my father's church told me that there were certain Highland districts in Scotland where it was difficult to make people believe in the importance of conversion, because they took the view: 'If I'm saved, I'm saved, and if I'm tamned, I'm tamned.' I do not think, however, that the majority of believers in the theory of predestination ever interpreted it in this sense. I was myself brought up in Calvinistic surroundings, but nobody that I knew believed that the elect could commit all the sins they liked without forfeiting salvation or that thousands of their fellows were born outside the scope of God's mercy. 'Shake them over Hell, but shake them in marcy' is a prayer I heard of uttered by a local Calvinist on behalf of his sinful neighbours; and the general view seemed to be summed up in the lines of the hymn:

> And while the lamp holds out to burn
> The greatest sinner may return.

The creed in which the chief character in *The Justified Sinner* was trained by the repulsive Presbyterian minister, Mr. Wringhim, is summed up in the paragraph which tells us:

Wringhim's whole system of popular declamation consisted, it seems, in this—to denounce all men and women to destruction, and then hold out hopes to his adherents that they were the chosen few, included in the promises, and who could never fall away. It would appear that this Pharisaical doctrine is a very delicate one, and the most grateful of all others to the worst characters.

Under the guardianship of this perverted preacher and a perverted mother, Robert grows up to believe himself one of the chosen and to feel himself justified in hating his lawful father and his brother (or half-brother) as reprobates consigned to everlasting destruction.

With great imaginative power Hogg depicts the crazy hatred of the young man that grows to such a pitch that, when he is tempted by the Devil in human form to murder his father and brother as a duty to God, he at last consents to do so.

There is an unforgettable scene in which he meets his doomed brother in a mist on Arthur's Seat, and the scene in which the Devil brings the brother within reach of his dagger in an Edinburgh green by night fills the mind with horror. Then comes the fear of retribution with the knowledge that the secret of the murder is out and that no mercy can be expected from the laws of man. Robert is too vile a creature to win our sympathy even to the extent to which Macbeth wins it. None the less, we feel appalled by his fate as that of a fellow human being who has given his soul to the Devil, deceiving himself the while into the belief that he was serving the will of God.

The story is divided into two parts—a plain and sane account of the crime and what led up to it by the editor, and a second account of what took place by the demon-possessed criminal himself. One of the extraordinary feats of Hogg in this book is his presentation of the normal world of likable people such as the father and the elder brother side by side with a supernatural world in which Satan the Tempter assumes a human shape. Realism and fantasy mingle and both seem credible as we read. There have been few more impressive studies of evil disguised as righteousness and used by the Powers of Darkness for the destruction of a human soul.

How Hogg came to write such a book is hard to understand. Scott and his circle appear never to have suspected that he possessed the Tartarean imagination that we find here at work on page after page. This is an account, not of everyday Pharisaism, but of the lowest hell of self-righteousness. That so imaginative a study of religious aberration should have come from a man of Hogg's character and ways is astonishing. Perhaps a fuller knowledge of his character and ways would throw some light on the mystery.

Hero-worship
(1944)

THE recent death of a friend who was a born hero-worshipper set me wondering at what age I myself began to indulge in what is surely one of the supreme pleasures of life.

I am not thinking of heroes in books, like Jack the Giant-killer, but of heroes whom one could see walking along the streets in real life. With most of us, I imagine, the earliest hero to be worshipped was a soldier. English children, I have been told, sometimes make a hero of a policeman; but in Belfast the police brought down their batons indiscriminately on the brains of Orangemen and Nationalists, and that did not seem quite fair. As a result, I regarded policemen with awe rather than reverential devotion.

Soldiers were different. Their very uniforms marked them out as heroes as they trod the pavements—the red coat of the common private or the swinging kilt of the Gordon Highlanders and the Black Watch. One had heard of their deeds, in battles still within living memory—of a battle in the Crimea in which the Russians, seeing a regiment of kilted Highlanders advancing on them, had laughed at them, thinking they were women in petticoats.

The soldier, too, walked the earth haloed—that was the shape of his cap—in fame brought from India and Afghanistan. My nurse's brother had been through the siege of Kandahar, and I often sat on his knee, when he was on leave, with his medals pinned on my chest. He never talked of his experiences, but my nurse filled my imagination with the story of the relief of Kandahar, when men burst into tears as the music of Roberts's approach told them they were free. I do not think I ever wished to be a soldier—the man I envied rather was the Orange drummer with his bleeding wrists—but every soldier was to me a hero—a man from whom a passing nod could put me into an ecstasy.

As heroes, soldiers were succeeded by Rugby footballers—

footballers playing for the school that I loved for years before I had entered its austere portals. There was a half-back—now called a three-quarter—who, while still at school, became an international player—a man with legs as dangerous as were Wooller's in pre-war Wales. To see him passing in the street was to turn and look after him with adoration such as Dante must have felt for Beatrice. And that is one test of hero-worship —excitement in the presence as though a heavenly vision had been vouchsafed to one. One felt that there were great men on earth—men to point out with awe, saying 'There goes So-and-so,' as many of the young in a later generation said on catching sight of Bernard Shaw in the Strand.

Politicians I regarded with interest and even enthusiasm, but I doubt whether I ever put them on a level with soldiers and Rugby players. I stood in discomfort for hour after hour looking at Arthur Balfour as he watched a procession of 100,000 Unionists marching past displaying such misleading mottoes as 'Defence, not Defiance,' and I climbed some high railings to see Lord Salisbury looking rather nervous as tumultuous shipyard workers, having got rid of the horses, dragged his carriage through the streets. But I never idolized Arthur Balfour or Lord Salisbury. Joseph Chamberlain was my only hero among statesmen; and him I did not see till I came to London and happened to be in His Majesty's Theatre one night when he was sitting in a box. Even then, though I no longer followed him in politics, the old thrill half returned as I watched him talking and laughing during the interval with an acquaintance from the stalls. How human, and yet how like a god!

From a fairly early age, I liked seeing people who wrote, even if I did not worship them. Ours was not much of a writing city, but occasionally someone would point out a writer—a barrister, for example, who occasionally appeared in *Punch*— and I would turn my head to look after him with a certain awe.

Journalists, too, seemed wonderful people. MacBride of the *Whig*, chief reporter, was an eminent and never negligible figure in the streets; and when Jacques MacCarthy came from Dublin to describe a football match, he, too, was pointed out as a man of genius—a king of comedy and good nature. And was he not a man of genius? Who else could have described how an

Irishman scored a try in an international Rugby match against England in such a sentence as: 'He fell over the line, festooned with Saxons'?

Actors and actresses came next in the progression of hero-worship. To be stage-struck is to regard almost any actor or actress as a person belonging to another and more wonderful world. Like many other people, I enjoyed a good spell of the pleasure of being stage-struck, and, so long as this lasted, it was an event that temporarily brightened the day to see even a minor member of Benson's Shakespearian company getting on to a tramcar. Perhaps the fact that the stage had been so long associated in Puritan circles with sin added to the glamour; but I think the chief attraction of actors and actresses was that they were artists—artists in an art which one loved and in which one would have given almost anything (except hard work) to excel.

Before painters I never felt awestruck in the same fashion. This may have been because painting was an art of which I was profoundly ignorant and which I had no desire to practise. It was probably also due in part to the fact that a number of my friends were painters in the making, and one does not stand in awe of one's friends.

Later years, I am afraid, slightly dilute the capacity for hero-worship. I fancy the last time I found myself trembling with excitement in the presence of genius was when I was taken up to be introduced to Mr. Shaw.

I still love great men and venerate them; but they seem a little less god-like than they used to be. The declension of worship probably began when one became critical of that god of one's boyhood, Rudyard Kipling. I saw him for the first time at the Thomas Hardy funeral service in Westminster Abbey, and I regret to say that I felt no more emotion than if he had been the mayor of a London borough. The loss was undoubtedly mine.

What set me thinking about hero-worship was news of the death of Frederick Niven—a literary hero-worshipper if there ever was one. It is more than forty years since I first met Niven. I had read one of his novels, *A Wilderness of Monkeys*, and reviewed it with enough enthusiasm to lead to our acquaintance. It was obviously the work of a writer, and by a 'writer' I mean a man who enjoys shaping his sentences and has the capacity to do this. Niven with his reddish brown hair, his lean face, and his burning eyes—brown with a reddish flame in them—was marked for a devotee, and, though he was past his schooldays, he still had something of an initiate's veneration for those who practised the art of letters. I found that he had a book of press cuttings into which he pasted all the contributions of Edward Thomas to the *Daily Chronicle*. Not many young men can have foreseen in those days that Edward Thomas, engaged in what he regarded as hackwork, was a writer who would become famous—and, indeed, immortal—as one of the English poets. Niven, however, was sensitive to the quality of the prose. And he had a piety with regard to good writing that never left him till the end of his life.

I remember his telling me of the excitement he felt in his youth when he was an assistant in a Glasgow reference library and a visitor, wishing to borrow a book, signed his name 'W. Romaine Paterson.' Some of the young readers of to-day may not know that this is the name of the Scottish novelist who acquired an enviable reputation in the nineties with *Nancy Noon* and other books, writing under the pseudonym, 'Benjamin Swift.'

As Niven described his emotions on first seeing an author—and a good author—whose books had actually been published, one felt that he could scarcely have been more excited if Robert Louis Stevenson had walked in.

I have said nothing of Niven's love of the great writers of the past, for in that thousands of others resembled him. It was his capacity for enthusiasm about the work of his contemporaries, not all of them living in a blaze of fame, that made one think of him as the perfect hero-worshipper.

The last time I saw him, he was lying in bed dangerously ill in a cottage in the Rocky Mountains district of Canada, and, though unable to rise, he still burned with all his boyish curiosity about what the new army of writers was doing. Happy though he was in his life in Canada, he could not do without the latest news of books from England, and many of the London literary papers were in his room.

Canada he loved, and he was devoted to the Red Indians, whom he knew intimately, and whom he defended from the common accusation of decadence; but books, and authors, I fancy, were the supreme objects of his idolatry.

As I was standing at the gate on my way from seeing him, a blue bird flew past—the first specimen of the Canadian blue bird that I had seen. It seemed like a symbol of Niven's happiness—the happiness of a man, himself a hero of letters, who, in spite of a life of many struggles that might well have taken the heart out of him, preserved his youthful gift of hero-worship till the end.

Falseness in Literature

(1946)

WHILE I was staying in Belfast recently, I found among the books in my bedroom a Penguin edition of George Moore's *Confessions of a Young Man*. It was many years since I had last read the book; this, indeed, must have been before the First World War; and I wondered how its audacity would taste after so long and tragically clouded an interval. On the whole, it seemed to me, the taste was no longer pleasant. Reality has played havoc with the real or affected frivolity of George Moore as it has played havoc with the more serious philosophy of Nietzsche. We have seen what all this superman's morality has led to in Europe, and the egoist with his supermorality is no longer amusing.

In 1888, when Moore published his *Confessions* at the age of thirty-six, the poor were distant foreigners to many of the comfortable, and, in times of disturbance, even wicked foreigners. The social conscience was less sensitive than it has since become, and it was possible to find Podsnaps among the intellectual as well as among the more stupid rich. Hence cultivated writers could find amusement in George Moore's selfish lamentations over the failure of starving Irish peasants to pay his rents and enable him to live in comparative luxury in Paris. He was not satirizing himself, as you might imagine, when he wrote:

That some wretched farmers and miners should refuse to starve, that I may not be deprived of my *demi-tasse* at Tortoni's, that I may not be forced to leave this beautiful retreat, my cat and my python—monstrous. And these wretched creatures will find moral support in England; they will find pity!

Pity, that most vile of all vile virtues, has never been known to me. The great pagan world I love knew it not. Now the world proposes to interrupt the terrible austere laws of nature which ordain that the weak shall be trampled upon, shall be ground into death and dust, that the strong shall be really strong—that the strong shall be glorious, sublime.

Moore, indeed, seems to have been genuinely convinced that there was nothing the matter with a scheme of things in which the weak would be trampled on in order that he and others like him—'the strong'—might pursue art and luxury without impediment. He even held that injustice was for artists a desirable thing in itself:

Injustice we worship; all that lifts us out of the miseries of life is the sublime fruit of injustice. Every immortal deed was an act of fearful injustice; the world of grandeur, of triumph, of courage, of lofty aspiration, was built up of injustice. Man would not be man but for injustice. Hail, therefore, to the thrice glorious virtue injustice! What care I that some millions of wretched Israelites died under Pharaoh's lash or Egypt's sun? It was well that they died that I might have the pyramids to look on, or to fill a musing hour with wonderment. Is there one amongst us who would exchange them for the lives of the ignominious slaves that died? What care I that the virtue of some sixteen-year-old maiden was the price paid for Ingres's 'La Source'? That the model died of drink and disease in the hospital, is nothing when compared with the essential that I should have 'La Source,' that exquisite dream of innocence, to think of till my soul is sick with delight of the painter's holy vision.

According to Moore, injustice is not only necessary to the production of works of art, but is actually a source of pleasure to a right-minded aesthete:

Nay more, the knowledge that a wrong was done—that millions of Israelites died in torments, that a girl, or a thousand girls, died in the hospitals for that one virginal thing, is an added pleasure which I could not afford to spare. Oh, for the silence of marble courts, for the shadow of great pillars, for gold, for reticulated canopies of lilies; to see the great gladiators pass, to hear them cry the famous 'Ave Caesar,' to hold the thumb down, to see the blood flow, to fill the languid hours with the agonies of poisoned slaves! Oh, for excess, for crime! I would give many lives to save one sonnet by Baudelaire; for the hymn, 'À la tres-chère, à la tres-belle, qui remplit mon cœur de clarté,' let the first-born in every house in Europe be slain; and in all sincerity I profess my readiness to decapitate all the Japanese in Japan and elsewhere, to save from destruction one drawing by Hokusai.

It may be argued that all this is the mere swagger of a young man of brilliant talent eager, like Baudelaire, to shock the respectable: Walter Pater seems to have regarded it as merely Moore's fun. At the same time, there are jests which to a sensitive imagination are intolerable, and, as we think to-day of George Moore gloating or pretending to gloat over the condemnation of gladiators to death and over the thought of seeing their blood flow and filling 'the languid hours with the agonies of poisoned slaves,' the joke—if it is a joke—seems in as poor taste as a joke about the agonies of Belsen.

Defenders of George Moore might retort that even so humane a writer as Charles Lamb made a joke about the Massacre of the Innocents. But Lamb did not even pretend to be speaking seriously, as he did not indulge in prolonged praise of cruelty in general. Never for a moment as we read him is the reality of the Massacre brought home to us. Moore, on the other hand, dwells with pleasure on the sufferings of the victims of injustice and brings the reality of these sufferings home to us by his advocacy of injustice to living peasants and miners.

Unlike Lamb, he was more of an egotist than a humorist; and, if he expressed shocking opinions, it was not so much in a comic spirit, as in order to draw attention to himself. He undoubtedly loved art and laboured at it with a devoted selflessness; but he was only half an artist. The other half of him, it seems to me, was a notoriety hunter, and he himself maintained that the love of notoriety was a universal characteristic of men and women and confessed that he sought notoriety at almost all costs:

Out with you liars that you are, tell the truth, say you would sell the souls you don't believe in, or do believe in, for notoriety. I have known you attend funerals for the sake of seeing your miserable names in the paper! You, hypocritical reader, who are now turning up your eyes and murmuring 'dreadful young man'—examine your weakly heart, and see what divides us; I am not ashamed of my appetites, I proclaim them, what is more I gratify them; you're silent, you refrain, and you dress up natural sins in garments of shame, you would sell your wretched souls for what I would not give the parings of my finger-nails for—paragraphs in a society paper. I am ashamed of nothing I have done, especially my sins, and always boldly confess that I desired to make a noise in the world.

In the Paris that Moore loved so well, eminent figures in the arts were, perhaps, more addicted to notoriety hunting than artists have ever before been in the history of the world. Balzac had advertised himself with a wonderful cane, Gautier with a wonderful doublet, and Baudelaire, rightly or wrongly, was said to have dyed his hair green. It is true that in England Sir Joshua Reynolds had made it a policy to draw attention to himself by driving about in a carriage and pair; but in France self-advertisement reached a point of eccentricity unknown in England, and George Moore became one of the eccentrics, his chief eccentricity being the utterance of shocking opinions.

It always seems to me that in nineteenth-century Paris many of the artists continued to behave like art students when they were old enough to know better. It is natural for the artistic youth to enjoy shocking the respectable: but the worst of shocking the respectable is that the respectable ultimately cease to be shocked, as is shown by the change that has come over literary fashions in the past half-century even in respectable England.

Yet it is surely no bad thing that human beings should be shocked by a false philosophy. The falseness of a pose does not matter if it is merely an affectation meant to amuse us. But false philosophy is a poison that may have dangerous consequences, as we have seen in modern Europe.

Moore became a man of genius, indeed, only when he all but forgot himself and his philosophy. Few prose-writers of our time have painted more beautiful landscapes, and his portraits of Yeats and Edward Martyn in *Hail and Farewell* are masterpieces. The Yeats is a portrait painted in malice, and reveals little of the Yeats who has written great poetry, but it is an amusing caricature.

What prevented him from becoming a great writer, I fancy, was a deficiency of wisdom. In all great writers there is a fundamental wisdom. You feel its presence in Boswell and Anatole France as well as in Johnson and Wordsworth. But George Moore never seems even to have sought wisdom, and one constantly distrusts his opinions, either because one suspects them of being insincere or because they are the fruit of personal prejudice.

As a critic, no less than as a moralist, he was among the eccentrics; and he seldom had a very good word to say for his English contemporaries. Towards the end of his life, if I remember right, he became enamoured of Stevenson, but in the *Confessions* he wrote of him with a curious wrong-headedness.

I think of Mr. Stevenson as a consumptive youth weaving garlands of sad flowers with pale, weak hands, or leaning to a large plate-glass window, and scratching thereon exquisite profiles with a diamond pencil. His periods are fresh and bright, rhythmical in sound, and perfect realizations of their sense; in reading him one often thinks that never before was such definiteness united to such poetry of expression; every page and every sentence rings of its individuality. But Mr. Stevenson's style is over-smart, well-dressed, shall I say, like a young man walking in the Burlington Arcade? Yes, I will say so, but I will add, the most gentlemanly young man that ever walked in the Burlington.

Did any other human being, I wonder, ever think of the writer of *Treasure Island*, *Kidnapped*, and *The Wrong Box* as 'a consumptive youth weaving garlands of sad flowers with pale, weak hands'? If it had not been known that Stevenson was consumptive, who could have deduced that he was from his stories?

At the same time, Moore's literary opinions are usually enjoyable, even when they are eccentric, though I have heard that he once dismissed Thomas Hardy as 'pudding,' and his note on Hardy in *Confessions* is gross enough. The name, he said, prejudiced him against Hardy from the first. 'A name so trivial as Thomas Hardy cannot, I said, foreshadow a great talent; and *Far From the Madding Crowd* discovered the fact to me that Mr. Hardy was but one of George Eliot's miscarriages.'

Many great men have uttered opinions as preposterous; but Moore stopped short of greatness. There was wisdom in Hardy, however, the wisdom of pity, and for want of it much of George Moore's work—though even he fell a victim to it in *Esther Waters*—has lost its vitality to-day.

The Reputation of T. S. Eliot

(1932)

THERE is no living writer whose reputation is more difficult to explain than Mr. T. S. Eliot's. Those who admire him try in vain to show those who do not admire him why the publication of Mr. Eliot's *Waste Land* was an important event in the history of English literature. Those who doubt this find it equally impossible to understand why anybody else should believe it. They see in his work only the shapeless beginnings of the delight of poetry and are sincerely convinced that it will be regarded by future ages as little more than a curiosity of minor Georgian verse.

If Mr. Eliot were merely the idol of a fashionable coterie the case for not admiring him would be simple enough. Fashion in literature is as arbitrary as fashion in dress, and the more obscure a writer is the more likely is he to become the object of a fashionable cult among the intelligentsia. Mr. Eliot, however, like Browning, Meredith, and the later Henry James, has been enthusiastically praised by intelligent men and women who cannot be suspected of swimming with the fashionable stream. In intelligence, in sensitiveness to beauty, in literary seriousness, those who like his work are no more deficient than those whom, in a very real sense, it leaves cold. How, then, is the extraordinary difference in the estimates of his talents to be explained?

Some of his disciples would, no doubt, say that those who are indifferent to Mr. Eliot's poetry are men and women who have lost the capacity for recognizing genius in a new form. This is an assumption that is commonly made when the reputation of a new and original writer is questioned, and has been made even in regard to those who doubt the significance of the work of Miss Gertrude Stein. There is, perhaps, something in the assumption—just as much, let us say, as in the assumption that those who praise a new writer are largely swayed by the passion for novelty. It seems more sensible, however, to assume that there is a case both for and against almost any writer, apart altogether from the age of those who make it, and to try to discover what the case for each side is.

Mr. Hugh Ross Williamson, in *The Poetry of T. S. Eliot*, has stated the case for Mr. Eliot. He writes with exceptional intelligence and is obviously sensitive to the fine things in literature; more than this, he possesses that very desirable quality in a critic—imaginative ardour. Every one who wishes to understand Mr. Eliot should read Mr. Williamson's book. The ordinary writer will certainly find him a useful guide through many obscurities. At the same time, I must confess that, after reading the book, I remain as unconvinced as before that '*The Waste Land* of 1922 is comparable with Wordsworth's and Coleridge's *Lyrical Ballads* of 1798, both as a turning point and as a force,' or, indeed, that it is great poetry at all.

Those who praise a poet ought to be able to prove their case to a reasonably sensitive sceptic by means of quotation. This was Hazlitt's test, and I have known sceptics to be convinced of the genius of Mr. Yeats by this means. Now, Mr. Williamson quotes freely, but I cannot find among his quotations a single one that would be likely to surprise a sceptic into the discovery that it was great poetry. He quotes, for example, the often-quoted passage:

> White bodies naked on the low damp ground
> And bones cast in a little low dry garret,
> Rattled by the rat's foot only, year to year.
> But at my back from time to time I hear
> The sound of horns and motors, which shall bring
> Sweeney to Mrs. Porter in the spring.
> O the moon shone bright on Mrs. Porter
> And on her daughter;
> They wash their feet in soda-water
> *Et O ces voix d'enfants, chantant dans la coupole!*

It is true that the passage depends for its effect on the context; but the great poets all contain passages which, however much they gain from their context, are beautiful even apart from it. Mr. Williamson can explain the allusions in the passage, but, even when everything is explained, it reads more like the work of a writer who is trying to say something than of one who has triumphantly said it.

Mr. Williamson describes *The Waste Land* as 'a poetic cryptogram,' and there is intellectual excitement to be had from solving a cryptogram as from solving a Torquemada cross-word puzzle. Those who look on *The Waste Land* as great poetry, however, obtain more important excitement from it than that. They see in it the imaginative record of a profound spiritual experience—the bitter experiences of a soul engaged upon the ancient quest. One may agree that it is all this while doubting whether Mr. Eliot is articulate enough to write good poetry. His obscurity seems to me to be due not to the difficulty of his materials, but to the fact that he is not sufficiently a master of his medium, words.

We realize this when we read such a passage as Mr. Williamson quotes from an early poem:

> I mount the steps and ring the bell, turning
> Wearily, as one would turn to nod good-bye to Rochefoucauld,
> If the street were time and he at the end of the street,
> And I say, 'Cousin Harriet, here is the *Boston Evening Transcript*!'

Mr. Williamson says that this expresses a number of things, and, no doubt, it is meant to express them. But it produces the effect of an amateurish shot that misses the mark.

Mr. Eliot's prose, as may be seen in *Selected Essays*, suffers from the same lack of mastery of the medium. As a result he often says a quite simple thing in prose that makes it look either profound or obscure. Consider, for example, a passage referred to by Mr. Williamson:

> The only way of expressing emotion in the form of art is by finding an 'objective correlative'—in other words, a set of objects, a situation, a chain of events which shall be the formula of that *particular* emotion; such that when the external facts, which must terminate in sensory experience, are given, the emotion is immediately evoked.

Everything in this passage is clear except the statement of it. I imagine that the difficulties in Mr. Eliot's work are the result, not of intellectual subtlety but of intellectual mistiness. The effects of this mistiness are to be seen in his reading as well as in his writing. One wonders at times whether he understands what the author he reads is getting at.   Thus, after quoting Shelley's lines:

> The earth doth like a snake renew
> Her winter weeds out-worn,

he says that it is not so easy to see propriety in an image which divests a snake of 'winter weeds.'   He could scarcely have made this remark if he had understood that by 'weeds' Shelley meant not plants but the garment of skin sloughed by the snake.

Again, he quotes Swinburne's

> Before the beginning of time,
> There came to the making of man
> Time with a gift of tears,
> Grief with a glass that ran,

and comments:

It is effective because it appears to be a tremendous statement, like statements made in our dreams; when we wake up, we find that the 'glass that ran' would do better for time than for grief, and that the gift of tears would be as appropriately bestowed by grief as by time.

But Swinburne did not mean us to need to be woken up in order to realize this.   He meant us to realize this as we read, and deliberately transposed the 'gift of tears' and 'the glass that ran,' turning what would have been clichés into a moving imaginative statement.

Traces of the same lack of clearness in the understanding of the exact meaning of words are to be seen in Mr. Eliot's appreciation of Marie Lloyd, that mistress of the low-comedy wink, that cornucopia of ribald hilarity, an actress of supreme genius on the saturnalian stage.   Mr. Eliot startles us by contending that her superiority over other music-hall artists was a 'moral superiority': 'it was her understanding of the people and sympathy with them, and the people's recognition of the fact that she embodied the virtues which they genuinely most respected in private life that raised her to the position she occupied at her death.'   And he offers the opinion that the 'lower class' find in the music-hall comedians 'the expression and dignity of their own lives.'   Is it not clear from this that Mr. Eliot uses words, not as things that mean what other people think they mean, but as shadowy counters with a meaning that is entirely arbitrary?

I am quite willing to concede that every critic has 'blind spots' in his appreciation of literature, and that Mr. Eliot's writings may be one of mine. But I should like to see the arguments of the sceptics more frankly met by the answers of those who regard him as a major writer. That he is a sincere and able and scholarly writer is beyond question; but where in his discussion of other artists has he triumphantly communicated his delight or compelled us to understand more lucidly our own delight? It is chiefly because he fails to do these things that he seems to fail as a critic of literature.

The Learned Sailorman

(1947)

ROBERT LOUIS STEVENSON somewhere speaks of
Herman Melville as 'the first and greatest genius to touch the
South Seas'; and in one of his letters, in which he tells Charles
Baxter that he means to write a book on the South Seas himself,
he says: 'I . . . will tell you more of the South Seas after very
few months than any other writer has done—except Herman
Melville, perhaps, who is a howling cheese.'

This is high praise, written in 1888, when Melville, though
still alive, was a half-forgotten author. To-day, when he is more
famous than he ever was during his lifetime, we find Mr. Montgomery Belgion in a new edition of Melville's masterpiece *Moby
Dick* sounding a still louder note of praise, going so far as to
rank it among the 'great books of the world.' Ever since a
critic rediscovered *Moby Dick* in 1914, indeed, it has become an
object of all but idolatry to a widening circle of readers. On
the strength of having been the author of it, Melville is one of
the few American authors who have been included among the
immortals in the English Men of Letters series.

There, John Freeman, a fine poet and critic, presents him as
'the most powerful of all the great American writers,' compares
him with Blake, speaks of 'Hamlet-like soliloquies'; and declares
that 'the never-to-be-ended combat typified by Milton's Lucifer
and Archangels is typified as boldly by Melville's Moby Dick
and Captain Ahab.'

How different this is from the reception given by the critics
to *Moby Dick* when it was first published in 1851! It was
received, says Freeman, with 'a little respect and a great deal of
derision.' And he quotes the verdict of the *Athenaeum* critic:

Mr. Melville has to thank himself only if his horrors and his heroics
are flung aside by the general reader as so much trash belonging to
the vast school of Bedlam literature, since he seems not so much
unable to learn as disdainful of learning the craft of an artist.

If this condemnation, written nearly one hundred years ago,

HERMAN MELVILLE

was likely to decide the general reader against reading *Moby Dick*, I doubt whether the enthusiasm of some later critics is of a kind to make the book seem more inviting. D. H. Lawrence, for example, affirmed rhapsodically that Moby Dick is 'the deepest blood-being of the white race; he is our deepest blood-nature. And he is hunted, hunted, hunted by the maniacal fanaticism of our white mental consciousness. . . . Hot-blooded, sea-born Moby Dick. Hunted by monomaniacs of the idea.'

Again, a scholarly American critic quoted by Mr. Belgion has written of the book:

Man—man sentient, speculative, purposive, religious, standing his full stature against the immense mystery of creation. His antagonist, Moby Dick, is that immense mystery. He is not the author of it, but is identical with that galling impartiality in the laws and lawlessness of the Universe, which Isaiah devoutly fathered on the Creator.

Well may an author pray to be saved from his interpretative friends.

Mr. Belgion, in his appetizing introduction, wisely brushes all such jargon and symbol-hunting aside with the remark:

If, for a monomaniac but individual Ahab pursuing a definitely given whale over the everyday sea, we substitute Man pursuing the mystery of creation over the tossing waters of truth, we shall not have made the plot of *Moby Dick* more exciting to us; we shall have made it less exciting. It will have been impoverished.

Most of us, I am sure, are excited by *Moby Dick*, not as an allegory or philosophical work of any kind, but as a story—a story of a voyage—a story, partly fiction, partly autobiography, and partly science, transmuted into art by a terrific imagination —for the lore of the whale forms as essential a part of it as the novelistic tale of the vengeful pursuit of the white whale that has cost Captain Ahab the loss of a leg. If the book had been merely a novel about Captain Ahab and the hunting of the whale, it could have been written in a quarter of the space, and most of the chapters, as we now possess them, would have to be dismissed as inartistic digressions. Ahab's story, indeed, gives unity to the book and leads it towards a magnificent and tragic goal; but it is only a part of the greatness of *Moby Dick*.

Moby Dick is to my mind Ishmael, the narrator's, story, to a greater degree than it is Ahab's story. Ahab is but one figure in Ishmael's many figured world. Nor do his frequent soliloquies seem to me to be 'Hamlet-like,' rather do they border at times on the fustian of melodrama, as when he addresses the quadrant:

Foolish toy! babies' plaything of haughty Admirals and Commodores and Captains, the world brags of thee, of thy cunning and might; but what after all canst thou do but tell the poor pitiful point where thou thyself happenest to be on this wide planet and the hand that holds thee? . . . Science! Curse thee, thou vain toy; and cursed be all the things that cast man's eye aloft to the heaven whose live vividness but scorches him as these old eyes are scorched with thy light, Oh Sun! Curse thee—thou quadrant, no longer will I guide my earthly way by thee . . . thus I trample on thee thou paltry thing that feebly pointest on high, thus I split and destroy thee!

The less eloquent Ahab is, indeed, the more impressive he is, as when, a slave to his monomania, he refuses the petition of the captain of another whaler to help in the search for a lost boat containing the captain's little son.

The book rises most assuredly to greatness, it seems to me, not in the soliloquies, but in its descriptions of the ocean and the figures human, and other, that frequent it. Both Freeman and Mr. Belgion inevitably quote from the chapter 'The Great Armada'—in which we are told how the ship's boat moves unharmed in a vast meeting-place of thousands of sperm whales in the Straits of Sunda, where the whales, 'like household dogs . . . came snuffing around us, right up to our gunwales, so that Queequeg could lean over and pat their foreheads.'

But far beneath this wondrous world upon the surface, another and still stranger world met our eyes as we gazed over the side. For, suspended in the watery vaults floated the forms of the nursing mothers of the whales and those that by their enormous girth seemed shortly to become mothers. The lake, as I have hinted, was to a considerable depth exceedingly transparent; and, as human infants while suckling will calmly and fixedly gaze away from the breast, as if leading two different lives at the time; and, while yet drawing mortal nourishment be still spiritually feasting upon some unearthly reminiscence—even so did the young of these whales seem looking up towards us, but not at us, as if we were but a bit of gulf-weed in their new born sight.

As for the accounts of battles with whales, each of them is a masterpiece, unsurpassed by any traveller's tale ever told about the wonders of earth and sea.   And each of them differs from the other in glory: the pitiful story of the killing of the aged whale with one fin missing is no less memorable than the picture of the ultimate duel with which ivory-legged Ahab and his ship are swallowed down out of sight, victims of the satanic whale.

The creative energy of Melville, as he recounts the story of the whaler's voyage, is enormous.   He endows every character, from Queequeg, the harpooner and ex-cannibal prince, to the briefly appearing ship's carpenter, with individual life, and makes his experiences our own, whether he describes the removal of a whale's blubber or the play of the monster's tail.   He himself had in early life served on a whaler under a harsh captain, and afterwards declared that the whale-ship was his 'Yale College or his Harvard.'   Seldom has there been a more propitious university education.

One of the astonishing things about Melville is that, though he ran away to sea at the age of eighteen and after an interval at home went to sea again in a whaler and later in a man-of-war, he nevertheless acquired such mastery of a tumultuous vocabulary as suggests constant intimacy with great books from his youth up. It is said that his early writings—contributions to a local paper —show little promise.   It may be that his genius developed late, and that his sensitiveness to the wonder of words came only after his sensitiveness to the wonders of experience had been awakened.   That he at some time of his life became a gluttonous reader is clear from the multitude of quotations about whales from all manner of books with which he prefaces *Moby Dick*. Here and elsewhere he reveals himself as an unconventionally learned man, whose learning comes mainly from life, but also in part from literature.

It would be absurd to think, however, that even when he set out on his adventures, he was merely or mainly a youth in quest of adventure.   He tells us in the person of his other self, Ishmael, that he was but a negligent hand on the whaler 'with the problem of the universe revolving in me.'   And he pointedly warns the owners of whaling ships:

Beware enlisting in your vigilant fisheries any lad with lean brow and hollow eye, given to unseasonable meditativeness; and who offers to ship with the Phaedo instead of Bowditch in his head.   Beware of such a one, I say—your whales must be seen before they can be killed,

F

and this sunken-eyed young Platonist will tow you ten wakes round the world and never make you one pint of sperm the richer.

The spirit of the sunken-eyed young Platonist broods over *Moby Dick*. It is this that has misled some critics into reading the book as a philosophic allegory. The philosophic vision certainly enriches the story; but how ineffectual it would be if it were not paired with the vision of mortal men adventuring away the mysteries of the deep and of the wonders day after day to be found there!

James Joyce and a New Kind of Fiction

(*1935*)

JAMES JOYCE is the only writer in English who has become world famous as a result of writing a book the sale of which was meanwhile forbidden in England. A few—a very few—other authors have had their works suppressed, but none of these has owed the chief part of his fame to his suppressed work. Joyce had undoubtedly won the attention and the praise of critics even before the enormous bulk of *Ulysses* created a sensation among both those who liked it and those who loathed it. But it was only after *Ulysses* appeared that critical circles began to speak of Joyce as a man of genius who had created a new kind of fiction or, alternatively, as one of the literary monsters of a decadent age.

It was only to be expected that on the publication of *Ulysses* Joyce would become the centre of a raging battle of acclamation and denunciation. It was evident to anybody who read him that he was a perfectly sincere artist, in love with truth as he saw it, and no exploiter of obscenity for commercial ends. It was equally undeniable, however, that much of the language that he reproduced in his transcripts from life, or whatever you like to call them, was of a kind that must inevitably shock and outrage ordinary men and women. There are things that even hardened war veterans do not like to see in cold print. This, I think, is the result, not of hypocrisy, but of an instinctive feeling that if this sort of thing goes too far, the baser sort of writers will mingle obscenity with their work for base ends and so lower the code of civilization.

As for Joyce himself, how are we to explain his passion for breaking the conventions of written speech? He is no Rabelais rioting in buffoonery. When he quotes an obscenity he seldom quotes it with hilarity. He quotes it without prejudice on one side or the other, as an anthropologist might quote the saying of an African tribesman. He has been described as a martyr to truth, a sensitive spirit in love with beauty and therefore doubly wounded by the ugliness of the world around him, compelled

to make a faithful report of that ugliness. He may be thought
of as a predestined protestant (with a small initial letter)—a
protestant who, with the most dutiful zeal in the world, sets to
defacing images and wrecking the lovely glass of tradition.

It was once said of Ibsen that he had had a Pegasus shot under
him in early life, and Joyce, too, has had a Pegasus shot under
him. He began his literary career with a volume of poems,
Chamber Music, and even his last experiment in language (*Finnegan's Wake*) is full of the echoes of poetry. At the same time,
as we read *A Portrait of the Artist as a Young Man*, we find that
even in Joyce's youth the lyric rapture had to struggle hard for
existence against the anger and disillusion of the Ishmaelite.
Much of *A Portrait of the Artist* might truthfully be described as
a school story. But how little we feel in it of the ecstasy of
boyhood. The physical delight of being young, the warmth of
hero worship or of friendship, the innocent adoration of first
love, the happy holiday laughter—these form a peculiarly small
part of the background of the life of the hero, Stephen Daedalus.
When the boys laugh, it is not with the infectious laughter of
the boys in *Stalky & Co.*; the laughter in *A Portrait of the Artist*
is harsh and like the crackling of thorns under a pot. It may
seem absurd to compare Kipling's schoolboys with Joyce's; but
I sometimes wonder whether, if Kipling had gone to Joyce's
school, and Joyce had gone to Kipling's school, Kipling would
not still have written a book more or less like *Stalky & Co.* and
Joyce a book more or less like *A Portrait of the Artist*. Art, it
has been said, is life seen through a temperament, and the
temperament contributes as much to the result as the life seen.

Stephen, however, is an infinitely more sensitive boy than
any of the young barbarians described by Kipling. He is pre-
cocious both intellectually and emotionally, and being brought
up in a religious school, he has a profound consciousness of the
sinfulness of sin. Like the character mentioned in *Lavengro*,
however, who felt compelled to commit the sin against the
Holy Ghost, Daedalus regards sin with a mixture of fascination
and repulsion. Flesh and spirit wage a cruel war in him—
now the enticement of sin, now the fear of hell dominates his
imagination. He is tormented as Bunyan was tormented in the
days described in *Grace Abounding to the Chief of Sinners*. Joyce
gives a very remarkable account of the spiritual crisis in the life

JAMES JOYCE

of Stephen Daedalus—a crisis that ended in proud Ishmaelitism, in rebellion alike against faith and fatherland, in courage begotten by despair. 'Look here, Cranley,' he says, towards the end of the book,

you have asked me what I would do and what I would not do. I will tell you what I will do and what I will not do. I will not serve that in which I no longer believe, whether it call itself my home, my fatherland, or my church; and I will try to express myself in some mode of life or art as freely as I can and as wholly as I can, using for my defence the only arms I allow myself to use, silence, exile, and cunning.

That is obviously meant to be read as the confession of an Irishman who could find no rest for his spirit either in the old religious faith or in the new political faith of his country. It is the confession of an Irishman who saw Ireland, not through the eyes of romance, but through the eyes of what is called realism. Stephen Daedalus, it seems to me, was a boy who was so sensitive to things that were unpleasant to the touch and unpleasant to the sense of smell that he could scarcely enjoy the other things that were pleasant to both senses. Similarly, he was more keenly conscious of the flaws than of the virtues of his traditionalist fellow countrymen. Yeats could write sorrowfully of a world in which 'all things uncomely and broken' are an outrage on the ideal beauty. But in his verse he remained a praiser of the ideal beauty. Joyce could not forget the things that were uncomely and broken. They make up the world in which his characters have their being.

Yet, in the volume of short stories called *Dubliners*, we get glimpses of a more normal country—a country in which sympathy and pity and disinterested love have their due places. The story called *The Dead* is remarkable not only for its realism but for the beautiful spirit that hovers in the atmosphere that surrounds it.

As for *Ulysses*, Joyce has described it as 'a modern Odyssey.' He has also said of it that it is the 'epic of the human body.' And in Mr. Frank Budgen's book, *James Joyce and the Making of Ulysses*, from which these quotations are taken, he has added: 'I want to give a picture of Dublin so complete that if the city one day suddenly disappeared from the earth, it could be reconstructed from my book.' I do not know how many readers have gone through *Ulysses* and the *Odyssey* in search of parallels, but I imagine they must be few.   After all, a work of fiction must stand on its own legs, so far as the ordinary reader is concerned, and only scholars have either the time or the taste to pursue remote parallels.   Even as a complete picture of Dublin's pre-war life, *Ulysses*, it is probable, will seem grossly libellous to the majority of the inhabitants of Dublin.   This would not necessarily prove it untrue, but even in the great funeral scene Joyce has been content to describe grotesque surfaces, and he leaves out of the picture some of the profoundest emotions that make life worth living in Dublin, as well as in other cities in other lands.

It has been said that he merely sets down life without praise or blame, but it seems to me that he cannot help writing as a critic.   As a picture of a whole city, *Ulysses* was bound in a measure to be incoherent, and, for the ordinary reader, even the character of Bloom cannot give it a unity that prevents it from seeming at times a bewildering maze.   It is difficult to believe that it could ever become a work generally understood, even in a world able to wander from the surface into the sub-conscious more cunningly than the men of to-day, and more indifferent to the shock of blasphemy and obscenity.   The ordinary man, I imagine, will always feel, if he tries to read it, like a man exploring the depths of the Cheddar caves with the aid only of a box of matches.

Joyce has a sense of humour and a sense of beauty; but he is also a determined psychologist.   'I try,' he declares, 'to give the unspoken, unacted thoughts of people in the way they occur.'   In this matter he has been followed by other writers; but one cannot help wondering at times whether the unspoken, unacted thoughts occur in real life in the way in which the novelists represent them as occurring.   I have my doubts about Mrs. Bloom.

After writing *Ulysses*, Joyce engaged on an experiment in a new language, called *Finnegan's Wake*.   I confess that when I looked at the first parts of it, I could not make head or tail of it.   The sentences seemed to mean nothing.   I had only the vaguest notion of what the characters were doing or talking about.   And yet when I heard a gramophone record of Joyce's own reading of a passage from *Anna Livia Plurabelle* I confess I was attracted, like someone listening to a beautiful foreign language that he does not understand. Spoken by Joyce, the queer, meaningless sentences touch the imagination both in their humour and their music. They can suggest longing and sorrow. I doubt, however, whether, except under the spell of Joyce's incantation, *Anna Livia* will ever convey the musical beauty which his voice gives it. Take the last passage, for example—a passage which a fine modern poet declared in my hearing to an eminent statesman had finally converted him to a belief in the genius of the new Joyce:

Can't hear with the waters of. The chittering waters of. Flittering bats, fieldmice bawk talk. Ho! Are you not gone ahome? What Tom Malone? Can't hear with bawk of bats, all the liffeying waters of. Ho, talk save us! My foos won't moos. I feel as old as yonder elm. A tale told of Shaun or Shem? All Livia's daughtersons. Dark hawks hear us. Night! Night! My ho head halls. I feel as heavy as yonder stone. Tell me of John or Shaun? Who were Shem and Shaun the living sons or daughters of? Night now! Tell me, tell me, tell me, elm! Night, night! Telmetale of stem or stone. Beside the rivering waters of, witherandthithering waters of. Night!

That, I assure you, if read rhythmically, sentence by sentence, has a most musical sound. I cannot explain its meaning. It is obviously meant to touch us through suggestion, not through the intelligence. Whether it is worth while writing like this I do not know. It is, at least, the work of a born experimenter of genius.

Logan Pearsall Smith

(1946)

WHEN Logan Pearsall Smith died I took down such of his books as I could find on my untidy shelves, and was reminded by one of them that, when he published *Trivia*, his friend Robert Bridges said of it that it was 'the most immoral book in the world, though every word could be read in any drawing-room.' Pearsall Smith was certainly not a moralist of the edifying kind.

Brought up in Quaker and Evangelical surroundings in America, he was as a small child canonized in a tract by his father, who told the story of the seven-year-old boy's conversion and, according to the family legend, helped to convert thousands of Red Indians by means of this. His father, however, seems to have been extruded from missionary circles as a result of mixing religion with heresies about sex, and his mother lost her faith as a result of her experiences of religious fanaticism. It is small wonder that Logan grew up a sceptic and cynic, though a cynic of the kindliest sort with ardours of his own.

He tells us that, as he grew older, he 'became more and more haunted by a sense of the oddity of existence, of the fact that, as Plato hinted, this universe is not one which should be taken too seriously'—not the popular view of Plato's teaching, perhaps. It was this sense of the oddity of existence that kept him in a perpetual state of what might be described as good-natured, malicious amusement.

There is a reasonable amount of wisdom, however, sparkling from his cynicism. For example: 'There are two things to aim at in life: first, to get what you want; and, after that, to enjoy it. Only the wisest of mankind achieve the second.' That is certainly a summary of the experiences of many successful people. Again, there is a good deal of sense in the epigram: 'Solvency is entirely a matter of temperament and not of income.' 'Entirely,' however, is rather an exaggeration.

Occasionally his wit is mere persiflage of the school of Oscar Wilde, as when he says: 'An improper mind is a perpetual feast,' or 'If you want to be thought a liar, always tell the truth'; but most of his epigrams are the fruit of observation of life. There is a Chestertonian echo in: 'What could be more enchanting than the voices of young people when you can't hear what they say?' A philosopher, too, reveals himself in the sentence: 'There is more felicity on the far side of baldness than a young man can possibly imagine.'

As a philosopher, Pearsall Smith was a sceptic, not only about other-worldliness, but about worldliness. He laughs at Mammon worship in the sentence: 'The spread of atheism among the young is something awful; I give no credit, however, to the report that some of them do not believe in Mammon.' In his autobiography he returns to the subject of Mammon worship and suggests that it is the chief cause of the decline of good writing among the young. He asks:

Can one imagine any one of the younger literary lions polishing a phrase to make it perfect, or searching dictionaries for the word he wants? They are much too busy setting the world to rights and earning comfortable incomes as they do so.

The need for money, and plenty of it, is, I think, one of the main reasons that the younger generation write so badly. They no longer find the charm, pure as a mountain spring, as Proust describes it, of being poor.

At the same time, he admits his own warm appreciation of the virtues of money, and tells us that he no longer preaches that 'it is a waste of time procuring that commodity.' 'If there is a struggle in the mind of the literary aspirant between God and Mammon,' he writes, 'I advise that the service of the god of money should be followed—as it certainly will be followed in any case.' Such candid cynicism could hardly have appeared anything but immoral to Robert Bridges.

At the same time the moralist constantly peeps out from his aphorisms, and it is no advocate of worldly success who writes: 'It is the wretchedness of being rich that you have to live with rich people,' and 'A best seller is the gilded tomb of a mediocre talent'—a gross exaggeration, needing to be modified in the interests of truth by the word 'often,' as the career of Dickens shows.

Pearsall Smith, however, was a zealot in the cause of good writing. He spoke truth about himself when he wrote that his

*F

last faint message to the world would be: 'You cannot be too fastidious.'

One would have expected the author, whose rather cynical epigrams I have quoted from *Afterthoughts*, to reveal his particular kind of fastidiousness in a love of the clear, unidealistic prose of such writers as Swift.   On the contrary, however, Pearsall Smith revelled in the rhetoric of the great preachers and affirmers. In his anthology, *A Treasury of English Prose*, the authors whom he quotes most lavishly are Donne and Milton and Thomas Browne and Jeremy Taylor; and among the nineteenth-century writers his favourite is that master of decorative sentences, Charles Lamb.   Perhaps this is partly to be explained by the fact that, when he abandoned religion and discovered a new religion in literature, the first poet who became a great influence in his life was Whitman of the barbaric yawp, and that, when he came to England as an Oxford undergraduate, the literary god of the hour was the ornate Walter Pater.

The truth is, he inherited a great deal of the idealism of his ancestors in another form.   Destined to succeed his father in a highly successful glass-blowing business, he decided to sacrifice the prospects of great wealth and to settle in England, where he could pursue a life of reading and writing on what most people would consider a small annuity.   He was no less a hot-gospeller because of his unbelief; but the gospel he believed in was the gospel of art.   For the rest of his days, the pursuit of perfection in literature or one of the other arts seemed to him to be the one thing that rescued life from ignominy.

It is the intermingling of this idealism with pleasantly derisive laughter at the expense of himself and others that makes him so attractive a writer.   He had the heart of an enthusiast and the head of a satirist.   He himself wrote in the book which I have quoted from already: 'Hearts that are delicate and kind and tongues that are neither—these make the finest company in the world.'   He may be said to have realized in his own life his ideal of what constitutes a good companion.

He wrote comparatively little, and his masterpiece *Trivia* is one of the tiniest masterpieces of modern prose.   But he was untiring in seeking the company of good writers, whether in their books or face to face, and he remained young among the young till the last, even though he felt that he had survived the generation that cared for the things he cared about. Commenting on this, he wrote sadly: 'I find that I now prefer the company of idlers and ne'er-do-wells and scallywags'—not a description of his younger friends that need be taken literally, by the way.

Much as he liked the company of the young, he was not one of those elderly sages who sentimentalize over lost youth and who regard youth as more to be praised than old age. Most of the arguments about the respective merits of youth and age are rather foolish; but if we must have such arguments, Logan Pearsall Smith, who thought of his own youth as a time of ignorance and folly, has written a pretty passage which might be quoted in defence of grey hairs:

The debt of our civilization to the ancient Greeks is, of course, beyond all calculation, but in one respect we have no cause to thank them. Their adoration of the youthful human form, in contrast to the Eastern idealization of venerable age, has put a kind of blight on human life; our progress, as we grow older, in wisdom and humanity is thought of in terms of the physical decay which accompanies that luminous advance. We feel ashamed, instead of feeling proud, like the Chinese, of our accumulating years; we are always trying in vain to seem younger than we really are; and in our Western world it is by no means a compliment, as it is in the wise East, to attribute to others a greater age than their appearance might suggest. . . . Our bones are ripening, it is true, for their ultimate repose, but how small a price, after all, is that to pay for the knowledge we have acquired of the world and men, for the splendid panorama of literature and the arts which years of travel and study have unrolled before us, and above all for those adequate conceptions in whose possession, according to Spinoza's wisdom, true felicity consists.

This is the prose of one who had attained serenity through a philosophy that would not satisfy many people and that seldom goes perhaps with 'the gift for being,' in his own phrase, 'kidnapped into heaven' by a lovely line of verse. Like the *Rubáiyát* of Omar Khayyám, however, *Trivia* will remain an abiding source of pleasure to many of those who do not accept its philosophy. I agree with those who count it among the minor classics of our time.

Jean Valjean

(1932)

NOVELS seem to rise and sink in fame to a more remarkable degree than books of any other kind. One generation finds it impossible not to read Sir Walter Scott: another generation finds it impossible to read him. In the course of a lifetime Thackeray shrinks from a giant's stature to the level of a minor classic. Even the same reader frequently fails to discover in a famous novel the genius that it possessed for him twenty years earlier. D. H. Lawrence confesses in his last book his disappointment on re-reading Tolstoy's *War and Peace.* Arnold Bennett was similarly disillusioned when he re-read Flaubert. There is scarcely one of the gods of fiction, indeed, who may not at any minute be dethroned and despised.

Among the novelists Victor Hugo has suffered more than ordinary loss of reputation. There is probably no critic writing to-day who would say of him, as Swinburne once did, that he was 'the greatest writer born in the nineteenth century.' His rhetoric has faded with time; his propaganda is the propaganda of a past age; his characters belong to melodrama rather than to the fiction of human nature; and his sentimentality is as unpalatable to many modern readers as that of a tract. As a result, though long critical studies of most eminent novelists, ranging from Balzac to Peacock, appear from time to time, it is difficult to imagine one of the younger critics spending his labour on a study of Victor Hugo.

Even so, when I re-read *Les Misérables* recently I found it as enthralling as ever. As one reads it, one feels certain that, if Hugo had been born in the present century, he would have been one of the greatest of all writers for the films. He is a master of suspense: he is also a master of the scenic; and the superabundance and variety of his imaginative force are among the most remarkable products of nineteenth-century literature.

Les Misérables, by Hugo's own confession, is an attack on three great evils—'the degradation of man by poverty, the ruin of

VICTOR HUGO

woman by starvation, and the dwarfing of childhood by physical and spiritual night.' 'So long as ignorance and misery remain on earth,' he declares in his preface, 'books like this cannot be useless.'

At the same time, Hugo aims at our conversion, for the most part, not as a preacher but as a story-teller. He sets out to win our sympathies for his merciful creed by compelling us to sympathize with three human beings—Jean Valjean, the convict; Fantine, the outcast woman; and Fantine's daughter, Cosette, the enslaved household drudge, who at length brings sweetness into Valjean's life.

At first, it is true, it is a little difficult to believe in Jean Valjean. We can easily believe that more than a hundred years ago it was possible for a man to be sentenced to five years in the galleys for stealing a loaf of bread to feed his sister's children. We can believe that, because he made four attempts to escape, his sentence was prolonged to nineteen years. We can believe that, owing to his past, he was turned from the doors of even the meanest lodging-houses, and was refused permission to sleep in a stable. What we can scarcely believe, however, is that when the Christ-like bishop of D—— took him into his house, fed him at his table, and gave him a bed, Jean rose in the night and stole his benefactor's silver. Being what he was, a fundamentally honest man, who could not even tell the bishop a lie about himself, Jean could not, in my opinion, have committed that particular crime.

Imaginative writers, however, must be given a certain licence to strain our credulity. Shakespeare strains it by allowing King Lear to behave as he does to Cordelia at the beginning of the play, and, in the result, we do not complain. Similarly, Jean Valjean's theft is artistically justified by the noble behaviour of the bishop when the convict is brought back by the police. It is not surprising that the scene in which the bishop pretends that he has given Valjean the silver, and adds the silver candle-sticks to the haul, remains as vividly and as movingly in the reader's memory as almost any scene in fiction.

Without the theft, this Tolstoyan charity would have been impossible, and without the Tolstoyan charity of the bishop, Jean Valjean would not have been transformed from an embittered ex-convict into a saint and martyr.

Jean Valjean, when we meet him first, is a man of forty-six or forty-seven:

He was a man of middle height, stout and hardy . . . a slouched leather cap half hid his face, bronzed by the sun and wind, and dripping with sweat. His shaggy breast was seen through the coarse yellow shirt which at the neck was fastened by a small silver anchor; he wore a cravat twisted like a rope; coarse blue trousers, worn and shabby, white on one knee and with holes in the other; an old ragged grey blouse, patched on one side with a piece of green cloth sewed with twine: upon his back was a well-filled knapsack strongly buckled and quite new. In his hand he carried an enormous knotted stick. His stockingless feet were in hobnailed shoes; his hair was cropped and his beard long.

When we meet him next, after his two revengeful crimes, the robbery of the bishop and of the little boy, he is transformed into a successful manufacturer who, in spite of his attempts to avoid distinction, has been appointed mayor of his town. This, too, is a little difficult to believe, but it is necessary for Hugo's titanic fable of the inhumanity of justice. Living under the name of M. Madeleine, Valjean is widely loved and respected, not only as a successful man, but as a supremely good man and the friend of the poor and miserable. Thus, it is not merely a rich man but a saint whom the law pursues with its lust for destruction.

The law is represented in Valjean's town by the ruthless police inspector, Javert. The rest of the story is, in great measure, the story of a man hunt, Javert being the hunter and Valjean the prey. Yet, though Javert has suspected Valjean's identity, it is Valjean himself who, by an act of self-sacrifice, throws himself once more into the arms of the law. The police have arrested another man on the charge of being that notorious robber, Jean Valjean, and Valjean appears in court to save an innocent man from the galleys by his confession. Even then the law has no mercy. Javert will not permit Valjean to bring Cosette to her dying mother's side as a last act of humanity before returning to a living death.

When Valjean once more escapes from the galleys in circumstances which convince everybody that he is drowned, he again finds himself Javert's quarry. The story of his having kidnapped Cosette puts Javert on his track, and we find another great flight along with Cosette, in which impossible walls are scaled, and Valjean has to allow himself to be carried out of a nunnery in a coffin and listen to the earth being flung on the lid in the graveyard in order to escape. Again a little incredible. But we believe it as we read, and are as apprehensive for the safety of Valjean as though he were not fabulous. We feel the terror of Javert's pitiless eye more than Valjean felt it.

There is no development in Valjean's character after his conversion: there is development only in his adventures. He is really a magnificent Henry Irving character conceived in the spirit of Dickens and Tolstoy. Or, if there is any development in his character, it is a greater softening that comes with his love for the child, Cosette. Possibly he ceases to be an entirely perfect saint for the moment, when Cosette grows up and he grudges her her happiness with her young lover. But on the whole he is a static figure representing innocence in the toils of justice—goodness hounded down by civilized society. It is because of the beauty of his character that we read with such excitement the story of his ceaseless perils—of his capture by the murderous robbers when, to show his indifference to pain, he brands his flesh with a hot iron; of his fight at the revolutionary barricades, when as a reward for his bravery he asks to be allowed to shoot the captured Javert with his own hand, and takes his old enemy away and lets him go; and of that last extraordinary fight along the sewer of Paris in which he carries the body of Cosette's lover into safety.

Possibly the novel that is half a tract and half a 'thriller' belongs to an outworn convention. The modern world does not seem to produce writers who are at once great preachers and great sensational story-tellers, as Victor Hugo and Charles Reade were. Among all the novels written with this double genius Les Misérables is surely the greatest; and among all the characters who have been created in such novels the most memorable, it seems to me, is Jean Valjean, the ex-convict.

Uncle Toby

(1928)

Of all the masterpieces of English fiction there is none about which the opinions of the mass of readers are more widely divided than about *Tristram Shandy*. It is a book which you will either read again and again or never be able to read at all. Most women, it is said, can see no fun in it, and to many men it is a mere rigmarole of indecency. That it is both a rigmarole and indecent must be admitted. I do not know whether any one has ever tried to tell the plot of the story: there is no definition of a plot according to which *Tristram Shandy* could be said to possess one.

As for the improprieties of Sterne, they are so inseparably interwoven with his writing that to remove them would leave the fabric of his work in shreds and tatters. It is possible to bowdlerize many great authors without doing any great violence to their genius. A bowdlerized Shakespeare is not noticeably less in stature than Shakespeare in the full text. Even Chaucer —though he would suffer more—would emerge with most of his genius left from the pious attentions of Dr. Bowdler. Expurgate *Tristram Shandy*, however, and the lifeblood ebbs out of its veins. It is as though the book were written by a truant imp, climbing over walls to trespass in forbidden grounds, peering into forbidden windows, ringing bells at forbidden doors and running away, and turning round to make mocking faces at the wrathful butler Propriety who stalks out in pursuit. Sterne's fun would lose half its point if he were not perpetually conscious of the imposing and threatening presence of Propriety. His humour is largely a game of hide and seek with decency.

One curious result of this impishness of Sterne's imagination is that scarcely anybody, even among those who read and re-read his writings, likes him very much. Nine out of ten of his admirers speak ill of him and enthusiastically of his characters. Sterne, they say, was a nasty fellow, and a sniggerer, but they become rapturous over the characters of Corporal Trim and

Uncle Toby.   Possibly they are right in disliking Sterne, but at
the same time, by some curious freak, he has contrived against a
background of impropriety to paint a number of figures who are
among the best company in English fiction.   Mr. Shandy, Uncle
Toby, Mrs. Shandy, Trim, and Yorick, they are all people we
should like to have met.   There is not, in fact, a single character
in *Tristram Shandy* whom we should not like to have met.   We
should like to have met even Dr. Slop with his fierce theological
prejudices.   Few novelists but Dickens give us so strong a desire
to have shaken hands with their characters.   It seems to me
that Sterne must have been more likable than he is generally
portrayed since he was the inventor of Uncle Toby.

It is possible that, if one met Uncle Toby in real life, one
would think him a bore.   But even if one thought him a bore,
one would love him.   He undoubtedly contributes little to the
conversation except misunderstanding—misunderstanding and a
general atmosphere of goodness.   He never says a witty thing,
and, though he is a comic character, he has no sense of humour.
He is a man of one idea almost as much as Mr. Dick in *David
Copperfield*.   How he must have bored his neighbours as he
attempted to explain to them what exactly happened at the siege
of Namur, especially as he got so muddled himself in the course
of explanation!   Who could have endured many visits to the
bowling green where he and Corporal Trim defended and
besieged their toy towns and reduced the wars of Europe to a
child's game?   Yet who, reading about them, does not enter
into the spirit of the game, and long to take part in their innocent
make-believe?   There is nothing more charming in the world
than innocence, and, apart from children and saints, what
human beings are more charming than innocent old soldiers?

Uncle Toby, indeed, has all the virtues.   There is not a
beatitude in religion of which he is not deserving.   He is kind,
courageous, generous, and modest.   His imagination is full of
war, but his idea of war is almost saintly in its simplicity.   'For
what,' he demands, 'is war?   What is it, Yorick, when fought
as ours has been, upon principles of liberty—and upon principles
of honour—what is it but the getting together of quiet and
harmless people, with their swords in their hands, to keep the
ambitious and the turbulent within bounds?'   Satirists in our
own time have written as though every one who advocated war

were possessed of the demon of blood-lust, but I think they overlook the Uncle Tobys who still exist with such an angelic conception of honourable war as 'the getting together of quiet and harmless people with their swords in their hands.' Certainly, whatever he may have done in the field of battle, Uncle Toby was, in private life, as his nephew said, a man who 'had scarce a heart to retaliate upon a fly.' In that famous passage in which he refused to kill a fly we have a summary of his gentle character.

'Go,' says he, one day at dinner, to an overgrown one which had buzzed about his nose, and tormented him cruelly all dinner time, and which, after infinite attempts, he had caught at last, as it flew by him; 'I'll not hurt thee,' says my Uncle Toby, rising from his chair and going across the room with the fly in his hand, 'I'll not hurt a hair of thy head. Go,' says he, lifting up the sash and opening his hand as he spoke, to let it escape; 'Go, poor devil, get thee gone; why should I hurt thee?—This world is wide enough to hold both thee and me.

Many critics complain of the sentimentality of Sterne, but this is sentimentality in comic extravagance. We love Uncle Toby not only for the gentleness but for the absurdity of his address to the fly.

Uncle Toby, however, was seldom so eloquent as upon this occasion. He was a man of few words, except on the subject of bastions, escarpments, and the details of sieges, and, if he made a remark, it was as often as not because he had misunderstood something that somebody else had said. He had, we are told, 'a tear at every one's service,' and would interrupt a kindly sentiment with 'Here's a crown for thee, Trim, to drink with Obadiah to-night,' but on the whole he is one of the least articulate characters in English fiction. We remember him less for anything he said than for the way in which he whistled 'Lillibullero' to himself on critical occasions. His protesting blush, as his brother kept referring to the story of how their sister, Dinah, had at the age of sixty married the coachman, impresses him on our memories better than his speech. His brother, Mr. Shandy, indeed, the philosopher with the bee of knowledge in his bonnet, and with the sense of low humour that Uncle Toby lacks, is with Trim the orator of the story, and the contrast between the knowing fool who goes on talking during a childbirth or any other domestic crisis and the innocent fool who goes on misunderstanding the talk produces a continually comic effect through the book.

What happened to Uncle Toby in the end we do not know. Whether he married Widow Wadman or not is as great a mystery as the end of *Edwin Drood*, and the curious thing is we do not wish to unravel it.   This may seem to suggest that we do not care for Sterne's characters in the way in which we care for the characters in the novels we like best, but I do not think that this is the true explanation.   The truth is that while we like them, we are not perturbed about their fate.   We know that whatever happens to them—even if Uncle Toby marries Mrs. Wadman—he will go on smoking his pipe, limping out to his sieges and counter-sieges on the bowling-green, whistling 'Lillibullero' in emotional moments, always remaining as innocent of the ways of the world as he was when Mrs. Wadman came and sat by him in his sentry-box, and asked him to look for the mote in her eye.   We know that, while she is not worthy of him, he will always be able to forget her existence as he did the very moment after he had proposed marriage to her, and asked her to share his hand and his heart.   'When my Uncle Toby had said it,' we are told, 'he did not care to say it again; so, casting his eye upon the Bible, which Mrs. Wadman had laid upon the table, he took it up, and, popping, dear soul, upon a passage in it, of all others the most interesting to him, which was the siege of Jericho—he set himself to read it over —leaving the proposal of marriage, as he had done his declaration of love, to work with her after its own way.'   I am sure that, if he married Mrs. Wadman, he went on forgetting her in the same fashion, as he won his campaigns on the bowling-green and in the kitchen garden with his ivory pipe in his hand, and that he was oftener to be found sitting in the white-painted sentry-box than by the domestic hearth.

A Brontë Portrait

(1928)

OF all the great English novelists of the nineteenth century, the Brontës, perhaps, created the fewest characters whose names have entered like proverbs into the general speech. Rochester in *Jane Eyre* is probably the best known of their characters, and even he owes a large part of his fame to his unintended absurdity. Yet it cannot be denied that the Brontës had a powerful sense of life, or that they were capable of great portraiture. *Villette*, for example, has the reality of a book of memoirs filled with brilliant portraits of people who have really lived. In the whole range of fiction there are few characters that stamp themselves more vividly on the memory than M. Paul Emanuel, the jealous, despotic, bitter-tongued, angelic-hearted professor of literature.

Lucy Snowe, the English heroine of *Villette*, tells us that M. Paul 'had points of resemblance to Napoleon Buonaparte.' Though she speaks as a devoted Napoleon worshipper of the little schoolmaster, she contrives at the same time to paint him with all his faults and with his virtues flashing from them like lightning from thunder clouds. 'Once and again,' she says towards the end of the story, 'I have found that the most cross-grained are by no means the worst of mankind,' and few good men outside novels have ever been more cross-grained than this 'small, dark, and square man in spectacles.'

He was the sort of schoolmaster who is a terror not only to evil doers, but to the virtuous. As a colleague he was about as comfortable to live with as a thistle. He rejoiced in the humiliation of his fellow teachers at Madame Beck's school, and trampled on them at every opportunity. He had the unscrupulous ambition of Satan. At the annual examinations he swept all the other teachers aside and insisted on carrying out the examinations single-handed, a vain little emperor of the school. 'He, this school autocrat, gathered all and sundry reins into the hollow of his one hand; he irefully rejected every colleague; he would not have help.' It is a proof of Charlotte Brontë's

164

genius that she has made the ambition of M. Paul as exciting to us as though his aim had been, not the conquest of a Belgian girls' school, but of the kingdoms of the earth.

We get a first glimpse of the insanity of his ambition when, owing to his ignorance of the English language, he has to leave the English examination in the hands of Lucy Snowe.   He does not do this without a struggle.   On the eve of the examination, Lucy meets him walking in the garden, smoking a cigar, while 'his black whiskers curled like those of a wrathful cat; his blue eye had a cloud in its glitter.'   He abruptly accuses her of ambition, of savouring in advance the joys of authority, of aiming, in fact, at being his rival.   He had seen her playing a part in a vaudeville at the school fête, and tells her: 'I watched you, and saw a passionate ardour for triumph in your physiognomy.'

When she assures him that she did not enjoy playing the part and that she looks forward to the examination with so little pleasure that she only wishes it were well over, he disbelieves her and suggests in order to test her: 'Shall I take it out of your hands?'   'With all my heart,' she replies, 'if you do not fear failure.'   'But I should fail,' he admits gloomily, and then another brilliant notion strikes him.   'My opinion is,' he declares, 'that it would be better to give up the thing altogether; to have no English examination; eh?'   She agrees at once. 'Heartily?' he asks, suspiciously.   'Very heartily,' she assures him.

It is only when he is at last convinced that there is no love of glory in her attitude to the examination that he suddenly seizes her hand, 'and the spite and the jealousy melted out of his face, and a generous kindliness shone there instead.'   'Come,' he says, 'we will not be rivals, we will be friends. . . .   After all, you are solitary and a stranger, and have your way to make and your bread to earn.'   The scene is as incredible as many a scene from the life of Napoleon.   Yet somehow we believe in the reality both of Napoleon and of M. Paul—partly, perhaps, because they were both foreigners.

And not only do we believe in M. Paul: we even like him. After all, is not M. Paul an imaginative portrait of M. Héger, the teacher whom Charlotte Brontë had so passionately adored while she was his pupil in Brussels?   Charlotte Brontë herself had known all the despair of Lucy Snowe as a poor girl alone and without prospects in a foreign city when life seemed 'a hopeless desert: tawny sands, with no green fields, no palm-tree, no well in view,' and she found in M. Héger a demi-god whose presence had turned the desert into a demi-Paradise.

Hence the very faults of M. Paul are steeped in the light of passionate affection, and we do not resent his gross behaviour when in a paroxysm of outraged propriety he drags Lucy away from the picture of Cleopatra in the gallery, or his rudeness to her at the concert, or his insults to her before the class, or his rummaging as a spy among the papers in her desk. We are shocked, but we are not alienated. We have a premonition early in the story that M. Paul is a lover disguised in furious outbursts of temper. He is, to some extent, an anticipation of the twentieth-century sheik, and all the world loves a sheik. 'Decidedly,' he admits, when he has reduced Lucy and an entire class to tears, 'I am a monster and a ruffian.' His very confession convinces us that he is neither.

We learn, too, in time of his secret good deeds, of his sufferings as a lover and his devotion to the memory of a dead woman, of his sacrifice of three-fourths of his income to charities and to the support of the dead woman's relatives who had darkened his existence. 'There never was a man like him,' says Madame Beck, 'for laying on himself burdens greater than he can bear, voluntarily incurring needless responsibilities. . . . Oh, you would laugh could you but know half M. Emanuel's crotchets and eccentricities!' The contrast between secret virtues and glaring faults in the same human being is always charming to fallible mortals; and so we even sympathize with M. Paul when he behaves so monstrously to Lucy on the occasion of his fête.

It is a day on which each of the girls and mistresses is expected to bring a little gift to the great professor of literature, and M. Paul arrives, dressed for the occasion, and with 'a clearness and amity in his blue eye, and a glow of good feeling on his dark complexion, which passed perfectly in the place of beauty.' Every girl in the school has presented her bouquet, and Lucy is about to present her little gift of a box, when a tactless remark of Mlle St. Pierre suddenly makes her as obstinately dumb and impotent as Cordelia. 'Est-ce là tout?' asks M. Paul, in hollow tones, conscious that one gift is missing. 'Est-ce là tout?' he repeats, and then again, 'in really tragic tones,' 'Est-ce là tout?' as Lucy's present is not forthcoming.

Lucy continues silent and M. Paul, casting his dignity and self-control to the winds, breaks forth into a violent and unpardonable denunciation of *les Anglaises*, abusing not only their minds, manners, and morals, but 'their tall stature, their long necks, their thin arms, their slovenly dress, their pedantic education, their impious scepticism, their insufferable pride, their pretentious virtue.'

'Oh,' cries Lucy Snowe, 'he was spiteful, acrid, savage, and, as a natural consequence, detestably ugly.' 'Little, wicked, venomous man!' she thought to herself. But do you and I think so? On the contrary, we regard the man as a tender-hearted little Napoleon, who has so little talent for hiding his feelings that he cries out when he is hurt. And so we are positively glad when we catch him surreptitiously ransacking the papers in Lucy's desk later in the evening, since this leads him to discover the little present she had meant to give him and so is the means of bringing about a reconciliation.

In the course of *Villette* Lucy Snowe observes that she always preferred books 'on whose style and sentiment the writer's individuality was plainly stamped.' *Villette* itself is a novel on whose style and sentiment the writer's individuality has been stamped with a plainness rare in fiction. It is as personal as a lyric. It is one of those novels in which the author is the most important character in the book. These, we feel, are scenes in which Charlotte Brontë herself took part; these are people who humiliated her and were kind to her, whom she hated and loved.

The weakness of the close of the book is due to the fact that she could no longer write as an autobiographer, telling of a love that had been put aside, but wrote as a novelist, telling of lovers whose love was stronger than death. M. Paul, bereft of his ill nature and his livid jealousy, becomes only half himself in those last pages in which, having established Lucy in a school of her own, he asks her to marry him on his return from his travels.

We do not believe that the plottings of priests or of dependants or of Madame Beck could have persuaded him to face those years of separation from Lucy in Guadaloupe, even for the most charitable purposes. We might not object to his being tamed by Lucy, but we object to his being tamed by Père Silas and Madame Beck. We have learned to love him as a toad with a jewel in its head, and we resent his appearance as a too submissive Prince Charming. 'Abrupt, whimsical, and irate'—we would not have him changed. In fiction, we like a hero to achieve virtue without losing his character.

Squire of the Squirearchy
(1948)

THE appearance of Sir John Squire's *Selected Poems* reminds me of a time when Sir John was regarded as the leader of a school of poetry as Mr. Auden is commonly regarded to-day. In those days he and his fellow poets were nicknamed 'The Squirearchy'; and the still younger poets who revolted against the domination of the Squirearchy seemed to think of its members as traditional to the point of lifelessness or as nature poets whose intimacy with nature was confined to week-ends in the country.

Those who are still vaguely of this opinion would do well to get hold of *Selected Poems*, and compare it with the work of the 'modern' poets of to-day. They will find that there, however ardently Sir John may have upheld the great literary traditions as a critic, he was far from being a slave to tradition in his verse. His diction is seldom what is called poetic diction: he often gets his most poignant effects in language that is almost colloquial. His rhythms are dictated by his emotions, not by conventions. And as for subjects, it was not a mere week-end nature poet who wrote the long poems—not included here—on a Rugby football match and the Chicago stockyard and chose 'In a Restaurant' as a theme for an ode.

His emotions are no more responsive to the songs of birds than to the spectacle of a deserted Regency house in the country, flaking and peeling in the rain; and how imaginatively he re-creates the eerie desolation of the scene as he speculates on the old retired colonel who is said once to have inhabited it!

> Was it wet when he lived here,
> Were the skies dun and hurrying,
> Was the rain so irresolute?
> Did he watch the night coming,
> Did he shiver at nightfall,
>   Before he was dead?
> Did the wind go so creepily,
> Chilly and puffing,

> With drops of cold rain in it?
> Was the hill's lifted shoulder
> So lowering and menacing,
>   So dark and so dread?
>
> Did he turn through his doorway
> And go to his study,
> And light many candles?
> And fold in the shutters,
> And heap up the fireplace
>   To fight off the damps?
> And muse on his boyhood,
> And wonder if India
> Ever was real?
> And shut out the loneliness
> With pig-sticking memoirs,
>   And collections of stamps?

And how well the landscape and the mood of the poet are matched in the final verse!

> And I leave him behind me,
> For the straggling, discoloured
> Rags of the daylight,
> And hills and stone walls
> And a rick long forgotten
>   Of blackening hay:
> The road pale and sticky,
> And cart-ruts and nail marks,
> And wind-ruffled puddles,
> And the slop of my footsteps
> In this desolate country's
>   Cadaverous clay.

There you have poetry that, hovering at times on the edge of prose, never ceases to be poetry, and that to me at least gives the same imaginative pleasure that it gave when I first read it thirty years or more ago.

A poem more obviously poetic in content is 'The Birds,' in which the unchangeable life of the birds is contrasted with the ever-changing phenomenon of human life:

> A million years before Atlantis was
> Our lark sprang from some hollow in the grass,
> Some old soft hoof-print in a tussock's shade;
> And the wood-pigeon's smooth snow-white eggs were laid,

High amid green pines' sunset-coloured shafts,
And rooks their villages of twiggy rafts
Set on the tops of elms, where elms grew then,
And still the thumbling tit and perky wren
Popped through the tiny doors of cosy balls
And the blackbird lined with moss his high-built walls;
A round mud cottage held the thrush's young,
And straws from the untidy sparrow's hung.
And, skimming forktailed in the evening air,
When man first was were not the swallows there?

This is the writing of one who has been moved to the centre by the miracle of creation, and how finely this is celebrated in the closing lines of the poem:

O delicate chain over all the ages stretched,
O dumb tradition from what far darkness fetched:
Each little architect with its one design
Perpetual, fixed and right in stuff and line,
Each little ministrant who knows one thing,
One learned rite to celebrate the spring.
Whatever alters else on sea or shore,
These are unchanging: man must still explore.

To illustrate the virtues of a lyric poet one ought, of course, to quote, not excerpts, but complete poems. Most of Sir John's best poems, however, are too long to quote in full, though 'An Epitaph' shows how he can pack riches into four lines:

Shiftless and shy, gentle and kind and frail,
    Poor wanderer, bewildered into vice,
You are freed at last from seas you could not sail,
    A wreck upon the shores of Paradise.

In 'The Stronghold,' again, he conveys morality touched with emotion in a brief space; and in a sonnet, 'The Seldom-Flowering Tree,' he writes his apologia as a poet of only intermittent utterance. After celebrating the loveliness of the annuals and perennials of the flower garden, he concludes:

I envy not these flowers so often seen,
    For I am of those trees, coiling and dark,
Which year-long stand in shrouded sombre green,
    But sprouting from whose patient iron bark
A few large, shapely, glimmering blooms appear,
Burning in darkness, every seventh year.

I fancy, however, that the intermittency of Sir John's inspiration is due largely to his extraordinary versatility. When I met him first not very long after he had come down from Cambridge, he had published verse translations of Baudelaire, a historical biography of William the Silent, and a volume of brilliant parodies and burlesques, *Imaginary Speeches*. Not long afterwards he became the first literary editor of the *New Statesman* under Clifford Sharp and contributed to it a delightful weekly causerie over the pseudonym Solomon Eagle. These causeries were afterwards collected into three volumes entitled *Books in General*, and when I re-read them the other day I found them as entertaining as ever.

It was during this period that he wrote most of the verse by which he is best known; and it was largely in order to encourage the younger poets that he founded the remarkable literary monthly, *The London Mercury*. As editor, he devoted his space not only to literature but to architecture and to the saving of national treasures, such as Stonehenge, and he extended his propaganda on behalf of a comelier England by founding the Architecture Club. He then tried his hand at fiction, and the result was a very enjoyable book of short stories, *The Grub Street Nights' Entertainments*—a book which would be well worth adding to the Penguin series.

Nor does this complete the list of his activities. In *The Gold Tree* we meet him as an essayist. In *Essays on Poetry* he is a literary critic in more serious vein than in Solomon Eagle's causeries. He was the presiding spirit on the Hawthornden Committee, founded by Miss Warrender for the encouragement of young authors and, more important than this, became editor of the new English Men of Letters Series for Messrs. Macmillan. And, as if this were not enough to keep a man busy, he stood on three occasions as a candidate for Parliament and founded the Invalids Cricket Club which provided A. G. Macdonell with some of the material for *England, Their England*.

And even now I was nearly forgetting some things. He collaborated on a stage version of *Pride and Prejudice*. He has written two volumes of a most enjoyable autobiography almost as capricious in its arrangement as *Tristram Shandy*. And he busied himself in producing a little newspaper during the General Strike.

All this suggests an exceptional energy and variety of character, and to what unselfish ends that energy has often been devoted! Never did a writer welcome with greater enthusiasm a younger writer in whose talent he believed.   I remember how eagerly he talked many years ago of a young man called J. B. Priestley, who had just come down from Cambridge.   He prophesied that this young man would in twenty or thirty years' time become as eminent a figure in literary London as Dr. Johnson once was, and indeed nominated him for the part of literary dictator. Well, Mr. Priestley has turned out somewhat differently, but, as I listened to his broadcasts during the war, I sometimes marvelled at the foresight with which Sir John had chosen him—then a tyro with only a few squibs, essays, and reviews to his name—as a coming national figure.   I think that was a pretty good shot.

Di Vernon

(1926)

DIANA VERNON is the most charming of Sir Walter
Scott's heroines. Most of us fall in love with her in our teens
the moment she gallops into the wild landscape of *Rob Roy*,
'mounted on a beautiful horse, jet-black, unless where he was
flecked by spots of the snow-white foam which embossed his
bridle.' A heroine is never so much a heroine as when on
horseback, and never had a heroine on horseback a more
romantic setting than in the native glen of the Osbaldistones.
Mr. Francis Osbaldistone, coming from London on a visit to his
uncle, lost his heart at once as she rode past, while 'her long
black hair streamed on the breeze, having in the hurry of the
chase escaped from the ribbon which bound it.'

She not only moves our admiration as 'the fair Amazon,'
however: she also moves our sympathy and our eager curiosity
as beauty in distress, beauty in the toils of a mysterious fate.
Her cousins, the Osbaldistones, were as savage as any Doones—
all except Rashleigh, schemer and plotter, who was bent upon
marrying her, and he was a 'bandy-legged, bull-necked, limping
scoundrel,' who is portrayed as 'Richard III in all but his hump-
back.' Diana herself described the whole family as 'the Orang-
Outangs, my cousins.' Drunken, barbarous, ignorant, they
were the sole companions of her girlhood, and the only means
of escape from them that lay before her seemed to be the
convent.

She owes a great part of her appeal to us to the fact that she
did not submit tamely to these circumstances. She had what
men flatter themselves by calling a masculine independence of
spirit. 'I belong,' she once told Francis, 'in habits of thinking
and acting, rather to your sex, with which I have always been
brought up, than to my own.' She refused to be less than a
man in the exercises either of body or of mind. She could
saddle and bridle a horse, clear a five-barred gate, and 'fire a
gun without winking,' and, rivalling her savage cousins in these

accomplishments, she also made herself master of Latin and Greek with the assistance of Rashleigh. 'Science and history,' she told Francis, 'are my principal favourites; but I also study poetry and the classics.' There are not many heroines of eighteen in fiction who could talk like this without being suspected of priggishness. But Diana is never priggish: she is too passionate for that. Her learning is not the ornament of self-satisfaction but the flag of a rebel.

Diana, indeed, is a rebel in more senses than one. She is not only a learned lady among wild beasts: she is also a beautiful young Jacobite in days when it is still possible to lose everything by following the Stuarts. Francis Osbaldistone, himself a Whig and a Presbyterian, tries to quench his love for her by telling himself that she is 'a Catholic, a Jacobite, a termagant into the boot.' But, no doubt, the romance of the lost cause cast a golden light round her for him as it does for us. She is everything that is rare, strange, and heroic—'a wild slip,' as Andrew Fairservice called her—one of the most beautiful women of action in literature.

If a fault can be found with her, it is that Sir Walter Scott does not give her enough to do. He is content to describe her beauty and to picture her situation. But in the end he gives us the portrait of a heroine rather than a narrative of her heroic deeds. She does, indeed, rise to the occasion and act with masterly decision, when the treacherous Rashleigh so contrives things that Francis is accused of having played the highwayman and robbed a King's messenger of important documents. It is she who takes Francis up the little hill and, drawing up her horse under the birch-trees, points to the Scottish border eighteen miles off and bids him fly for his life. When Francis refuses to go till his reputation has been cleared, it is she who accompanies him to old Squire Inglewood, the Justice, and forces the reluctant and angry Rashleigh to produce Rob Roy himself as a witness to the innocence of the young Whig from London. Everything that she puts her hand to she carries through magnificently, but for the most part she has little more to do than domineer over her cousins. 'I am a girl, and not a young fellow,' she tells Francis on one occasion, 'and would be shut up in a mad-house if I did half the things that I had a mind to.' Sir Walter is content to give us these brief glimpses of the lovely Diana's lovely character. But he does not sufficiently show us her character in action.

It is true that the chief activities of her life go on behind the scenes. We have a hint of them in the mysterious figure whose shadow is seen walking beside hers across the windows of the old library. This is her secret, and it is because he has discovered it that Rashleigh hopes to be able to force her to marry him. Here, again, the romantic imagination glows for Diana as we learn of all that she is enduring through hiding and watching over her father, the Jacobite refugee with a price on his head. More than ever she seems to be doomed either to marriage with a beast or to the convent, and, were it not that her secret has been discovered, we feel that she would fly to the convent with a sense of joyful escape. She is, she says herself in a burst of indignation at the way in which Rashleigh talks of her coming marriage, 'like the poor girl in the fairy tale, who was betrothed in her cradle to the Black Bear of Norway, but complained chiefly of being called Bruin's bride by her companions at school.' What reader does not feel in an agony of anxiety when Francis is compelled to leave her— 'a princess deserted by her subjects and deprived of her power' —surrounded by perilous mysteries to which it is not in her power to give him the key. She can only warn him that the secrets are not hers to give away, and beg him to believe that she is 'a plain true-hearted girl, who would willingly act openly and honestly by the whole world, and fate has involved me in such a series of nets and toils and entanglements, that I dare hardly speak a word for fear of consequences—not to myself, but to others.'

'We never meet more,' she tells him as she holds out her hand to him, and, as she disappears into her room from his farewell embrace, she seems doubly beautiful under the doom that overhangs her.

The second half of the story is Rob Roy's as the first half is Diana's. And yet, in a sense, the second half is Diana's too, for, though she scarcely appears in it, she is the goddess who directs events. It is she who gives Francis the sealed packet, only to be opened in the last extremity, that in the end enables him to recover his father's fortune, which has been brought to the verge of ruin by the treachery of Rashleigh. If Rob Roy is there in the cathedral crypt in Glasgow to whisper 'You are in danger in this city' in Francis's ear, it is as Diana's messenger. And the adventures of ambush, battle, and murder among the hills in the company of Rob Roy, Andrew Fairservice, and Bailie Nicol Jarvie are all the outcome of Diana's plan for the salvation of a young man and his father's house.

At the same time, we grudge her absence from the scene. With what delight we ultimately discover that one of the two horsemen who come up with Francis in the moonlight in the solitude of the Highland hills is Diana Vernon in a man's cloak! Here, again, she is the goddess of events, for she is now able to give Francis another packet that restores him the family fortune. 'You see, my dear coz, I was born to be your better angel,' she says. It would be unbearable if the eternal farewell she again speaks on this occasion were indeed to be eternal. And, when the 1715 rebellion is over, and Diana and her father are both fugitives under the protection of Francis at Osbaldistone Hall, we are at last assured of a happy ending.

What Diana's adventures were during those terrible days—days all the more terrible because Rashleigh had turned traitor to the Jacobite cause and assisted in its ruin—Scott does not tell us in detail. But Diana's father, Sir Frederick, tells Francis a little of them. 'She has,' he says, 'endured trials which might have dignified the history of a martyr; she has faced danger and death in various shapes; she has undergone toil and privation, from which men of the strongest frame would have shrunk; she has spent the day in darkness, and the night in vigil, and has never breathed a murmur of weakness or complaint.' Has there ever been a heroine with fewer faults? Has there ever been a heroine with more entrancing virtues than Diana Vernon?

A Hardy Heroine

(1928)

EVEN during the lifetime of Thomas Hardy, if you took a seat on a charabanc going westward from Bournemouth, there was usually a guide who kept shouting through a megaphone to the passengers all sorts of information about what he called 'the 'Ardy Country.' On one such occasion, on the way back from Lulworth Cove, I remember the guide's pointing to a certain lane and telling us in a deafening voice: 'Ladies and gentlemen, up this little lyne to the left is the cottage w'ere 'Ardy wrote 'is fymous novel, "Aw'y from the Maddeneen Crahd."' He had got the name slightly wrong, and I do not know whether he was any more accurate in the rest of his information, but the number of things he told us about 'Ardy and his characters during the journey afforded evidence at least that Hardy had made a country-side blossom with new associations as no other modern novelist has done. His characters are now a part of the legend of Wessex, equally with its greatest historic inhabitants.

The truth is, though Hardy wrote chiefly about the men and women of his own time, he wrote about them in the spirit of legend. Despite the melancholy cast of his temperament, the sun of the Heroic Age rises again in his pages, and Achilles, Hector, and Helen are reborn in the farmhouses and the labourers' cottages of the West Country. The increasing pessimism of his later works has blinded many readers to the fact that the novels of Hardy, no less than the stories of Conrad and Mr. Kipling, are in the tradition of heroic literature.

And of them all *Far from the Madding Crowd*, the name of which the man on the charabanc so sadly mangled, is perhaps the most heroic in its material. Bathsheba Everdene, Gabriel Oak, and Sergeant Troy are all of the line of the demi-gods in some of their qualities. It is difficult, I admit, to accept as a demi-god a man of whom we are told on the very first page:

When Farmer Oak smiled, the corners of his mouth spread till they were within an unimportant distance of his ears, his eyes were reduced

178

THOMAS HARDY

to mere chinks, and diverging wrinkles appeared round them, extending upon his countenance like the rays in a rudimentary sketch of the rising sun;

but we have only to read on—to read of the terrible night on which all his sheep were driven to their death over the cliff by a foolish dog, of his beginning a new life in a labourer's smock after the ruin of his ambitions, of the way in which he saved Bathsheba's sheep after her cruel treatment of him, of his super-human energy in the midnight of lightning and tempest in which he preserved from destruction her £750's worth of stacked wheat and barley while her newly married husband and her men lay in a drunken stupor—in order to realize that, if he had lived in the morning of the world, he would have been a prince in the *Iliad*.

As for Bathsheba, if she did not love Gabriel Oak immediately, as he loved her, it may have been because the demi-god in him was at first too efficiently disguised. He, with his grin and his rustic manners, might easily have been mistaken for an ordinary mortal. She, from the moment at which he first sees her, sitting in the yellow two-horse wagon with the caged canary among the pots of geraniums, myrtles, and cactuses, is a being apart. We can never forget the picture of her, with the sun lighting up her black hair and her scarlet jacket, as she takes out the swing-mirror in the wagon and smiles at her reflection, not knowing that Gabriel is watching her.

She never ceases to be feminine in her frailties, but her beauty, her courage, her independence set her as high above the multitude of women as Gabriel Oak is above the multitude of men. Towards the end of the story Hardy tells us that 'she was of the stuff of which great men's mothers are made.' The greatness of her character is no more obscured by the occasional foolishness of her conduct than is the greatness of Gabriel's character by the occasional foolishness of his smile.

She is in a great part of her being a piece of wild nature, unsubmissive to the slavery of rules. 'She was going to be a governess once, you know,' her aunt tells Gabriel, when he comes to woo her, 'only she was too wild.' Later, when she was mistress of a farm, we are told that her beauty belonged 'rather to the demonian than to the angelic school,' so that 'she never looked so well as when she was angry,' and even this seems to emphasize a certain wild demoniac energy in her character.

In the admirable nineteenth-century fashion, however, she combined innocence with wildness and 'demonian' beauty. Until she met Sergeant Troy, according to Hardy, 'she had been proud of her position as a woman; it had been a glory to her to know that her lips had been touched by no man's on earth— that her waist had never been encircled by a lover's arm.' Her wildness ran for the most part to feats of horsemanship, indeed, and to such freaks of playfulness as sending the valentine to Mr. Boldwood that was the first seed of the murder of Sergeant Troy and was to bring Boldwood himself within a hairbreadth of the gallows.

Few novelists would deduce such a train of tragedy from a valentine sent in jest, and it must be admitted that Hardy in his plots is no more realistic than the teller of a fairy-tale. Yet how seldom in this book does he lose hold of reality! His countryside scenes—the lambing ewes, the fire in the rickyard, the sheep-shearing—have the reality of history as well as of poetry, and his characters are bathed in the reality of their setting.

Even the handsome and devilish Sergeant Troy emerges as a real person from the scarcely credible scene in the hollow amid the ferns in which he gives Bathsheba the demonstration of swordplay, flashing his sword round her head in the evening sunshine, and bringing it so close to her at each cut that at the end of the demonstration he assured her: 'More precisely speaking, you have been within half an inch of being pared alive two hundred and ninety-five times.' Sergeant Troy's sword dazzles us into conviction as Bathsheba's courage dazzles us; but Hardy had already created an entire landscape of conviction for the scene.

We may hesitate to believe that Bathsheba would have yielded so easily to the flatteries of the wicked sergeant with the earl's blood in his veins, but after all her other lovers were the gloomily persistent Boldwood and Gabriel, a ruined farmer reduced to a shepherd's smock. Troy, moreover, had a wildness answering her own, and a masterfulness such as she demanded in a husband. 'I want,' she had once said to Gabriel, 'somebody to tame me; I am too independent; and you would never be able to, I know.'   Gabriel, she was to find later, was masterful in everything except love, but Troy was masterful in love. Even so, as she confessed to Gabriel while they toiled during the lightning storm to save the cornstacks, she would not have married Troy but for the fear of scandal and the fact that on a fatal day at Bath Troy had boasted that he had seen a more beautiful woman than herself and heightened her love with jealousy.

It was an irony of fate that such a thing should happen to a woman of strong character who in her girlhood 'had always nourished a secret contempt for girls who were the slaves of the first good-looking young fellow who should choose to salute them,' and it must be admitted that Bathsheba was a curious mixture of weak woman and heroine.   In the story of her marriage to Troy she appears as a woman to whom things happened rather than as a woman who made things happen. She is heroic chiefly because of the greatness of her sufferings.

And Hardy spared her no suffering.   He devised many painful and improbable coincidences in his novels, but not many more painful or improbable than that which brought the coffin containing the dead bodies of Troy's victim, Fanny Robin, and of her baby to rest for the night in Bathsheba's house.   I cannot quite believe in the scene in which Bathsheba opens the coffin, is convinced of her husband's guilt, and Troy enters and, falling to his knees beside the dead woman, kisses her while Bathsheba flings her arms round his neck and cries: 'Don't—don't kiss them!   Oh, Frank, I can't bear it—I can't!   I love you better than she did; kiss me, too, Frank—kiss me!   You will, Frank, kiss me too!'   And yet it is the dialogue rather than the scene itself that leaves us incredulous.   Hardy nearly always persuades us when he describes; it is when he makes his characters talk that he fails most often, when he does fail.

There is certainly no lack of descriptive and inventive power shown in the episodes that bring the book to a close—Troy's heartless abandonment of his wife, his swim and supposed death, his return as a performer in a circus to the old neighbourhood, his unexpected appearance at the Christmas Eve party where Boldwood believes that Bathsheba will at last promise to marry him, his murder, and, ultimately, Bathsheba's proposal to Gabriel when she thinks she is going to lose him for ever.   Up till the last Bathsheba has been passive, though magnanimously and heroically passive.   In going to Gabriel's house to propose to him she is a heroine in action.   And, when we read of this, we like her the better for it, and Gabriel Oak none the worse for it.   For, in reading her saga, we have been following the fortunes of a queen.

Mr. Polly

(1926)

MANY people like Mr. Polly best of all H. G. Wells's characters. The appeal of Mr. Polly, I fancy, is at bottom much the same as the appeal of the hero of a Harold Lloyd film. His story is the comic fable of a failure who makes good—of a butter-fingers who at a crisis is transformed into a hero. There is no better fighting of the knockabout kind in fiction than the fighting in *The History of Mr. Polly*. It is as a fighter that this little man who does not know how to fight remains in our memories and affections.

Until he was nearly forty years old, nothing had even happened to Mr. Polly except indigestion. He was born and he married, it is true, but these were trifling events compared with his daily attacks of indigestion. He seems never to have fallen in love and never to have formed a lasting friendship. Once he had nearly fallen in love with a red-haired girl sitting on a wall, but that was only the romance of a sentimental passer-by. Why he married it would be difficult to explain. In his marriage, as in the rest of his life, he was more of a helpless victim than the master of his fate. He was then and afterwards merely an inconspicuous drop in the great 'stream of human failure.'

He was even a failure at his business. He was, we are told, 'not naturally interested in hosiery and gentlemen's outfitting,' and the little shop in Fishbourne was—naturally—not paying. Apart from his love of books, there was not a single thing in his life that seemed to make it worth living. And the indigestion that resulted from his wife's cookery seemed to make it decidedly not worth living. At the same time, it was his indigestion that in the end turned him into a famous character in fiction. It drove him into revolt, brought about the bad temper that led to the first fight with Mr. Rusper, the ironmonger, made him set his house on fire, and so brought about his flight from home and all those desperate battles with Uncle Jim in the neighbourhood of the Potwell Inn.

Nowhere else in literature, I think, has indigestion been made the principal theme of a novel. Mr. Polly's indigestion is as important in its way as Othello's jealousy or Shylock's vengefulness. Mr. Polly had no passions that were not directly attributable to it. His life was a little epic of indigestion. When Wells wishes to tell us what sort of man Mr. Polly was, he describes him as 'a battleground of fermenting foods and warring juices'—as 'not so much a human being as a civil war.' In appearance, Mr. Polly was 'a short, compact figure, and a little inclined to localized *embonpoint*'; but that does not tell us as much about him as we learn from a description of his Monday dinner—cold pork, mixed pickles, cold suet pudding, treacle, cheese, bread, and a jugful of beer. 'Wonderful things must have been going on inside Mr. Polly,' says Wells, after telling us of this unholy meal. 'Oh! wonderful things.' It is little wonder that he slammed his way out of the house, 'a figure of sinful discontent,' in a mood of 'violent rage and hatred against the outer world.'

Even indigestion so extreme as this did not, however, immediately incite Mr. Polly to heroic deeds. He was at first content merely to hate his neighbours and to say sharp things about them behind their backs, as when he called Hinks, the sporting saddler in the check suit and tight trousers, the 'chequered careerist,' and spoke of his patterned legs as 'shivery shakys.' But when Mr. Hinks heard about it and threatened him with physical violence, Mr. Polly made no heroic response to the large freckled fist that was shaken under his nose. 'You been flapping your mouth about me, I'm told,' said Mr. Hinks:

Mr. Polly suddenly felt spiritless. 'Not that I know of,' he answered.

'Not that you know of, be blowed! You been flapping your mouth.'

'Don't see it,' said Mr. Polly.

'Don't see it, be blowed! You go flapping your silly mouth about me, and I'll give you a poke in the eye. See?'

And Mr. Polly saw.

Perhaps it was because Mr. Rusper, the ironmonger, whose head 'was the most egg-shaped head he had ever seen,' was of a less sporting figure that Mr. Polly ventured on a physical tussle with him on the day on which he fell off his bicycle among the ironmongery on the pavement and began to behave like a bull

in a china shop. Even here, however, the incompetence of
Mr. Polly as a fighter, rolling about among the pails, was more
conspicuous than his daring:

There on the pavement, these inexpert children of a pacific age,
untrained in arms and uninured to violence, abandoned themselves to
amateurish and absurd efforts to hurt and injure one another—of which
the most palpable consequences were dusty backs, ruffled hair, and
torn and twisted collars. Mr. Polly, by accident, got his finger into
Mr. Rusper's mouth, and strove earnestly for some time to prolong
the aperture in the direction of Mr. Rusper's ear before it occurred
to Mr. Rusper to bite him (and even then he didn't bite very hard),
while Mr. Rusper concentrated his mind almost entirely on an effort
to rub Mr. Polly's face on the pavement. (And their positions
bristled with chances of the deadliest sort!) They didn't from first to
last draw blood.

That, however, was a beginning, and when Mr. Polly
deliberately sets his house on fire, and forgets to cut his throat
(as he had intended to do) when his trousers begin to burn,
and saves the deaf old woman next door, and emerges from the
scene of his crime 'amidst a tempest of applause,' we feel that
never again will he have cause to regard himself as 'the faintest
simulacrum of man that ever hovered on the verge of non-
existence.' A nobody has suddenly become a somebody.

He is still a futile enough figure when he runs away from
home and begins a new life as odd-job man at the Potwell Inn
on the river.

His first efforts with a punt-pole as the inn ferryman, when
he splashed his elderly fare with waterweed and hit him twice
with the pole, were just as incompetent as had been his manage-
ment of the shop. But, when Uncle Jim, the landlady's brutal
and drunken nephew, arrived, there came a testing-time for
Mr. Polly that proved him a hero. 'He's the Drorback to this
place,' said the landlady of Uncle Jim. 'That's what he is.
The Drorback.' And one of the things that made him a draw-
back was that he couldn't stand strangers about the place,
needing all his aunt's money for himself, and had driven Mr.
Polly's various predecessors away by threats of violence and even
of torture. When he arrived he at once told Mr. Polly to
clear out, presenting him with a number of blood-curdling
alternatives, ''Orrible things . . . kick yer Ugly . . . Cut yer

* G

—— liver out. . . . See? I don't care a dead rat one way or the uvver.'

It is as fortunate for the rest of us as it was for himself that Mr. Polly, after trembling on the verge of flight, decided to stay and defend the landlady and the little girl in the inn. For, as a result of that decision, we have three of the most glorious comic fights in English fiction. They are fights in which the weapons are beer bottles, boat-hooks, pig's pails, and anything else that comes handy, and it must be admitted that when the 'mad drunk' Uncle Jim knocks off the bottom of two beer bottles with a view to their use in battle and goes forth to destroy Mr. Polly, Mr. Polly takes to his heels and runs like a hare. Happily, in the tussle for the broom that follows the breaking of the bottles, Mr. Polly finds himself able to drive the broom home under Uncle Jim's ribs, pushes him into the river and nearly drowns him, and thus brings the first campaign to an end 'in an insecure victory.'

In the second campaign Uncle Jim mistakes a muscular young camper-out for Mr. Polly, and having come up behind him and assaulted him, finds himself once more ducked in the river, after having his face smacked with raw steak and a parcel of lump sugar burst over his head.

Wells has invented in these scenes a rich world in which almost everything can be used as a weapon of assault. It is a world of whirling words, whirling legs and arms, and the wild whirl of the chase. If Mr. Polly appears armed with a poker, it is to find Uncle Jim holding a dead eel 'by means of a piece of newspaper about its tail,' and passionately swiping a spectacled hotel guest under the jaw with it. You will have to go to *Don Quixote* for more fantastically hilarious fights than these. It is true that in the end a more normal weapon is introduced, and Mr. Polly in his night-shirt has to hide among the nettles in the churchyard while Uncle Jim tries to pot him with a rook rifle. But the fighting as a whole is magnificently incompetent, and Mr. Polly remains to the last a futile little man, though a hero. In his story Wells has given us a comic modern version of the defeat of Goliath. His book is a farcical fable of the triumph of the bottom dog.

Robinson Crusoe

(1927)

ROBINSON CRUSOE is as familiar a figure in the general imagination as Jack the Giant-killer. He is, I think, the only hero of a long novel who has frequently been the centre of a Christmas pantomime. I do not suppose one person in a hundred reads *Robinson Crusoe* after the school age. Even so, most people feel that they know Robinson Crusoe, with his dog, his cats, his parrot, and his man Friday, as one of the immortal legends.

And there could be no better adventure story to read at any age. Compare it with the travel books that are so popular nowadays—(and *Robinson Crusoe* is largely a travel book in the form of fiction)—and how many of them approach it in variety of excitement, observation, and interest? It would be the perfect travel book if it were true, and while we read it we believe that it is in fact true. We enjoy in it at once the excitements of fiction and of the old voyagers' tales.

Never elsewhere in popular fiction, I think, have we had a hero who, during at least half the story, never even speaks to another human being. (I am referring, I should say, only to the first volume of *Robinson Crusoe*, which is all that is published in many editions, and which is all that most boys read.) Yet seldom for a page do we cease to follow the alterations in the life of the solitary castaway with fascinated curiosity. There are some people who maintain that Robinson Crusoe is not a very real character, and that it is in his adventures rather than in himself that we are interested. I do not agree with them.

Robinson Kreutznaer—Bob Crusoe, as his schoolfellows called him—seems to me to use the very speech of reality from the time when first, without his father's consent, he leaves Hull on a ship bound for London. In his follies, his hopes, and his fears, he reflects moods that all human beings know, and, all through his life, from the time of his capture and enslavement by the Moors, he moves in the light of the sun, an ordinary human being flung into extraordinary circumstances.   A hundred attempts have been made to explain the spell of *Robinson Crusoe*, but none of them can be successful which ignores the reality of Crusoe himself, and the fact that even from a psychological point of view he is more truly observed and created than the heroes of most of the so-called psychological novels of modern times.

The truth is *Robinson Crusoe* is an exceedingly deft mixture of several of the elements of good fiction.   It is at once about a real person and a figure in a fairy-tale; it is both realistic and sensational; it fulfils the dream of every child about a little island of its own and at the same time excites all the inherited fears of solitude and danger.

Without some such variety of imaginative appeal, the story would have been bound to be monotonous.   Some critics, indeed, have under-estimated the imaginative quality of Defoe's writing: they even complain that he has not brought the scenery of Crusoe's island clearly before our eyes.

I wonder, however, if any other scenery in fiction is much more vivid in the memory than the long level of the sandy beach of the island on which the ship was wrecked.   It is brought home to us in sentence after sentence, as Crusoe swims and staggers through the shallow water with the great breakers pursuing him.   A retreating wave leaves him almost dry, and he scrambles to his feet.

Struggling towards the land, he looks back apprehensively, and 'I saw,' he says, 'the sea come after me like a great hill, and as furious as an enemy, which I had no means or strength to contend with. . . .   The wave that came upon me again buried me at over twenty or thirty feet deep in its own body, and I could feel myself carried with a mighty force and swiftness towards the shore a very great way; but I held my breath, and assisted myself to swim still forward with all my might.' Clearly, Defoe himself saw that shallow shore as vividly as though it had been outside his study window, and he makes us see it with the same vividness.

He is a master, indeed, of the kind of detail that brings a whole scene to life.   How well he brings home the loneliness of Crusoe, and his sense of the loss of his comrades when he makes him write of them: 'As for them, I never saw them afterwards, or any sign of them, except three of their hats, one cap, and two shoes that were not fellows.' Those 'two shoes that were not fellows' might be used as a text for a sermon on the secrets of good writing.

Robinson Crusoe is the oldest novel in the English language that has survived for the general reader, and it has survived largely through Defoe's genius for particularity. The realist of to-day gives us plenty of insignificant detail. Defoe gives us only significant detail. He loves making catalogues of things, like a child writing a letter about the Christmas presents it has received; and everything that Crusoe recovers on his journeys to the wreck before it finally disappears—the three bags full of nails and spikes, the great screw-jack, the seven muskets, the three large runlets of rum, and the pair of large scissors—becomes as interesting to us as a Christmas present in the nursery. Descriptions of the utensils in a large English house might well become wearisome, but even a bagful of stale chicken food is treasure trove on a desert island when, on being thrown out as worthless, it may sprout into crops of corn and rice. For *Robinson Crusoe* is a story of magic as well as of character.

Magic alone would not have made a great story, as readers of *The Swiss Family Robinson* will agree; and character might have resulted merely in a tragic story of a miserable wretch, if there had not been good fairies to provide Crusoe with the wherewithal to shoot, to cook, to till the ground, to build boats, to surround himself with a small menagerie of pets, and even, till the ink ran down, to write. All the offices of the good fairies, however, do not detract from the moral triumph of Crusoe (during the twenty-four years before he rescued Friday from the cannibals and so added a second human being to the population of the island) in housing, feeding, and clothing himself, and maintaining not only sanity, but a kind of cheerfulness. 'I had never handled a tool in my life,' says Crusoe, and yet, as builder, farmer, slaughterman, tailor, and carpenter, he had in the course of time achieved an all-round success surpassing anything recorded in Smiles's *Self-Help*. Even if we did not sympathize with him, we should respect him as (in the modern phrase) 'the man who made good.'

But we do sympathize with him at every turn of his fortunes —when his boat is carried out to sea on the current, and, thinking he is lost, he longs for the island as 'home'—when, seeing the print of the naked foot in the sand, he flies to his castle and passes a sleepless night in terror—when, having observed the cannibal visitors at their orgies, he meditates wrathfully on putting five or six pounds of gunpowder under the place when they made their fire to blow them up, and then begins to wonder whether it is right to murder even cannibals —when he has rescued Friday and taught him English and the Protestant religion, and finds it difficult to answer his objection: 'If God much strong, much might as the devil, why God no kill the devil, so make him no more do wicked?' Defoe is not much praised for humour, but there is a quiet smile in the story at times that lights up Crusoe and makes him a more than ever attractive figure. We like him the better even for laughing at his grotesque appearance in his goat-skin cap, goat-skin jacket and breeches, with the 'great clumsy, ugly, goat-skin umbrella' over his head, and wondering what would be thought of him if he travelled in such a dress through Yorkshire. We like him immensely in the comical description of himself and his 'little family' sitting down to dinner—the dog sitting at his right hand, the two cats at opposite sides of the table, and the parrot, 'the only person permitted to talk to me.' Here he becomes an oddity as well as an ordinary man. There are few more irresistible combinations in fiction.

Mrs. Thrale in her *Anecdotes* quotes Dr. Johnson as saying: 'Alas, Madam, how few books are there of which one can even possibly arrive at the last page! Was there ever yet anything written by mere man that was wished longer by its readers, excepting *Don Quixote*, *Robinson Crusoe*, and the *Pilgrim's Progress*?' That is a tribute with which everybody would agree if Defoe had not written the second part, and with which most of us agree, even though the second part falls short of the interest of the first.

R. S. Surtees

(1933)

THE name of Jorrocks is even to-day, I imagine, more widely known than the name of Robert Surtees, who created him. Surtees is, from the point of view of the ordinary reader, a one-character novelist. If he had not in a lucky hour invented Jorrocks his work might by this time have ceased to be read.

One is all the more surprised to learn that the original publisher of *Handley Cross* looked on Jorrocks and his misadventures as the blot on the book. Jorrocks had already appeared in *Jorrocks's Jaunts and Jollities* without setting the Thames on fire; and so little did the publisher like him in *Handley Cross* that he begged Surtees either to tone him down or to 'eliminate him altogether.' When it first appeared, in 1843, *Handley Cross* was 'rather a frost,' and it was not till ten years later that Surtees became a successful novelist with the publication of *Mr. Sponge's Sporting Tour.* He was then forty-eight years old.

Born in Northumberland in 1803, he spent most of his early life at Hamsterley Hall, in County Durham, where foxhunting was all but the local religion. Surtees tells how, as a child, during his holidays from school, he used to steal from the dining-room to the servants' hall to listen to the 'marvellous stories' of an old huntsman, whose name 'Matthew' had been altered to 'Methusalem' by the other servants on account of his immense age. When Matthew was a very old man and very ill a coffin was made for him, but 'he rallied and went out with a pack of foxhounds.' Such was the picturesque background of heroic characters against which Surtees passed his boyhood. Stories of foxhunting did more to feed his imagination than the Border ballads.

At the age of sixteen he was taken away from Durham Grammar School and articled to a solicitor in Newcastle. Six years later, in 1825, he was 'further articled' to a solicitor in London, and came to him, at 27 Lincoln's Inn Fields. He 'beguiled the time,' we are told, 'in attending court and hunting.   An insatiable habit of observation and a pleasant vein of satire, led him to "scribbling," as he modestly puts it, and what better subject than the Law Courts?'   There was at that time plenty of hunting to be had within a few miles of London, and the Cockney sportsman on his horse was a familiar figure. It was during his years of companionship with Cockney sportsmen that Surtees discovered the comic and heroic grocer, Jorrocks.

His first book, however, which appeared in 1831, had no comic intention.   It was entitled *The Horseman's Manual: being a Treatise on Soundness, the Law and Warranty, and generally on the Laws Relating to Horses*.   Meanwhile he had become an occasional contributor to the sporting periodicals of the time, and in 1831 he helped to found the *New Sporting Magazine*—'established by gentlemen who,' according to the advertisement, 'carried it on more for amusement than profit'—and was its editor for the following five years.   His editorship is interesting for two reasons.   It was to his own magazine that he contributed the Jorrocks papers which were afterwards collected into a book as *Jorrocks's Jaunts and Jollities*.   Here he found a literary medium for the expression of his youthful delight in foxhunting—in such extravagant sentences as:

What true-bred city sportsman has not in his day put off the most urgent business—perhaps marriage, or even the interment of his rib, that he might 'brave the morn' with that renowned pack, the Surrey subscription foxhounds?

Surtees's years of editorship are also interesting, however, because they bring out the vein of Puritanism in his nature which is repeatedly apparent in his life and opinions.   Among those who applied for work on the magazine was Pierce Egan, the elder, one of the most famous of sporting journalists.   Surtees refused to employ him, however, because of his association with bull-baiting and cock-fighting, which he regarded as 'low and de-moralizing.'   Surtees was no humanitarian, but there were many points on which humanitarians would have agreed with him. 'To Surtees,' as Frederick Watson says in his *Robert Smith Surtees*, 'sport was only defensible when it preserved the decencies.'   In foxhunting, itself, 'he believed the fox should be hunted like a gentleman.'   He disliked bag foxhunts.   'One may take it that

Surtees would have disapproved of digging out foxes except as an occasional method of destroying some notorious robber to appease the farmers.' He detested the battue in shooting.

He loathed coursing. 'Coursing,' he declared, 'should be made a felony.' And he made Jorrocks remark: 'Now, of all slow-starvation, great-coat, comforter, worsted-stocking, dirty-nose sorts of amusement, that same melancholy coursin' is to me the most miserably contemptible. It's a satire upon racin'.' He objected to the hunting of carted deer, when 'a great fat lubberly thing, after being well shaken up for some miles in a close-covered cart, is turned out, half stupefied, to be mobbed by all the foot people and perhaps by half the horsemen.'

To him, indeed, foxhunting was almost the only sport— foxhunting carried on under the conditions in which he had known it as a boy. He found some reason for condemning almost every other form of sport. He denounced horse-racing, for example, as heartily as Canon Peter Green, and looked on the race-course as a mere resort of gamblers, blacklegs, and pickpockets. 'As a general principle, Surtees suspected sport immediately it encouraged cruelty, betting, and drunkenness.' I fancy, however, that the strongest reason Surtees had for condemning other sports was that he agreed with Jorrocks that 'all time is wasted that is not spent in hunting.'

Probably it was due, at least in part, to the underlying censoriousness of Surtees that his books did not immediately captivate the sporting public. The sporting public does not like to have its amusements criticized even by a foxhunter. And, in regard to the foxhunting world itself, while Surtees loved the sport, he was the satirist, not the sentimental belauder, of those who pursued it. He 'exasperated and estranged the fox-hunting and country-house public by his failure to treat the whole social structure, from the landowner to the stable boy, with reverence or sentiment. 'He was destitute of romance reverence, and sentiment. He hit one nail on the head, and that nail was satirical comedy.' Thus, we cannot be surprised that, in the romantic and sentimental age of the Victorians, he did not become immediately popular. Of one of his books, *Hawbuck Grange*, his publisher wrote to him : 'The sales are small by degrees and grow beautifully less'; and half the edition remained unbound. Who could have predicted in the year in which *Handley Cross* was published, that in 1928 a first edition of the book would fetch £440 at a sale?

Surtees seems to have lacked the gifts that make for easy popularity in private life as well as in the novel-reading world. At the age of thirty-three, on his father's death, he abandoned the law and became, like his ancestors, a foxhunting squire; but he was far from being the jovial, easy-going foxhunting squire of tradition. At the age of thirty-five he even gave up hounds, and in the following year he married. For the rest of his life he continued to write and went through the routine of his duties as a country gentleman, but his life was marked by 'an increasing loneliness of spirit . . . and a deepening sensibility to the disappointments and petty irritations of daily life.' 'Sensitive even to the point of irascibility, he had always been a man of few friends and suspicious of casual acquaintanceships. His intense desire for anonymity, his refuge in solitude, his rigid propriety of behaviour and thought—all point to an austerity of temperament which tradition has, perhaps, too lightly labelled taciturnity.'

He dreaded notoriety, and published his books anonymously. He did not make friends even with his fellow authors, except Thackeray, whom he tried to persuade to illustrate *Mr. Sponge's Sporting Tour.* As a result, he is, as a man, one of the least known of the eminent Victorians. His contemporaries did not gossip about him, and so little was he gossiped about after his death even the compilers of literary histories have frequently forgotten about him. Gradually, however, the foxhunting world lost its distaste for his satire and began to recognize in his work the most faithful and exhilarating picture of the life they loved. The County has long since taken him to its heart, and to-day it is more likely to be heard quoting Jorrocks than Hamlet. His satire is now accepted as almost sympathetic, and he might be described as the foxhunter's Dickens.

During his lifetime he was abused by Trollope for misrepresenting the character of foxhunting society. But everything has been forgiven him because of Jorrocks. There is a certain irony in the fact that the full-blooded hunting world should have chosen as its prose laureate a man of whom it is said: 'Surtees was never young in spirit, and age did not mellow so much as sadden him. With his masked, sensitive face he looked out upon a world he had found an interesting place for a traveller, but not for a resident.' When he died at Brighton, at the age of sixty-one, no one seems to have realized that a writer of any importance had gone. Surtees himself would probably not have objected to this. His vanity, it is said, ran to dandiacal dress, but it does not seem to have run to the desire for fame.

Dislike of Professors

(1939)

I READ an article by an able critic the other day in which he spoke rather contemptuously of professors and their work. I gathered from it that he looks on professors as the enemies of literature. After commending the logic of the Nazis from their own point of view in making a bonfire of books, he added: 'A well-endowed professorship of literature would have done the job better and less ostentatiously.'

Hostility to professors is, I think, on the increase just now. A professor is widely supposed to be a pedant who can appreciate a work of genius only when the author is dead. He is also supposed by his boring comments to make the work of genius seem almost as dead as the author.

Probably there are such professors. I knew one professor who made Virgil himself seem a mere wilderness of Latin grammar. At the same time, it is absurd to make generalizations about professors as a class as though they were all built on the same pattern. Generalizations about professors are as misleading as generalizations about women or Scotsmen. One professor differs from another as night from day. There is the dry-as-dust professor who is technically a great scholar but who is utterly incapable of imparting any pleasure he ever got from literature, if indeed he ever did get any. In youth he was a great passer of examinations, and he teaches merely for the purpose of helping others to pass examinations. On the other hand, there is the professor who loves literature as literature and who can communicate his delight in it. To listen to him is as exciting and, to my mind, as enviable an experience as to listen to a great conversationalist pouring out the riches of his mind.

Certainly, I should not like to have missed a nodding acquaintance with those two great professors, Sir Samuel Dill and Samuel James Macmullan, father of the brilliant dramatist,

Mr. C. K. Munro. Dill, with his noble Periclean head, brought a majesty of mind to the exposition of Greek literature that made the grandeur of Aeschylus doubly real to the imagination. Homer, Herodotus, Sophocles—how inviting a world he made of them and how much more enjoyable than most of us could have discovered for ourselves! I was never a scholar, but if any man could have persuaded me to become a scholar, it was Samuel Dill. His translations, spoken in his grave and beautiful voice—the voice of a man who seemed to have forgotten that he was in a classroom and to be absorbed in the sacred sentences he was reading—turned Greek literature, as one listened to him, into literature in English. While one was in his presence, Greek was no longer a dead language. One thought of him as a visitor from Plato's world who had come with a message from the master.

It may be that he was a little pedantic about Thucydides. So far as I could gather, some German scholar had discovered that the text of Thucydides was full of corrupt interpolations, and Dill compelled us to record them all. I cannot imagine what good this did to anybody, unless some member of the class was preparing to devote the rest of his life to textual criticism. Another thing that I objected to was being compelled to take notes; and Dill frowned on any member of his class who was not perpetually busy with his pencil and note-book. I have always hated taking notes; but, in order not to come under his reproof, I used to make illegible scrawls on paper, which I could throw into the fire when I got home.

In spite of his belief in the value of note-taking, however, Dill had a deep-seated hatred of the examination system. He regarded examinations as a kind of regrettable, recurrent accident with which he had nothing to do. He was there, he held, not for the purpose of helping an assortment of young men to become Bachelors of Arts, but in order to introduce them to the glories of Athens and the old Greek world. I remember how one day, when he saw a theological student yawning during a lecture that was perfectly useless for examination purposes, he turned to him wrathfully and said: 'Why do you *come* here? What is your object? Do you regard me as a mere grinder paid to help you to scrape through some wretched examination?' 'Yes, sir,' said the theological student with an honest grin. That was the only occasion on which I ever saw Dill deprived of the power of speech.

Samuel James Macmullan disliked examinations even more heartily than Dill. He was a man of equally noble presence— tall, white-bearded, and with cheeks that flushed easily under emotion. His appearance suggested a mixture of the last of the Vikings and the last of the Bohemians. I was glad to find that he disapproved of the habit of note-taking; indeed, he all but suggested that a young man who took notes could not expect to come to any good. As for the books that we were supposed to study for our examination, on some days he mentioned them and on some days he didn't. If Gray was one of the appointed authors, Macmullan was just as likely to lecture to us on Turgenev; and, when we were supposed to be studying *Macbeth*, he would digress into an hour's magnificent account of the most famous murder in the history of the North of Ireland. Students who were concerned only with passing examinations were some- times tempted to ask for their money back—especially mathe- matical students whom he frankly told that they were 'intellectual barbarians.'

Yet how great literature came to life under his touch! He had a divine gift for opening the eyes of the young to the divine gifts of the great writers. His voice enriched the meaning of a passage of prose or verse as he quoted it. He had some odd theories, such as that Shakespeare did not write the phrase, 'the primrose path to the everlasting bonfire,' because Shakespeare was not a man to make a jest of eternal punishment; but these seemed the pardonable eccentricities of a mind that had lived in the company of masterpieces and could illuminate them for others.

I cannot help thinking that professors of this kind keep the lamp burning no less than the poets and novelists. Indolent and hostile to lectures, I nevertheless came to love both Dill and Macmullan this side idolatry. And I have heard other men speaking of old professors with equal enthusiasm—of Sir Walter Raleigh, for example, and W. P. Ker. From this I conclude that the good professor, far from being the enemy of literature, is a lavish contributor to the imaginative enjoyment of it.

I also think that there is much to be said in defence of the other more academic kind of professor, who compiles histories of literature or goes to endless pains to provide us with the best possible texts of the great writers. I have seen more than one attack in recent years on school and university histories of English literature. It seems to me that it would be equally unreasonable to attack atlases. No one will deny that it is better to read Milton than to read about Milton—his dates, the names of his wives, and so forth—just as it is better to visit Florence than to trace the journey to Florence on a map. People who love maps, however, can get a great deal of true imaginative excitement from opening an atlas and going on imaginary travels.

In the same way the history of literature may give pleasure as a map of masterpieces and fill the reader with a longing to become acquainted with them. In our teens, the mere names of famous writers affect us like poems—Drummond of Hawthornden, Ben Jonson, Andrew Marvell, Walter Savage Landor. They call up a vision of realms of gold which we long one day to enter. There are some people, I know, who say that their love of literature was almost destroyed at the outset by the study of English literature at school. But I think this experience must be exceptional. For the most part, the professorial compiler of literary history is justified by results.

As for the professor who collates texts in his search after perfection, I feel sure that the great poets of the past would have been glad to know that reverent scholars would see to it that what they wrote was correctly printed. There are few things more exasperating to a writer than to see misprints in his work; and the perfect proof-reader is justly regarded as the author's friend and benefactor. If it is important to avoid misprints in an ephemeral newspaper, how much more so it must be in the works of an immortal poet! And it is only the professors who can save us from them.

On the whole, then, instead of damning them, I am inclined to praise professors of all sorts, shapes, and sizes. They seem to me to do very little harm and an enormous amount of good.

The Gentle Art of Idling

(1925)

IN reading the life of a writer of genius, you will often discover he was equally notable for two things—industry and idleness. Sir Walter Scott, one of the most industrious authors who ever lived, was a man whom visitors usually found ready to devote the day and the night to entertaining them; and, even at the end of a life in which he had poured forth many long narrative poems, a still greater number of novels, biographies, editions of great writers, and journalistic articles, as well as attending to his fairly arduous legal duties, he spoke of himself as one who was born with a 'determined indolence' and 'aversion to labour.'

Not that he praised idleness as Robert Louis Stevenson did. Looking back on his youth, he declared: 'It is with the deepest regret that I recollect in my manhood the opportunities of learning which I neglected in my youth; . . . through every part of my literary career I have felt pinched and hampered by my own ignorance.' One of his professors at the university was so greatly shocked by his mixture of indolence and ignorance that he declared one day: 'Dunce you are, and dunce you will always be'—a prophecy which he lived to withdraw, as Scott tells us with a chuckle, over a bottle of burgundy. Even in his adult life, Scott struck some of his friends as an author who did not take his work quite seriously enough. To Wordsworth it seemed that 'on the whole he attached less importance to his literary labours or reputation than to his bodily sports, exercise, and social amusements.'

The truth of the matter is, of course, that Scott both worked and idled twice or three times as energetically as an ordinary man, and that, if he had idled less, his work would have been the poorer. Idleness is often simply an occupation that the world does not admit to be work, though many men would learn quite as much in a class for idleness as in a class for algebra.

Dr. Johnson, another great worker, was also a great idler; and, like Scott, repented bitterly of his indolence. Even while he was writing his essays for the *Idler*, we find him writing in his private memoranda: 'This year I hope to learn diligence.' His example, on the whole, is not one that can be commended for universal imitation. A clerical friend describes him in 1770 as lying in bed till midday, or, if up, drinking tea and declaiming to his visitors.

He declaimed all the morning, then went to dinner at a tavern, where he commonly stayed late, and then drank his tea at some friend's house, over which he loitered a great while, but seldom took supper.

Yet, even in his youth, he had written in his notes: 'I bid farewell to Sloth, being resolved henceforth not to listen to her siren strains.'

No one, looking at the great volume of Johnson's work—his *Dictionary*, the *Lives of the Poets*, or the Essays—can doubt that he did his full share of work. To Carlyle, indeed, he was 'the hero as a man of letters'—'a giant invincible soul.' Yet in Boswell's *Life* it is the great idler as well as the great worker that the world has learnt to love. He is for us the man who 'walked the streets at all hours' and who rose from his bed in the small hours to go out for a 'frisk' with his friends.

Gray was an idler of a different kind. He was physically indolent to the point of taking no exercise. As an undergraduate at Cambridge, he also avoided the orthodox paths of learning, having an especial antipathy to mathematics. 'It is very possible,' he wrote to a friend, 'that two and two make four, but I would not give four farthings to demonstrate this ever so clearly; or if these be the profits of life, give me the amusements of it.' At the age of thirty, he speaks of himself as 'lazy and listless and old and vexed and perplexed.'

Nor was Gray producing in the intervals of indolence an immense volume of work, as Johnson and Scott did. He remained to the end, in his own phrase, 'a shrimp of an author.' He is the greatest poet in English who ever wrote so little poetry. His 'Elegy in a Country Churchyard' was not finished for seven years after it was begun. Yet what labour of genius was concentrated on the writing of this single poem! Who can say that the world would have been richer if Gray had idled less? On the whole, it may be doubted whether men of genius have got much happiness out of idleness.   At least, the more indolent they have been, the more they seem to have groaned under indolence as under a burden.   Coleridge, even in his twenties, portrayed himself as a man under the curse of sloth-fulness.   'My face,' he wrote, 'unless when animated by immediate eloquence, expresses great sloth, and great—indeed, almost idiotic—good nature.'   He spent a great part of his life planning large works and putting off writing them.   He did not always even turn up to deliver the lectures for which his audiences were waiting.   Yet, if you have the complete works of Coleridge on your shelves, they will probably seem to you to represent a reasonably full life-work, even for a busy writer.

Certainly, more of Coleridge has survived than of many a good writer famed for industry.   Industry, indeed, without some taint of idleness, does not seem to achieve the highest things in literature.   It is more likely to give us a Southey than a Coleridge—a Trollope than a Walter Scott.   There are exceptions to this as to nearly every other rule, but the lives of the poets and the novelist suggest that it is best for an imaginative writer to have the double capacity for work and for idleness. Chaucer has come down to us as a man of ceaseless industry— a man who, after his day's work at the Customs, went home and absorbed himself in study.   But there are passages in his poems which showed that he had also idled to advantage, especially among birds and flowers at the coming of spring. Shakespeare, again, undoubtedly gives us the fruits of idleness as well as of industry in *Henry IV*.   When, but in hours of idleness, could he have got to know Falstaff?

This is not to say that a youth with an ambition to write would do well to acquire habits of idleness.   If idleness does not come by nature, it is better to leave it to those who were born with it.   All the great idlers down to Thoreau and Stevenson were natural idlers.   Thoreau's idleness, however, was not mere indolence, but was a deliberate protest against the race for gold that was going on all round him.   From the point of view of an angel, if not of a business man, it is possible that Thoreau was one of the most efficient workers of his time in America.

Stevenson, again, who preached a gospel of idleness, resorted to idleness, not through laziness, but as a means of doing the work for which he believed that he was born.   He has told us himself how, when he played truant, he always carried two books in his pocket—a book to read and a book in which to write. If he idled, it was in order to educate himself as a writer instead of allowing himself to be educated as a lawyer. He was surely the most industrious idler of his century, and, if he preached a gospel of idleness in his youth, his later life gave an example of industry amid hampering circumstances that has earned him a place among the heroes of literature. He said himself that his success as a writer was due, not to genius, but to his capacity for taking pains.

And, indeed, if a novelist were to study the lives of authors, he would find himself driven to the conclusion that there are two sorts of idleness. First, there is the idleness that is an aid to work and makes men cheerful; and then there is the idleness that hinders work and makes man miserable. Either kind of idleness may be useful to a writer, if he has a conscience that compels him to work like a demon. But, if he is an Epicurean who wishes to enjoy the chief pleasures of life, he will be wise to turn to work rather than to idleness. Hard work, it seems to me, is the supremely satisfying amusement of mankind. The right kind of idleness is as good a recipe for the happy life as has yet been discovered.

III
Criticism and Critics

The Bounds of Decency

(1927)

THERE is nothing in which taste changes more than in the
matter of propriety. It seems incredible to us to-day that even
so innocent an author as Charles Lamb was once driven to complain: 'I have lived to grow into an indecent character.' Not
only, indeed, had he been told that *Rosamund Gray* was indelicate,
but his sonnet, 'The Gypsy's Malison,' was declined by the
Germ on the ground that it would 'shock all mothers.' It was
on the rejection of this sonnet that Lamb exclaimed in comic
disgust: 'Damn the age! I will write for antiquity!'

Obviously the capacity for being shocked varies, not only
from age to age, but from person to person. There is, we may
be sure, always an editor of the *Germ* alive, who needs no
Rabelais or Whitman to bring the blush of startled innocence to
his cheek. On the other hand, it would be a mistake to think
that the capacity for being shocked is a mark of the lower orders
of intelligence. Men of genius have suffered the pangs of outraged propriety as have their fellows. We are accustomed,
partly because of its fiction, to regard the middle of the eighteenth
century as a time of comparative licence of speech, but it was in
that easy age that Oliver Goldsmith wrote for the *Public Ledger*
his paper entitled 'The Absurd Taste for Obscene and Pert
Novels, such as *Tristram Shandy*, Ridiculed.' 'A bawdy blockhead,' wrote Goldsmith in this essay, 'often passes for a fellow
of smart parts and pretensions,' and he added:

A prurient jest has always been found to give most pleasure to a few
very old gentlemen, who, being in some measure dead to other sensa-
tions, feel the force of allusion with double force on the organs of
risibility.

The author who writes in this manner is generally sure, therefore, of
having the very old and the impotent among his admirers; for these he
may properly be said to write, and from these he ought to expect his
reward; his works being often a very proper succedaneum to can-
tharides, or an asafoetida pill.

An interesting problem in the psychology of decency is raised by the fact that Sterne himself does not seem to have realized that there were any just grounds for attacks on his book on the score of impropriety.   He was genuinely hurt by the suggestion that *Tristram Shandy* was a book that no clergyman ought to have written, and we need not doubt too gravely his sincerity in protesting, like Rabelais, that his chief object in writing was 'the hopes of doing the world good.'   Authors accused of scandal are all but unanimous in offering this defence, and of some we very reasonably suspect the good faith.   But Sterne has left us evidence of the honesty of his contention in the letter in which, while at work on *Tristram Shandy*, he refers to his sixteen-year-old daughter and says: 'My Lydia helps to copy for me—and my wife knits and listens as I read her chapters.'   We do not know whether Sterne allowed Lydia to copy out at random everything that he wrote, but we may presume from his readiness to associate her with *Tristram Shandy* that, far from acquiescing in Goldsmith's opinion that it was a bawdy book, he regarded it as a book of humour suitable for schoolgirls and for clergymen in their leisure hours.

As for Goldsmith's criticism, it is chiefly interesting, not as the expression of a personal point of view, but because it is symptomatic of a centuries-old sense of decency and serves to remind us that, in spite of the outspokenness of certain of the novelists, the eighteenth century was as capable of being shocked by impropriety as was the age of Queen Victoria.   Those who have the greatest scorn for the Victorian age speak at times as though it were the first period in history in which there was any demand for decorum in literature.   Rebellious Victorians themselves sometimes imagined that they were living in such a prison of the conventions as had never existed before.   Thackeray's outcry on the subject is famous.   'Since the author of *Tom Jones* was buried,' he lamented in the preface to *Pendennis*, 'no writer of fiction has been permitted to depict to his utmost power a MAN.   We must drape him, and give him a certain conventional simper.   Society will not tolerate the Natural in Art.'   The proprieties existed, however, long before the reign of Queen Victoria, and were by no means confined, even in the most outspoken times, to the Puritans and the Jeremy Colliers.   We have only to glance casually through the records in order to discover that, though men have differed considerably as to where the bounds of decency are to be traced, they are usually agreed that the bounds of decency do somewhere exist. Even Mr. Pepys, whose own writings are in places so indecorous that an entirely unexpurgated edition of the *Diary* has never yet been published, was offended by the indecorousness of Dryden's play, *An Evening's Love, or The Mock Astrologer*, and, after seeing it, wrote in his diary: 'I saw this new play with my wife yesterday, and do not like it, it being very smutty.' Again, we find in his *Diary* the characteristic entry: 'To the Strand, to my bookseller's, and there bought an idle, rogueish French book, *L'escholle des Filles*, which I have bought in plain binding, avoiding the buying of it better-bound, because I resolve, as soon as I have read it, to burn it, that it may not stand in the list of books, nor among them, to disgrace them, if it should be found.' Similarly Fielding, whose novels were once considered so indecent that they were withheld from general circulation in some Victorian libraries, was sufficient of a puritan in his turn to denounce Aristophanes and Rabelais for having made 'so wretched a use' of their talents, and to declare that the object of their works seemed to be 'to ridicule all sobriety, modesty, decency, virtue, and religion out of the world.'

The further we prosecute the inquiry, the more inevitably we are forced to the conclusion that everybody is shocked by somebody or something. Swinburne shocked the Victorian age with the first series of *Poems and Ballads*, but he himself was shocked by some things in Shakespeare—sufficiently shocked, at least, to praise Dr. Bowdler for having expurgated the plays and made them fit reading for the young.

All this goes to prove that the sense of decency is no pallid and unnatural growth of a too respectable age, but is an eternal and universal part of human nature. It is like the sense of right and wrong: we may differ from age to age and from person to person as to what is right and what is wrong, but every sane human being recognizes a distinction between right and wrong, and there are certain things which he will condemn in his neighbours and even himself for doing.

Morals may in some respects change with climate, but there is no climate without its standard of virtue. Pull down one moral standard, and you will find yourself compelled to set up

H

another in its place. And some standard of decency is equally essential. We can no more live a full and free life without it than without morals or manners. In ordinary affairs we all accept this as obvious. We should regard it as indecent now-adays to go about with black finger nails, or to become verminous through abstinence from bathing, or to spit in a church. Most people would even look on it as indecent for a man to walk naked along the street. And there are a number of habits unnecessary to mention which create among civilized people universal disgust.

Even those who denounce the decencies in literature demand some kind of decency in the conduct of their friends. For every one, be he ever so little fastidious, is capable of disgust. Disgust is merely the other side of good taste, and without it we should never have had civilization or the arts, nor could we continue to enjoy them.

This is so obvious that it would not be worth repeating if it were not for the fact that certain writers of our own time have made a virtue of being disgusting and their work has been praised by admirers as though it were extending the territories of literature. They go on the assumption that there is nothing that a man can do that is not fit to be written about, and that it is the business of the artist, not to make a selection of the facts of life for an imaginative purpose, but to guide his readers into every obscene nook and corner with a courageous indifference to everything that offends the senses, both physical and moral.

If literature were a chaotic catalogue of slimy and grimy things, and not an imaginative reconstruction of life in its most interesting aspects, there might be something to be said for this view. But literature depends on careful selection and omission as much as does the work of a good gardener. No good gardener will lead you to his beds and point out boastfully as his supreme achievement a wilderness of weeds, slugs, and leatherjackets. The ultimate test of literature is the quality of its flowers, or rather of its flowers and its fruits. And the greatest writers seem to have realized instinctively that these cannot be produced in perfection until the weeds, the slugs, and the leatherjackets have been to some extent eliminated. Homer is as instinctively decent as he is instinctively frank. Aeschylus is food for boys in their teens. And you will find as a rule that the greater the classic is, the less it stands in need of expurgation, *virginibus puerisque*, and the less it suffers from such expurgation if this happens to be made. The more 'minor' the classic is, the more likely it is to be indecent. There is more indecency in Petronius than in all the plays of Molière.

It would be absurd, of course, to pretend that all the greatest writers have observed the decorum required in a Victorian drawing-room, or to deny that many of them have gaily transgressed the bounds of decency. Man is naturally Rabelaisian in his comedy, and the comic writers contain many a passage likely to shock an old-fashioned clergyman. Even in comedy, however, genius only came to flower as the result of an escape into comparative decency. Aristotle makes this point emphatically in the *Ethics*. 'There is a difference,' he says, 'between the jocularity of the gentleman and that of the vulgarian. . . . The difference may be seen by comparing the old and the modern comedies; the earlier dramatists found their fun in obscenity, the moderns prefer innuendo which marks a great advance in decorum.'

We need not pause to inquire what exactly Aristotle meant by 'innuendo'—*hyponoia*, the word he used, is said by the scholarly not to convey the unpleasant shade of meaning that 'innuendo' conveys to the modern reader—but it is clear that he regarded comedy as having grown to perfection as a result of its having broken free from its original obsession with obscenity. In this he may have intended to disparage the humour of Aristophanes in comparison with the more subtle humour of his successors; but it is equally true that, in the hands of Aristophanes, Greek comedy, which appears to have been the child and nursling of obscenity, escaped from its mother's obscene apron strings to roam freely over life, politics, and literature. The comedies of Aristophanes survive to-day, indeed, not because of their obscenity, though their obscenity is often extremely amusing, but because they contain so much more than obscenity—a comic vision of the world as a poet of genius saw it.

It is possible, however, to enjoy the great comic literature of the past in its frequently Fescennine licence and yet to doubt whether we should gain as much as we should lose if we attempted to recover that licence. Manners have changed, and what Aristophanes could say without offence to the citizens of Athens

could not always be said without offence to the citizens of
London or New York. It is not that we have got beyond
Aristophanes in genius and virtue, but that the conventions of
speech are different in America and in England from the conventions that were accepted in Athens, and that to-day the
writers are addressing a mixed general audience such as, I
imagine, did not exist in the ancient world.

No sensitive writer can fail to be conscious of his audience.
In private life there are things that a man will say in the presence
of men and that he would not say in the presence of children.
Most of those who champion the artist's right to say anything
and everything ignore the fact of this enlargement of the audience.
But the little writer is likelier to ignore it than the great. Sir
Walter Scott and even Dumas certainly acknowledged it, and
claimed it as a virtue that they had respected the decencies in
their writings; and Anthony Trollope, who is at last being
generally admitted into the circle of the enduring writers, asks
in his *Autobiography*, after referring to six of the leading nineteenth-
century novelists: 'Can any one by search through the works
of the six great English novelists I have named, find a scene, a
passage, or a word that would teach a girl to be immodest, or a
man to be dishonest?'

We may, if we please, dismiss all this as prudery and priggishness, but he would be a bold perverter of words who affixed the
word 'prig' to authors at once so genial and so virile as Scott and
Trollope. They were guilty, indeed, of nothing worse than good
sense—the good sense to recognize the emergence of a great
mixed audience and their responsibility to it.

Literary manners have altered, however, not only as a result
of the enlargement of the audience—though that was bound to
have an important effect on literature—but as a result of changes
in the manners and customs of everyday life. The increase of
privacy, the improvement of sanitation, the growing custom of
cleanliness both of habits and of the body, and the abolition of
many gross usages, have resulted in making many things that once
were the comic *contretemps* of ordinary life seem now merely
offensive irrelevancies. Probably improved sanitation has had
more influence on literary manners than any one yet suspects.
You will notice that what its enemies call prudery is most general
in countries in which sanitation has made the greatest progress.

If Rabelais were to return as an Englishman or an American to-day, he would probably find himself blushing like a Victorian girl at some of his own jokes. This is not to belittle the jokes of Rabelais, but merely to recognize that the manners and conventions that were the natural soil of many of those jokes no longer exist to-day.

Decency, it need hardly be said, belongs for the most part to the realm of manners rather than of morals. Sir Thomas More and Luther jested in a fashion that would be accounted indecent by modern conventions, but no intelligent man would think of making use of the fact as an argument against the excellence of their characters. It is true that Chaucer—if we accept the prayer at the end of 'The Parson's Tale' as genuine—prayed near his death for divine forgiveness for having written *The Canterbury Tales*, but, when he expressed his sorrow for having written 'many a song and many a lecherous lay,' it is likely that he was thinking of his narratives of love—'endytings of worldly vanities' —at least as much as of the indecorous situations and speech in his comic poems. Certainly taste has changed to such a point that it is almost impossible to conceive a modern poet of genius who could write a poem in the happy, gross vein of 'The Miller's Tale.'

It is not that the moderns are either better men or better poets than Chaucer. It is simply that the genius of the age has changed its manners, and that manners natural in Chaucer's age would be artificial in this. Poetry, while it remains fundamentally the same, has altered its clothes, and it would be idle affectation to return to the ancient garments. Those who love Chaucer most would be the last people to think of adopting in their writings the manners of the fourteenth century.

And much the same is true of Rabelais. The greatest disciples of Rabelais who are writing to-day are as chaste in phrase as Louisa M. Alcott. We even find the modern Rabelaisian enthusiast solemnly discussing such things as the relation of Rabelais to biblical studies! (This, I fancy, would have amused Rabelais.) If the genius of Rabelais has descended to any modern author, it is not to the tittering imitators of his grossness, but to such a writer as Mr. Hilaire Belloc, who, instead of copying the mud on Rabelais's shoes, had brought back the soul of Rabelais into a twentieth-century body of good prose.

This is not to pretend that the modern intelligent man in all his moods talks like a character in *Daisy in the Field*. But, as the proverb says, there is a time for everything, and no one, however much he may delight in sitting in Rabelais's easy-chair among his fellow Rabelaisians, would, unless he were a fool, make it a principle to force Rabelaisian conversation on a company in which the code of manners was opposed to it. After all, the chief object of comedy is to amuse and not merely to shock. If you are dining with Catholics, you do not indulge in ribald jests about the pope. If you are dining with Christians of any creed, there are certain blasphemous levities of speech which, however much you may be inclined to them, you will avoid. It is all a matter of good manners, and in such things the sensitive—and all good artists are sensitive—find it easy to conform.

There is, of course, no clear line that can be permanently drawn between decency and indecency. One age may be so delicate that—though it is difficult to believe this—it will shrink from mentioning legs and will even speak of the 'limb' of a chicken. Another age will speak freely of every natural function. Every age probably tends either to an excess of refinement or to an excess of outspokenness. And the more extreme is the swing of the pendulum in one direction, the more extreme is the succeeding swing of the pendulum in the other. The only thing we can be sure of with regard to literature is that, in whatever direction the pendulum swings, great literature recovers and survives. Miss Austen is as sure of immortality as Rabelais, Charles Lamb as Montaigne, Dickens as Chaucer. No writer ever survived in the general love of mankind either because of his propriety or because of his impropriety. Sir Walter Raleigh once pointed out that there were many writers of Boccaccio's age who were more indecent than he, and that nevertheless they had been forgotten; and there are many writers to-day as decent as Charles Garvice, and they too will be forgotten.

Literature survives because of its morals rather than because of its manners—and by its morals I mean its fidelity to the author's vision of life, his sympathy with and understanding of his fellow creatures, and its service to an ideal that cannot be corrupted by money or applause, though the artist as much as any other man likes to have as much as possible of both. Talent is purchasable, but genius is not. There is no great book in literature which is not essentially the book of an honest man—a book of good faith. We realize this whether we are reading Mr. Pepys's secret confessions of his peccadilloes or the austere moralizings of Marcus Aurelius.

Even when we have accepted this fundamental truth of criticism, however, we have not yet settled the question whether, on the whole, literature gains from the taboos of decency or whether it is hampered and devitalized by them. There are critics who maintain that certain modern writers, in describing the progress of abnormal passions, have cultivated new and beautiful fields of literature in what was forbidden land to the Victorian novelists. They also regard James Joyce as having performed a service to truth in having dragged into the light of day thoughts and words that the ordinary adult man would not utter except in a delirium.

That, indeed, is the odd thing about the modern revolt against the old-fashioned notions of decency. It began in the nineteenth century as a kind of feverish religion and, instead of being a defence of laughter against the laughterless, it nowadays invites the imagination into a sanctuary of gloom. It is not only serious: it is solemn. There is nothing Rabelaisian or hilarious about it. There are still, indeed, writers who treat the physical life of man in the ancient comic spirit, though without the ancient gusto; but one of the eminent characteristics of most of the modern adherents of 'outspoken' literature is their laughterless enthusiasm and devotional awe. It is as though they seriously believed that it had been left to them to make the grand discovery of sex, both in its normal and in its abnormal manifestations, for the first time—that their ancestors, while marrying and bringing up families, had remained completely ignorant of sex, either through stupidity or as a result of not having the courage to open their eyes and face the facts. Everything that Freud and psycho-analysts announce about sex they regard as though it were a revelation from heaven.

It is as if a new sun had arisen and disclosed continents unknown to Shakespeare and the writers of old time. Shakespeare did not know that Hamlet was in love with his mother and had been homicidally jealous of his father, but the young disciples of Freud know. Dickens, when he wrote *David Copperfield*, thought that Mr. Dick was only an innocent eccentric, but the Freudian knows, as a result of reading one of the latest books on psycho-analysis, that Mr. Dick was really a case of sexual aberration.   I do not mean to suggest that psycho-analysis is the parent of all the earnestly sexual fiction of to-day, but undoubtedly it has loosed on the world a flood of theories about sex that has swept a great many writers and readers into morasses that their ancestors instinctively avoided.   It is important that psychologists and doctors should examine these theories carefully, sifting the true from the false, and giving the former its due and comparatively obscure place in the crowded paradox of human life.   But I have never yet seen any association between psycho-analysis and literature that was not injurious to literature.   This, indeed, is bound to be so, since, like any other theory that is carried too far, psycho-analysis is a bed of Procrustes into which men and women as we know them cannot be fitted without mutilation. We have only to look round among the people we know most intimately to realize that there is not one thing in a hundred that make them interesting human beings on which a psycho-analyst could throw the faintest glimmer of candlelight.

And the increasing absorption of novelists in the 'sexual' life of man is as likely to be barren in literary results.   There is nothing that fascinates the curiosity, especially of the adolescent, more than sex, and there is no kind of curiosity that provides less food for the imagination.   Here, perhaps, it is important to define one's terms.   By curiosity about sex I mean curiosity, not about men and women and their tragic and comic relations, but about their animal functions.   Obviously, in a broad sense, everybody must be curious about sex.   In this sense the poet, the novelist, and the moralist, as well as the most ordinary man, must be profoundly interested in it.   There is all the difference in the world, however, between the interest of Homer in Helen and the Peeping Tom curiosity of the adolescent.   Homer did not look at life through puritanical eyes, but he saw that the interesting thing about Helen was not what some people nowadays call her 'sex life,' but her beauty and the long train of tragedy and war that followed from Paris's love of her.

The great artists, like the great moralists, do not dwell on the descriptions of adultery, but on its consequences.   Their theme is a man or a woman in the toils of destiny, and not the animal functions; and, if any one replies that for some men and women the animal functions are themselves destiny, all one can say in reply is that the greatest writers have, in choosing their heroes and heroines, avoided characters of so limited an interest.

Take any of the great love stories of the world—the story of Paris and Helen, of Antony and Cleopatra, of Tristram and Iseult, of Paolo and Francesca—and everywhere you will find the story, not of a 'sex life,' but of the fate of a noble soul. Nowhere is there a description of commonplace sexual adventures. The lovers in all cases bear more resemblance to betrothed or married lovers on whom a doom has fallen than to the vaguely amorous nonentities who populate so many modern novels. The truth is, passion is interesting to the imagination only when it is more than physical passion and absorbs the whole being—when it is all but, in the ancient phrase, faithful unto death and for its sake there is no suffering too great to be endured.

George Moore once said that children are born of the marriage, stories of the adulterous, bed. It is an epigram that stops a long way short of the truth. Ordinary adultery has given us no great stories. It is the sufferings of lovers, their fidelity, and their desperate struggle in the hands of destiny, that fit them to be immortal figures in literature. The amours of uninteresting people are no more interesting in the world of the imagination than their meals or the symptoms of their illnesses. A writer cannot make an uninteresting person interesting in the literary sense merely by giving him a number of sexual adventures. One sexual adventure is very like another, and in the end even Paul Pry will complain of the monotony.

That is, I think, one of the surest safeguards against pornography. Normal intelligent people with any breadth of interest in life get tired of it. In comic pornography, indecency is a kind of *sauce piquante* which becomes infinitely wearisome as soon as we realize that the flavour is, as it is in nine cases out of ten, merely a means of concealing the flavourlessness of the wit and humour. In serious pornography it is a strong spice which as a rule is used to disguise the poor quality of the dish to which it is added. It is, to a large part of the present generation, something of a novelty in literature, and to many people it is still as exciting as a new dance or a new fashion in clothes. Let it become more general, however, and it will gradually seem as

* H

unattractive as if everybody were to give up washing or to take to going about with grimy hands and faces.

There is much the same argument for cleanliness of the mind as for cleanliness of the body. The plain fact is that most people, given the chance, enjoy being clean, and that they feel more comfortable in the company of people who are clean than in the company of people who are not. And, when once the habit of cleanliness had been established, no one would pay much attention to a man who argued: 'Greater ages than ours have been ages of dirt. Shakespeare never used a toothbrush: why should I? Villon was probably verminous: why shouldn't I be?' We should say to him, if we said anything: 'Can you imitate Shakespeare's genius, or only his teeth? Have you suffered like Villon and turned your sufferings into music like his, or do you forget that there were millions of verminous men in the Middle Ages, but only one Villon?'

There are some things, indeed, to which the world, if it remains reasonably sane, will never go back. It will never abandon soap for vermin, and it will never return to the insanitary conditions of Rabelais's day in literature any more than in ordinary life.

If there is a danger of the world's doing so, it lies, perhaps, in our making a fetish of cleanliness. Cleanliness is a convenience, as filth is an inconvenience, and it is chiefly that. Whoever said that it was next to godliness was neither a Christian nor a philosopher. A kind of negative cleanliness that becomes self-righteous as though it were a rival of the supreme virtues is scarcely less offensive than its opposite. Who would praise whited sepulchres, and who does not know that it is possible for a man to take a bath every morning and yet not to possess a single admirable quality? Similarly in literature there are hundreds of clean books that make the sensitive young impatient of cleanliness—books that are namby-pamby, empty-headed, empty-hearted falsifications. Imaginative readers are quick to detect the difference between truth and imposture, and they prefer the truth told grossly by Montaigne to shallow lies told by professional optimists.

At the same time, it is sometimes forgotten nowadays that truth is not merely an absence of reticence, and that a filthy lie is just as much a lie as a clean lie. The truth of the artist is widely different from the truth of the doctor or farmer or the man not engaged in the arts who looks at the world through the glasses of a particular trade or profession. The doctor, in his capacity of doctor, is bound to look on a human being largely as an assemblage of organs; and, if he were examining Julius Caesar himself, it would be his duty to take note more of the condition of Caesar's stomach than of Caesar's conquests. His report would be the truth about Caesar as the doctor professionally sees it, but Shakespeare can tell us infinitely greater truth about Caesar, while ignoring what may be called the doctor's truth. Shakespeare knew perfectly well that Caesar had a stomach, but he had no occasion to draw attention to it. Similarly, Wordsworth in his vision of the countryside ignores the manure that it would be criminal in a farmer cultivating his fields to forget. It is not that Wordsworth did not know about manure or that, in a conversation with a farmer, he would have shrunk from freely discussing the manuring of crops; but as a poet he was more interested in lambs and green linnets and daffodils.

Genius of any kind, whether in an art or in a profession or in a trade, is, it seems to me, largely the power to concentrate on relevant facts and to order them to a large purpose. Hence the writer of genius must give us a very much purified account of his vision of the world—an account purified, so far as it is possible, from everything irrelevant, whether it is decent or indecent. There are realists, on the other hand, who seem to think that, if only a fact is indecent, it ceases to be irrelevant. Incapable of delight, they find a perverted substitute for delight in disgust. It is true that, if it is their object to preach a gospel of disgust, their indecencies may be relevant to their propaganda; but in that case they must be content to be judged, not as artists, but as preachers of a gospel that seems to most people false.

I do not mean to suggest that it is impossible for a great writer to adhere to the gospel of disgust with life in general. But, if he cannot impart his vision of disgust in such a way as to afford more delight than disgust to his fellow creatures, his writings have no place in literature. The pessimism of Schopenhauer and Baudelaire, like the cynicism of La Rochefoucauld, is beautiful in its expression. The truth is, a writer of great intellect and imagination writes instinctively in obedience to certain laws of beauty which themselves overlap the ultimate laws of decency and of delight. We may regard his vision as evil and his creed as poisonous, and may believe that no man inspired by such a creed and vision has ever ascended to the highest peaks of literature; but, as we read his masterpieces, we have no sense of the dull tedium of disgust. It is the men of lesser talents—the men of half-genius and the men of no genius at all, but of abnormal vanity—who repel us with their deliberate indecorum. They are epicures of the unsavoury. They take pleasure in defiling life, and are scandalmongers about the soul and body of man.

Writers, of course, like other men, are commonly inspired by mixed motives, and it is seldom that a writer's only motive is a passion for indecency. Some of the Restoration dramatists almost achieved this single-mindedness, and the general oblivion into which their works have fallen is the inevitable reward of the single-minded bore in literature. If a number of modern writers outrage the decencies, however, it is usually only in patches. Some of them are merely escaped puritans. They are so self-satisfied as they dabble in their mud pies that you think of them as cracked and crazy little Jack Horners. They have none of the generous joviality and superabundant spirits of the great outragers of the decencies. Their error is the result, not of an excess, but of a deficiency, of vitality. Other writers of the kind are, as Stevenson said of Zola, 'diseased anyway and black-hearted and fundamentally at enmity with joy.' We can love almost any author who enjoys life, or even any noble author who does not enjoy it, but an author who can give us nothing but prying and joyless excursions into mud is a predestined bore, and literature will have none of him.

It would, I admit, be as absurd as it would be unjust to speak of Zola and certain other writers who have shocked the respectable as though they were obscene and nothing more. Zola in some of his novels all but achieved greatness, and there are one or two living writers with comparable preoccupations to whom, one feels, the divine gift of genius was offered at their cradles. The question at issue is not whether Zola and those others are worthless writers, but whether they may not have lost vastly more than they have gained by refusing to recognize the ordinary taboos of decency. I for one am convinced that they have chiefly lost.

The artist, after all, is a creator of life in its infinite variety. In him the whole range of human emotion is reborn for us. If he gives us disgust, it must be only as the shadow of our raptures. He takes us through child's play and April and sunshine, through friendship and love that challenges the grave and seems even in death to defeat it, through all the conflicts of ambition, greed, and noble disinterestedness, through laughter, tears, and the medicinal wisdom that makes laughter a release into charity, and tears a release into faith and hope, and so on finally to the calm sunset peace of Prospero.

If the artist is preoccupied with the indecent, he has not that free imagination out of which the greatest and most beautiful figures of literature have been born. He has become the slave of a fixed idea, and his imagination enjoys about as much liberty as the caged eagles on the Roman Capitol. If you want to see evidence of this, you have only to look at English lyric poetry. No Rochester, or man of Rochester's mood and mind, has ever soared to those heights to which Wordsworth and the great lyric poets have soared. I doubt, indeed, if a selection of the thousand greatest lyrics in the English language, made on purely aesthetic grounds, would contain half a dozen lyrics that would be gravely questioned on grounds of decency by a committee of bishops.

Much of the indecency of the present day, I fancy, is due to a feeling that the soil of literature is exhausted and that we can enrich it by digging deeper and working in the subsoil. Writers who take this view forget, unfortunately, that when you are digging a garden, while you are advised to dig deep, you are warned on no account to bring the subsoil to the surface. The subsoil is barren, and the great artists, if they refrained from bringing it to the surface, did so because they knew that nothing would grow in it. In ordinary life, if we buried the soil under the subsoil, we should find ourselves starving. Joyce seems to me to have buried the soil under the subsoil in *Ulysses*, and to have produced a vast waste in which the imagination starves.

There are things that Nature never meant us to drag into the light. Just as the gardener must dig down to the subsoil and break it up with his fork, so the artist may venture as deep as

he will with his curiosity, but he must be careful to leave hidden
what was meant to be hidden and to cultivate the same exuberant
earth that was cultivated by the great artists before him.   The
instinct of shame and reticence, in spite of its many absurd
manifestations, was implanted in him by nature as a means of
enabling him to distinguish between what was worth his doing
and what was not.   It goes deeper than superstition, though it
has often been accompanied by superstition, and we owe to a
hundred taboos our rise out of savagery, the progress of human
society, and the development of the arts.   For every great work
of art is a masterpiece of suppression no less than of expression.
Homer and Shakespeare knew a great deal about the animal life
of man and the quagmires of the human imagination that they
were not too great prudes but too great artists to put into writing.

As to where the bounds of decency are to be fixed, it is
impossible to lay down an absolute rule.   All we can be sure
of is that decorum of one sort or another is as essential to the
arts as it is to social life, and that without it the arts tend to
sink into a monotony of triviality or feverishness.   Rabelais and
Sterne may be cited as witnesses on the other side, and undoubtedly the laws of decorum are looser in comic than in more
solemn writing; but even of Rabelais Coleridge could say, as
could be said of few of the supremely indecorous authors: 'I
could write a treatise in praise of the moral elevation of Rabelais's
work which would make the Church stare and the Conventicle
groan, and yet would be truth and nothing but truth.'

To-day, however, it is, as I have suggested, not the comic
writers, but the writers who never make a joke, who seem
oftenest to transgress the bounds of decency; and it would be
difficult to write a treatise in praise of their moral elevation.
Some of them have imaginations that can scarcely rise above the
physical side of sex, and any uninteresting nobody making love
to any other uninteresting nobody is more fascinating to them
than Helen on the walls of Troy or the agony of Lear beside the
dead Cordelia.   They are more interested in love affairs than
in love, and, in opposition to the old Sunday-school tracts,
write what might be described as Witches'-Sabbath-school
tracts.   They too, however, have their own reticence.   They
too, like Homer and Shakespeare, leave things out; they leave
out, indeed, just those things that Shakespeare and Homer

thought important. It is as though they were trying to construct novels from the refuse-heaps of the artists of the past. But, after all, if a novelist can move us neither to tears nor to laughter, it does not very much matter whether he is indecent or not, since he has already written his epitaph with his signature on the title-page. And, if he can move us to tears and laughter, we shall take him to our hearts, however he may offend the conventions of the hour.

If a defence of decency in literature is necessary, it is not in order to denounce this or that writer, but in order to keep alive in a generation of fluctuating thought and opinion a sense of the eternal values in the arts. Readers too easily allow themselves to be herded into opposing camps of puritans and antipuritans, and in the result we often find the antipuritans, in the heat and enthusiasm of battle, trying to foist upon us as a work of exalted genius some third-rate book that has very little merit except that it is likely to shock the pious. The puritans, to do them justice, are less concerned to prove that a book with the morals of which they agree is great literature. They are content to enjoy a bad book of a morally good kind in the same illiterate mood in which most of us enjoy detective stories.

On the whole, there seems to be no necessity to join either of the camps. Literature needs to be defended alike against the deadly decorum of the extreme puritans and the equally deadly indecorum of the extreme antipuritans. But that a profound and noble decorum is all but an essential of great modern literature I am convinced. It was not altogether by accident that the most decorous age in English history produced the greatest novelist in English literature—Charles Dickens.

The Religious Background of Literature
(1928)

FEW people nowadays believe in the inevitability of progress as confidently as their grandfathers believed in it. The theory of evolution is still accepted by the majority of white men who understand it, and even of those who don't; but we no longer apply the theory generally to the affairs of mankind or see any certainty of an orderly progress in civilization itself. There has been steady progress, it is true, in the accumulation of knowledge and in the perfecting of inventions. There is no reason why science should not add storey upon storey to the tower of human knowledge till it has outgrown the tower of Babel. But in other spheres of human activity we feel increasing doubts about the future. Prophets who believe that European society will progress toward Utopia are balanced by those who maintain that it is already in the first stages, or even at an advanced stage, of decay. And when we come to the arts, which are the graces of civilization, not even the professional optimist can see traces of any law of progress at work. Painting, sculpture, music, and literature seem to flourish for a few generations or a few centuries, and then to wither. Golden ages are succeeded by silver ages. Pegasus loses his wings and ambles on his feet. Homer is not followed by greater writers of epics, but, after nearly three thousand years, is still without an equal. Three great tragic dramatists appear in Athens, and there is no other dramatist fit to be named with them till more than two thousand years later Shakespeare begins to write in England. Phidias is still the greatest sculptor, Plutarch the greatest biographer, as Bach and Beethoven—or so it seems to me—are the greatest composers of music. Nowhere in this sphere is there any sign of progress. 'If Art was progressive,' said Blake in his *Annotations to Reynolds*, 'we should have had Michelangelos and Raphaels to succeed each other. But it is not so. Genius dies with its possessor and comes not again till another is born with it.'

Blake, perhaps, went too far in his denial of progress in the arts. Undoubtedly the Greek drama progressed in the age of Aeschylus, and the English drama progressed in the age of Shakespeare. At the same time, it is true that in literature we do not inevitably pass from peak to higher peak of genius. Literature is as likely to take a downward direction as an upward. It is supposed to be the mark of a pessimist to say that anything is going to the dogs, and I should not like to say that literature is going to the dogs at present; but so many literatures have gone to the dogs in the past that it is worth inquiring what are the causes and whether any of these causes are perceptible to-day.

My own belief—and there is some evidence for it—is that literature begins to go to the dogs as soon as earth becomes restive and declares its independence of heaven. In the great ages of literature, earth was, if not a suburb of heaven, a subject kingdom. Heaven and earth were places on the same cosmic map; civilized men believed in the existence of heaven centuries before they believed in the existence of America, and believed in it just as firmly as we believe in the existence of America to-day. Possibly their ideas of heaven were even more mistaken than the modern European's ideas of America. But at least the life of mortals was lit up for them by the presence of the immortals, and the gods presided over human destinies. To me it seems incredible that it is a mere accident that all the supremely great epics, from Homer's to Milton's, were written by poets who not only accepted the heavenly background, but wove it into the theme of their narratives. The gods may not be the most interesting of the characters in the *Iliad*, but the mortal characters seem to borrow a radiance from them, and to take part in larger wars than those of which historians write in prose. Take the gods out of the *Iliad*, and you diminish the heroes. The battle-field of Greek and Trojan would, in the absence of the gods, seem as petty as a lamp-lit town over which hung no firmament of stars. We may not be able to explain why this is so, but we know that it is so. We know that in the presence of the stars we feel an exaltation and liberation of the spirit such as we do not feel in the light of the lamps in a street. It is as though the stars enlarged our world and gave us the freedom of the universe. If we could imagine the extinction of the stars, we should think of the world as an infinitely

impoverished place.   Literature, I believe, would suffer an equal
impoverishment as a result of the death of the gods.

There is, I take it, no need to prove by evidence the existence
of the religious background in epic poetry.   It is too obvious to
be overlooked, whether we think of the *Odyssey*, as Poseidon
drives Odysseus hither and thither, 'a wanderer from his native
land,' and Athene pleads with Zeus to permit his return, or of
Paradise Lost, in which the poet avows it as his object to 'justify
the ways of God to men.'   Virgil and Dante see life in the same
divine setting.   'Sing, Heavenly Muse'—so Milton invokes
inspiration as he writes, and the adjective is not meaningless.
There is no other muse but a heavenly muse that has ever
produced great epic poetry.   According to the Greek legend,
the muses were the daughters of Zeus, and thus song has a
heavenly descent.   Even in the legendary ages, however, there
appear to have been singers who disputed the supremacy of
heaven in poetry.   There was at least one mortal who not only
attempted to sing without the aid of the daughters of Zeus, but
who boasted that he could conquer them in singing, and Homer
in the Catalogue of the Ships tells us of his melancholy fate.
Thamyris, says Homer, 'averred with boasting that he would
conquer, even did the muses themselves sing against him, the
daughters of aegis-bearing Zeus; but they in their anger maimed
him, moreover they took from him the high gift of song and
made him to forget his harping.'   There, I think, we have a
fable of the eternal dependence of literature for its highest
inspiration on a world larger than a world inhabited by none but
mortal men and women.   I do not mean by this that a man who
is intellectually an atheist or an agnostic cannot write great
literature.   What I do contend is that the literary imagination
is akin to the religious imagination, and that literature, while it
has its roots in earth, flourishes in its greatest splendour when
its branches are stirred by some air from heaven.

And literature is not unique among the arts in having such
close associations with religion.   Architecture, sculpture, painting, and music, in at least as great a measure, seem to flower
most abundantly when they are in the precincts of the temple
of the church.   There are no buildings of the Christian era
which, either individually or in the mass, reveal imaginative
genius in the same degree as the great churches.   The age of

the most beautiful painting was the age in which men painted the Madonna and the Child.   Critics differ as to who were the greatest composers, but ordinary men find a pleasure in listening to the music of Handel and Bach, written when music and religion were closely associated, such as they do not find in listening to the music of to-day.   I know that there are critics who explain that the music of Bach is not spiritual, just as there are critics who explain that the poetry of Milton is not Christian. There are critics, again, who deny that there is anything spiritual in the architecture of St. Peter's.   Even if we admit this, however, we shall also have to admit that it is a remarkable coincidence that music like Bach's, epic poetry like Milton's, or architecture like that of St. Peter's, has never been pro- duced by artists indifferent to the religious tradition of mankind.

It may be contended that it is a mere accident that the great poets, the great painters, and the great composers belonged to an age more superstitious and less rational than our own, and that, naturally enough, these men of genius reflected in their work the theology of their time, as some novelists of our own time reflect the psychology of Freud.   There has never yet, it may be urged, been an age of reason, in which men free from the ancient superstitions have had an opportunity of producing work to rival the ancient masterpieces.   We constantly hear to-day of literature's breaking new ground and creating new forms, as though we had only to be patient in order to find a better Homer and a better Milton waiting for us round the corner.   All talk of this kind, I believe, is based on a profound illusion—the illusion of progress in the arts.   We shall never have another Homer until we have a great poet who believes in Olympus.   We shall never have another Milton till we have a great poet who believes in the war between heaven and hell.   It is arguable that these beliefs are superstitions, and that the human race will be both wiser and happier for having abandoned them.   But literature, at least, will be the poorer.   Literature will always have to return for inspiration to Olympus, though it may be to an Olympus transformed.

When Thomas Love Peacock wrote mockingly of poetry more than a century ago as a kind of literature unsuitable to men in an age of reason, he may have written in jesting fashion, but what he said was fundamentally true. 'A poet,' he declared, 'in our times is a semi-barbarian in a civilized community. He lives in the days that are past. His ideas, thoughts, feelings, associations, are all with barbarous manners, obsolete customs, and exploded superstitions. The march of his intellect is like that of a crab, backward. The brighter the light diffused around him by the progress of reason, the thicker is the darkness of antiquated barbarism, in which he buries himself like a mole, to throw up the barren hillocks of his Cimmerian labours.' There you have the truth put in a hostile fashion, but it is none the less truth. The march of a great poet's intellect is, like that of a crab, backward—or would be except for the fact that a crab walks sideways. If the belief in Olympus, or in something corresponding to Olympus, is the mark of a semi-barbarian, then a great modern poet will necessarily be a semi-barbarian. He will probably be more at home in the Dark Ages than at a contemporary meeting of shareholders.

This is not to say that either the great poets or the great prose-writers of the future will be occupied mainly with religious themes. Religion in itself, in the ordinary sense of the word, is no more likely to produce great literature than party politics. If you look around the shelves of a theological library, you will probably find even less good literature than on the shelves of a purely secular library. Glance through a hymn-book, and you will come on very few poems that you feel ought to be included in the *Oxford Book of English Verse*. One of the most astounding facts in literary history is, indeed, that while so many passionately sincere men and women have written religious verse, few of them have written poems as divinely inspired as the poems that other men have written about nightingales and daffodils. Words-worth declared that poetry is 'the spontaneous overflow of powerful feelings.' Well, here among the hymn-writers you have surely the spontaneous overflow of powerful feelings—feelings for which the writers would have been prepared to go to the stake—yet, as literature, their verses are little better than the sort of verses that could be written in favour of the policy of a party leader. This does not mean that hymns are not good for their own purposes, which are conceivably as lofty as the purposes of literature, or more so. It would be as absurd to complain of the literary quality of hymns as it would be to

complain of the literary quality of 'God Save the King.'   Hymns
move many of us as patriotic songs move us, but they seldom
give us the double delight of great poetry—the delight in the
thing expressed and the delight in the way in which it is
expressed.   It may be that the ordinary poet, in writing hymns
as in writing patriotic poetry, depersonalizes himself and writes
in order to express the emotions of human beings in general
rather than his personal vision of the world.   That, I think, is
the most reasonable explanation of the mediocrity of most
religious verse.   When we read Wordsworth's 'Daffodils,' we
feel that we have been admitted into the intimate secrets of
Wordsworth's soul.   When we read Bishop Heber's 'From
Greenland's Icy Mountains,' however, we do not feel that we
have been admitted into the inner sanctuary of Bishop Heber's
imagination.   He has not re-created the world for us; he has
only exhorted us.   We suspect him of writing, not in order to
communicate his vision of life to us, but in order to do us good.
He writes as the advocate of a cause, and not in the pure delight
of the imagination.   It may be said that the real failure of the
hymn lies in the fact that Bishop Heber was not a man of
consummate genius, whereas Wordsworth was.   And that is
partly the explanation.   But, apart from this, we have to face
the fact that a number of men of genius have written both
religious and secular verse, and that, while the secular verse is
beautiful poetry, the religious verse is almost always inferior.
Campion wrote both profane and religious verse, and, though
his religious verse is not negligible, how uninspired most of it
is compared with 'Hark all you ladies that do sleep,' or 'Follow
thy fair sun, unhappy shadow'!   Donne, again, though Dean of
St. Paul's, wrote with nobler inspiration of love than of Paradise.
Herrick, another clergyman, was happier when singing 'Gather
ye rosebuds' or 'Fair daffodills' than when singing the praises
of his Creator.   He did, indeed, write a charming thanksgiving
to God for his house—in which he recounts his blessings in
detail in such simple lines as:

> Thou mak'st my teeming hen to lay
> Her egg each day;

but the charm of the poem lies in the picture it gives us of
Herrick in his earthly house, rather than in opening up to us a

vision of the world transfigured by the light of Paradise.   It is
as though all these poets wrote of love and earthly things with
free imaginations, but of religion under some conventional
restraint.   You will find a parallel to this if you try to imagine
what would happen if all the living poets of genius sat down to
write poems about international peace.   Probably most of them
believe in the ideals of international peace, but however ardently
they believed in them it is almost certain that they would write
about it conventionally and without inspiration.   They would
write, not from the privacy of their souls, but like public
speakers, bent upon influencing an audience.   And no great
literature comes except from the privacy of the soul.   Genius,
indeed, demands the same freedom and fullness of expression in
religious poetry as in secular poetry.

Whenever a great writer tells us as much of the tumult of his
soul in a hymn as Shakespeare tells us of the tumult of his soul
in his sonnets, we have great religious literature.   This is no
mere prophecy; the miracle has happened in the past.   There
has been great religious poetry written in one century after
another, in which we wander in new fields of the imagination.
When we read Henry Vaughan's 'They are all gone into the
world of light' or 'My soul, there is a country, Far beyond the
stars,' we become sharers in the deepest experiences of a great
writer's soul.   Here, we feel, are his profoundest confessions,
his autobiography.   Here he does not disguise his 'powerful
feelings' in the language of convention and restraint.   He writes
of heavenly things, not as an intruder on his best behaviour,
but as one who is as familiar with them as Shelley with the song
of the skylark.   We find the same familiarity and fullness of
expression in Francis Thompson's *The Hound of Heaven*, and in
those verses in which he turns the eyes of men to the vision of

> . . . the traffic of Jacob's ladder
> Pitched between Heaven and Charing Cross.

The religious poets, as a rule, close their eyes to the fact that,
even to a religious man, Charing Cross is at least as real as
heaven.   They forget that, by making Charing Cross more real,
they also make heaven more real, and that a heaven that is not
related somehow to Charing Cross and the fields of earth is to
the imagination merely a vague formula.   Literature must be

human even when it is divine: otherwise it is not literature, but only divinity.

It is not only in religious poetry, but in religious prose, that you commonly find a deficiency of humanity.   The inhumanity of the mass of pious books is, as we say, 'notorious.'   Thackeray made fun of the worst kind of them in *Vanity Fair* in his references to Lady Emily Sheepshanks and her 'sweet tracts,' 'The Sailor's True Bivouack,' 'The Applewoman of Finchley Common,' 'Thrump's Legacy,' and 'The Blind Washerwoman of Moorfields.' It is possible, even probable, that works of this kind have helped tens of thousands of people to live happier and better lives, but no one has ever claimed that they possess literary value.   They are argumentative in purpose, not imaginative.   They are as little literary either in motive or in achievement as a pamphlet in favour of or in opposition to vivisection.   On the other hand, let an imaginative man begin to write of religion in terms of his own experiences, and immediately we are in a world as enchanting as the world of the great story-tellers.   Bunyan had an edifying, as well as a literary, motive in writing *Grace Abounding to the Chief of Sinners* and *The Pilgrim's Progress*, but he obeyed every rule of imaginative literature as he wrote.   He founded his books on human life, and on the passions and experiences that were the most wonderful things that he had known.   The ordinary religious story tells us that the salvation of a human soul is wonderful, but it does not make us experience the wonder in our own imaginations.   Bunyan does this, and he does it, not only because he is a man of genius, but because he can be true to heaven without being false to Bedfordshire. Like all great religious writers, he is the inhabitant of two worlds.   You see how naturally they interpenetrate one another in that beautiful sentence in *Grace Abounding* describing his conversion: 'But upon a day the good providence of God called me to Bedford to work at my calling, and in one of the streets of that town I came where there were three or four poor women sitting at a door in the sun, telling about the things of God.' How full of light, of grace, of the loveliness of earth, that sentence is, as well as of edification!   No one can read it without realizing that the human background is as necessary to religious literature as the religious background is to literature in general.

I have referred to the position of the hymn and the tract in literature chiefly in order to make it clear that, in urging the importance of the religious background in poetry and imaginative prose, I am not contending that men of letters are, or should become, the rivals of preachers, or that they have any kind of propagandist function. I am merely proposing an investigation of one of the chief tributaries that feed the river of great literature, and raising the question of how much literature owes to the acceptance of a larger world than the world we touch with our hands and see with our eyes. So far as epic poetry is concerned, the facts undoubtedly suggest that great epics cannot be written about a world deserted by the gods. The importance of the religious background is not quite so clear, however, when we turn from the epic to drama, lyric poetry, and the novel. Most critics affirm that modern literature flowered into genius largely as a result of breaking free from the authority of religion, and the movement of humanism is praised because it released the human mind from the despotism of theology and enabled it to think and to express itself boldly.

Literature, these critics hold, is essentially heretical, the opponent of the standards of priest and presbyter, and Walter Pater maintained that one of the strongest characteristics of the literature even of the Middle Ages was a 'spirit of rebellion and revolt against the moral and religious ideas of the time.' As evidence of the heretical and sceptical character of medieval literature, he quoted the passage in *Aucassin et Nicolette*, in which Aucassin, threatened with the pains of hell if he does not give up Nicolette, cries scornfully:

'In Paradise what have I to do? I care not to enter, but only to have Nicolette, my very sweet friend, whom I love so dearly well. For into Paradise go none but such people as I will tell you of. There go those aged priests, and those old cripples, and the maimed, who all day long and all night cough before the altars and in the crypts beneath the churches; those who go in worn old mantles and old tattered habits; who are naked, and barefoot, and full of sores; who are dying of hunger and of thirst, of cold, and of wretchedness. Such as these enter in Paradise, and with them I have nought to do. But in hell will I go. For to hell go the fair clerks and the fair knights who are slain in the tourney and the great wars, and the stout archer and the loyal man. With them will I go. And there go the fair and courteous ladies, who have friends two or three, together with their wedded lords.   And there pass the gold and the silver, the ermine and all rich furs, harpers and minstrels, and the happy of the world.   With these will I go, so only that I have Nicolette, my very sweet friend, by my side.'

That is certainly not an orthodox speech, but it is a speech made in a world that believed in heaven and in hell.   Again and again, even in those early days, we find the priest and the poet in conflict, but they carry on their quarrel against a background that contains other worlds than our own.   We see another example of this in medieval Irish literature, in the famous dialogue that took place between St. Patrick and Oisin, the long-dead pagan hero, who returns from the Country of the Young to Ireland to find all the heroes dust and Christianity triumphant.   To Oisin this Christian Ireland is an Ireland in ruins.   He weeps for the vanished pagan world that he had known, and Patrick reproaches him for mourning for heathen companions who are now in hell.

'Leave off fretting, Oisin,' says Patrick, 'and shed your tears to the God of grace.   Finn and the Fianna are black enough now, and they will get no help for ever.'

'It is a pity that would be,' replies Oisin, 'Finn to be in pain for ever; and who was it gained the victory over him, when his own hand had made an end of so many a hard fighter?'

'It is God gained the victory over Finn,' Patrick tells him, 'and not the strong hand of an enemy; and as to the Fianna, they are condemned to hell along with him, and tormented for ever.'

'O Patrick,' cries Oisin, 'show me the place where Finn and his people are, and there is not a hell or a heaven there but I will put it down.   And if Osgar, my own son, is there, the hero that was bravest in heavy battles, there is not in hell or in the heaven of God a troop so great that he could not destroy it.'

Here, again, we have a passage that seems to suggest that literature has an irreligious rather than a religious temper.   But the conflict in this dialogue is not really between religion and irreligion, but between two different kinds of religion.   Oisin, like St. Patrick, has a vision of a world that is on no earthly map.   He has the Country of the Young to set against the saint's heaven.   He cries to Patrick: 'The Country of the Young, the Country of Victory, and, O Patrick, there is no lie in that name. If there are grandeurs in your heaven the same as there are there, I would give my friendship to God. . . .' Not yet has literature reached that stage of post-humanism where the writer has no eyes except for the earth.

With the growth of the drama and the growth of the novel in later times, literature did undoubtedly become more exclusively human. But, even when it was reticent in regard to the religious life of man, it was at its greatest when it was written on the assumption that religion was true. Enthusiastic partisans have attempted to prove that Shakespeare was a Catholic or a Puritan, or that he had no religion at all. I do not know what his convictions were, but it is clear that his plays could never have been written except out of an imagination steeped in Christian conceptions, just as the *Oedipus Rex* could never have been written except out of an imagination steeped in Greek religious conceptions. That profound sense of sin which we find in the tragedies of Shakespeare is essentially a Christian sense. If Shakespeare had brought gods as well as ghosts on to the stage, he could not more clearly have made the life of man seem no trivial accident between life and death, but an event in a larger universe.

Take the religious conceptions out of *Hamlet*, and rewrite the play in terms of Freudian complexes, and you will lose almost as great a proportion of beauty as you would lose if you rationalized *Paradise Lost*. Hamlet's cry:

> 'O all you host of heaven! O earth! what else?
> And shall I couple hell?'

is no mere figure of speech. Hamlet's actions are again and again governed by his sense of the existence of another world. There is scarcely a great scene in the play in which the divine background of life is not taken for granted. It is all the more interesting to discover that Professor Gilbert Murray contends that the tragedy of Hamlet has even a quasi-religious origin and that it is the perfection of an ancient myth, as is the tragedy of Orestes—that, in fact, both tragedies are sprung from the same mythical seed. 'We finally,' he declares,

run the Hamlet saga to earth in the same ground as the Orestes saga: in the prehistoric and worldwide ritual battle of Summer and Winter, of Life and Death, which has played so vast a part in the mental development of the human race and especially, as Sir E. K. Chambers has shown us, in the history of medieval drama.

This is not to say, of course, that Shakespeare consciously wrote *Hamlet* as a fable of the ritual battle of Summer and Winter, of Life and Death, the conception of which is one of the sources of both religion and literature. But it is interesting to discover that the plot he chose can tentatively be traced back to its origin in a myth of the battles of the gods. If this is true, *Hamlet* has a doubly religious lineage, and it would probably not be going too far to say that without the religious imagination it would have been as impossible for *Hamlet* to have been written as it would for the books of the Bible to have been written. And, if we turn to the work of later men of genius who have used the dramatic form, we shall find that the greatest of them, however heretical, have for some reason or other been unable to dispense with, or escape from, the supernatural. If it is possible to write dramatic poetry as great as Goethe's *Faust* and Ibsen's *Brand* and *Peer Gynt* without the assumption of a supernatural background —be it only for dramatic purposes—to men's lives, how is it that no one has ever done so? My own theory is that without this assumption the doom of man loses most of its tragic grandeur, and that for this reason the dramatic, like the epic, poet is inevitably forced to return to a heavenly muse for inspiration. The more we consider the matter, indeed, the more we are compelled to the conclusion that literature, while often in revolt against orthodoxy, is inextricably bound up with the religious imagination. Literature might almost be said to be sprung from a seed dropped from the tree of religion.

The religious element in literature, of course, is much more obvious in poetry than in the novel. 'It utters somewhat above a mortal mouth,' said Ben Jonson of poetry, and the practice of the great poets has endorsed his saying. They see the world transformed by a 'light that never was on sea or land.' They release us from the actual, or lead us through it to the universal. 'Poetry,' declared Shelley, 'defeats the curse which binds us to be subjected to the accident of surrounding impressions.' Modern fiction seldom defeats this curse. Many modern novelists devote themselves entirely to the description of surrounding impressions. They are content to observe rather than to imagine, and, as we read their realistic novels about some uninteresting young man or woman in revolt against the uninteresting atmosphere of an uninteresting home, we feel the world growing emptier.   Life at its best in such novels is a Canterbury pilgrimage without Canterbury, and with the fun left out.

The aridity of most realistic—or, as it might be called, materialistic—fiction, I believe, is largely due to the fact that the realistic novelists are convinced that the world has outgrown Canterbury.   Possibly it has, as it outgrew Olympus, but, just as Homer could not have written the *Iliad* without Olympus in the background, and Chaucer could not have written *The Canterbury Tales* without Canterbury in the background, so, in my opinion, a religious background, either expressed or implied, will always be necessary to the production of great literature. It may be a mere coincidence that the greatest fiction of recent times, the Russian, sprang from what rationalists would describe as the most superstitious soil in Europe; but I do not think so. Some people would deny that there is any religious background in Hardy's work, but it is significant that in *The Dynasts* Hardy found himself compelled to imagine an overworld of spirits and angels as part of the setting of human hopes and fears.   As we read the plays of Bernard Shaw, who invented the life force, again we realize the truth of the old saying that 'if God had not existed, we should have had to invent him.'

Everywhere the imaginative man confronted with the mystery of life and death is forced to adopt a religious attitude to life——the attitude of awe before the eternal mysteries.   Without it there can be neither the greatest poetry nor the greatest prose —neither the verse of Milton nor the prose of the Bible and Sir Thomas Browne.   Great poetry will cease to be written when poets cease to be men for whom the invisible world exists. And if this is true of poetry, is it not reasonable to believe that it is also true of imaginative prose, which is only poetry in its weekday dress?

The Importance of Leaving Things Out
(1931)

WE live in an age in which authors are getting more and more into the habit of putting everything in. It is all the more necessary to emphasize the importance of leaving most things out. Putting everything in is one of the surest methods of dooming a book to oblivion.

One of the most delightful arts in literature is the art of biography. Yet not one biography in a hundred survives its author, chiefly because the author seldom has the gift of leaving things out. Those massive two-volume biographies which were favoured during the nineteenth century looked very impressive when they were new; but most of them were choked to death by the irrelevant matter they contained.

It is not that readers are prejudiced against a long book. There will always be plenty of readers for Gibbon's *Decline and Fall* and Macaulay's *History*. Gibbon and Macaulay, however, knew how and what to omit. They separated the grain from the chaff, and left nothing in their books that was not good food for the mind. If either of them had put all he had read or thought about his subject into his book it would have been as long as the *Encyclopaedia Britannica* without being as readable.

As regards readableness, it is a matter of no importance whether a book is as short as Plutarch's Life of Antony, or as long as Boswell's *Johnson*. It is not length but irrelevance that is tedious. Even Boswell, I fancy, would have been tedious if he had given us a verbatim report of everything Dr. Johnson had said in his presence, whether it was of interest or not. Full though his record is, however, Boswell, as we know, was a selective artist and had an extraordinary genius for fixing on those parts of Johnson's conversation which best revealed his genius and his character.

Many biographers—especially in the United States—still seem to be under the impression that it is their duty to fling into their books all the material they have collected, however dull

or unimportant.   It is as if an architect were to offer us a huge
heap of stones and rubbish instead of a house.   There is neither
arrangement nor selection.   Imagine what a biography of Gladstone would be like if it quoted the full text of every Bill
introduced into Parliament during his premiership.   It might
be a useful reference book, but it would be perfectly unreadable.

Besides the biographers who do not know how to omit
tedious facts we have the biographers who cannot control their
imaginations but must paint crowded pictures, not of things
that happened, but of things that may have happened.   This has
been the fault even of many able biographers.   Miss Amy Lowell
injured her Life of Keats by supposing all kinds of things about
him, when all that we wanted to read was what she knew
about him.

Walter Bagehot found the same fault with Masson's great
Life of Milton.   'Mr. Masson,' he declared, 'is fond of
telling us what he thinks may have happened,' and he gives as
an example the following passage about Milton's youth:

Look back, reader, and see him as I do!   Now, under the elms of his
father's lawn, he listens to the rural hum, and marks the branches as
they wave, and the birds as they fly; now in the garden he notes the
annual series of the plants and the daily blooming of the roses.   In his
walks in the neighbourhood, also, he observes not only the wayside
vegetation, but the whole wide face of the landscape, rich in wood
and meadow, to the royal towers of Windsor and the boundary line of
the low Surrey hills.   Over this landscape, changing its livery from
day to day, fall the varying seasons.   Light green spring comes with
its showers and its days of keener blue, when Nature is warm at the
root, and all things gain in liveliness; spring changes into summer,
when all is one wealth of leafage, and the gorgeous bloom of the
orchard passes into the forming fruit, summer deepens into autumn,
gathering the tanned haycocks and tumbling the golden grain; and, at
last, when the brown and yellow leaves have fallen and the winds have
blown them and the rains rotted them, comes winter with his biting
breath, and the fields are either all white so that the most familiar eye
hardly knows them, or they lie in mire, and in the dull brumous air,
the stripped stems and netted twig-work of the trees are like a painting
in china ink.   And these seasons have each their occupations.   Now
the plough is afield; now the sower casts his seed; now the sheep are
shorn; now the mower whets his scythe.   Look on then, glorious
youth, at star and trees, at the beauties of day, and the beauties of

night, at the changing aspects of the seasons, and at all that the seasons bring!

I have quoted the passage in full because, while it is a piece of eloquent prose, it is an excellent example of the sort of thing that ought to be left out. The reader, eager to progress, feels as if he were dragging his feet slowly through soft sand. The writer should be a road-builder making progress easy. Facts and fancies that impede progress are among the curses of literature.

It is one of the rules of good writing that no author should tell us either all he knows or all he thinks. He must from all he thinks and knows select those comparatively few facts and thoughts that are significant. Thus, if the day of the month on which an event happens, or even the hour of the day itself, is significant, it is the part of a good writer to mention it. But if we were told the exact day and hour of every event referred to in history, a library would scarcely be room enough to contain the full history of a single war. In conversation, the man who has not the art of omitting irrelevant detail is shunned as a bore.

Suppose, for example, you had been to Oxford to see a football match between Brasenose and Balliol. If you wished to tell a friend of this you would not begin: 'I got up at twenty-five minutes to eight. I put on my dressing-gown and slippers and went to the bathroom. First I brushed my teeth, then I shaved, using such and such a razor, such and such a soap, and a badger-hair brush for which I paid 17s. 6d. on the 3rd of March last year —I bought it at 1.22 p.m. Then I had a bath, first letting the hot tap run then the cold, just to make it tolerable.' And so on, with details of the breakfast, the taxi ride to the station, the railway ticket and journey, all leading laboriously up to the arrival at the football ground, and all part of the story of the day at Oxford, but a part that should be taken for granted. If conversationalists did not take the majority of facts for granted, conversation would become a form of torture. And what is true of the art of conversation is also true of the art of writing.

Most of the psychological novels that are being written to-day will, I am sure, perish chiefly because they are as boring as dull conversation. The psychological novelist, like the old-fashioned realist, usually believes that any fact at all is worth printing. The most tedious processes of thought of the most tedious young man or woman are to him a delight; and the dullest action stirs his pulses more than a golden deed. He puts in everything that the great writers left out, forgetting that the great writers left these things out because they were not worth putting in. He is sometimes praised as original, but he is original only as a novelist would be original who described every single movement of his hero's eyelids. You could fill a volume by recording every opening and shutting of the eyelids that occurs in a man's life in twenty-four hours. 'Then his eyelids shut; then they opened. Then they shut; then they opened.' And so on. Such a book would be full of facts. But they are facts of the kind that every sane novelist leaves out.

Much of the obscenity that appears in modern fiction is due to the belief that anything that is a fact is worth printing. The truth is, of course, that, from the point of view of art, only those facts are worth printing that heighten our delight or touch our imaginations. The artist does not see the same Hamlet that the family doctor sees. He looks for and discovers a different set of facts. Hamlet's temperature, the colour of his tongue, the sound of his chest when he says 'ninety-nine,' the state of his stomach, are all facts of immense interest if you are his family doctor; but, if you are a poet, you are after bigger game, and merely physical details, except on the rare occasions on which they happen to be artistically significant, are taken for granted.

There are hundreds of facts which would be significant in a medical text-book or an anthropological study but which would be utterly insignificant in a Greek tragedy. All the natural functions of the body are the proper study of the man of science, but to harp on them in a poem would reduce it to the dullest of prose.

It is, of course, arguable that a novelist should be permitted to give his book a scientific rather than an artistic interest, and to appeal to our curiosity rather than delight our imagination. The majority of readers, however, do not go to novels for information, and, apart from that, the majority of novelists are no better informed than their readers. Hence the novelist who clutters up his book with facts that in themselves are no more interesting than the numbers on bus tickets may interest his readers at first because he happens to bore them in a new way, but even the newest way becomes old in time and boringness that has lost its novelty becomes 100 per cent boring.

Those novelists who rely for the interest on saying all kinds of uninteresting things that Dickens left out will in time be generally recognized as bores, like the majority of the old two-volume biographers. It does not matter whether the things that should be left out are decent or indecent. If they are irrelevant, they bore us, and death is the punishment for the book that bores its readers.

Tolerant versus Intolerant Criticism

(1931)

ALMOST as regularly as the equinox comes the demand from somebody or other for a more ruthless type of literary criticism than is customary in the present century. These critics of criticism look back with longing to the good old days of the *Saturday* when authors were slashed as with knives and served up as the most delicious kind of mincemeat to the public. Only by the return of such merciless criticism, we are told, can the standards of taste be restored, and only by such means can literary criticism save its soul.

There is, indeed, a revolt against toleration in general in progress among a considerable section of the human race. In the nineteenth century it was commonly taken for granted that toleration in politics and religion was an essential characteristic of civilized human beings; but human beings grow tired even of toleration, and so we have numerous reactions in favour of despotism and the ruthless suppression of free speech. Toleration in the sphere of morals has immensely increased, but here, too, a reaction may set in because of the universal love of change. Toleration, moreover, is apt to become anaemic, and, when it does, men instinctively refresh their blood with the tonic of intolerance.

Schopenhauer, whose literary essays are among the most stimulating ever written, was strongly of the opinion that, however necessary toleration might be in the ordinary spheres of life, there was no room for it in literary criticism. 'It is quite wrong,' he declared, 'to try to introduce into literature the same toleration that must necessarily prevail in society towards those stupid, brainless people who everywhere swarm in it. In literature such people are impudent intruders; and to disparage the bad is a duty towards the good; for he who thinks nothing bad will think nothing good either. Politeness, which has its source in social relations, is in literature an alien and often injurious element, because it insists that bad work shall be called good.' But even Schopenhauer, with magnificent honesty, had to admit that the right kind of intolerant criticism was almost unattainable, for he added: 'This ideal journal could, to be sure, be written only by people who joined incorruptible honesty with rare knowledge and still rarer power of judgment, so that, perhaps, there could at the very outset, be one, and hardly one, in the whole country.'

The truth is, the case for intolerance in criticism breaks down on two very important considerations—good sense and good manners. Good sense is undoubtedly for ever counselling toleration. As a rule, the young with high artistic ideals tend to be intolerant because they cannot bear to think of thousands of books being printed every year that have not enough merit to keep them alive more than a few weeks. A conventional love story sickens them. They read with disgust and impatience a pasteboard historical novel, and denounce it because in imaginative riches it falls short of *Salammbô*. They have an ideal in their minds which makes even some of the best books of the year seem relatively tawdry and ill written. They feel that, by denouncing nearly everything that is published, they are clearing the Augean stables of literature.

If I remember right, Bernard Shaw once explained that this, or something like it, was his attitude in the days when he was a dramatic critic. He attacked various plays, not because the authors failed to do quite effectively what they set out to do, but because they were not the kind of plays which he himself wished to write and to see written. This attitude may be justified in an artist of genius, since it produces lively criticism of an original kind. But it is not every century that gives birth to a Bernard Shaw, and no critic could be a worse model for critics of smaller stature. For good sense tells us that, in the mass of books and plays, we have no right to demand genius of any kind at all. The ordinary book is not planned by its author as immortal literature, and is not published as immortal literature; and to condemn it for not being what it was never meant to be is foolish and off the mark.

Everybody knows, in fact, that there are two kinds of books published—books which exist more or less in the world of literature and books with little or no literary quality the object of which is merely to convey information or entertainment to the reader. The ordinary novel, for example, has merely an entertainment value. It has no more imaginative quality than the ordinary music-hall turn. It can while an hour away by appealing to our superficial sentimentality or exciting us with impossible sensationalism or making us laugh. It can be read once, or even read eagerly once, and may be commended to an imaginary tired business man and to the tired business man's still more tired wife. On its own level it may be an extremely efficient piece of work; it has entered for a pass and has passed creditably; it has not entered for honours and cannot fairly be examined on the assumption that it has.

The moralist, of course, may quite fairly hold the opinion that books of this kind ought not to be allowed to exist, that (as some people say of football and crossword puzzles) they merely waste our time and sap our intelligence. I do not take this view myself, but a case can be made out for it. At the same time, a man who believes that all sweetmeats are bad for the young is not invited to be a judge at a confectionery exhibition. And in the same way, the reviewer who is invited to judge popular literature has to remember that what he is asked to examine is not an exhibition of would-be masterpieces, but a show of generally acceptable toys and trifles. A critic will admire the Winged Victory none the less because he can see the merit of a little clockwork man who tumbles head over heels on the floor.

The real vice of criticism, indeed, is not the toleration of books of a rubbishy but harmless kind, but the praise of books of a pretentious kind. These he must measure by a severer standard. These attempt to deceive the reader into the belief that they are works of art, profound studies of psychology, and so forth; and it is the critic's duty to make it clear that they are not what they seem and to expose them as the species of solemn humbug they really are. Far more critics fail through being unable to distinguish between a real masterpiece and an imitation masterpiece than through an easy-going toleration of readable rubbish.

Even in exposing humbug, however, I hold that a critic should remain as tolerant as he possibly can. In the first place, he may be mistaken in his judgment, as the critics who attacked Keats were mistaken in theirs. In the second place, intolerance easily becomes a habit, and the intolerant critic finds himself so often in a rage that in the end few people take his rages seriously. Again, there is always the possibility that the critic will begin to take a positive pleasure in hurting the feelings of comparatively harmless authors, and criticism can easily degenerate into a blood-sport. Intolerance is best, in my opinion, when it is directed against established reputations. A really good writer cannot be injured by hostile criticism except in his suscepti-bilities; and the reaction against a fierce onslaught on him will probably increase the enthusiastic devotion of his readers. If the onslaught is unjust, it is the critic, not the author, who ultimately suffers in reputation.

Criticism at its best, however, is the praise of literature at its best; and here there is seldom room for intolerance. Even Schopenhauer, who called for intolerance of everything that was not genius in literature, protested against the nagging kind of criticism which is too much occupied with dwelling on the faults of writers of genius. 'In appreciating a genius,' he wrote, 'criticism should not deal with the errors in his productions or with the poorer of his works, and then proceed to rate him low; it should attend only to the quality in which he most excels. For, in the sphere of intellect, as in other spheres, weakness and perversity cleave so firmly to human nature that even the most brilliant mind is not wholly and at all times free from them.' This, it seems to me, is going a little too far. It is often necessary to point out the defects of an author in order to define his quality. Wordsworth lost nothing as a result of its being pointed out that there were limitations to his genius and that it was only within certain limits that his genius burned brightly. The good critic not only praises the author's best work, but carefully separates it from the worst. He is a gold washer separating the precious metal from the dross.

In the history of criticism, I think, however, it will be found that the greatest critics have been appreciators, not detractors. This may be due partly to the fact that they have written for the most part about the dead. For, in literature, we can know more about the dead than about the living, and the dead whose books have survived have generally some virtue worth praising. Faults that seemed intolerable to their contemporaries are mere motes in the sun to us. And it will be noted that this praise is not the outcome of lukewarmness, which is an eminent vice in criticism. Even intolerance is better than that, since a man in a temper is more interesting than a man who is apathetic. But intolerance, as a rule, is the result of petty egotism, and that, too, becomes dull in time. The only intolerance that is really tolerable is the intolerance of a critic who is as magnanimous as he is just. And such intolerance is rare.

Words and their Use

(1930)

To say that sincerity is the chief maker of style is, perhaps, to tell only a half truth. It is obviously possible for a man to be a passionately sincere Protectionist or Free Trader and yet to write the most atrocious English on his favourite subject. Most of the sincere people who have written about politics, indeed, like most of those who have written about religion, in the past three thousand years have lamentably failed to turn their sincerity into literature. It is clear that the sincerity that goes to the making of style is something different from the sincerity of the propagandist. It is not merely the sincerity of an emotion felt or of an opinion held: it is, beyond this, a sincerity in the use of words themselves—an instinctive desire to make words express as truly as possible what the writer sets out to express. The best writer, other things being equal, is he whose words convey his matter most truly to the intelligence and, in the greatest literature, to the imagination of his readers.

In this sense, a half-sincere cynic may use words more truthfully, because he is more sensitive to their precise meaning, than a superlatively sincere fanatic.

It is difficult to say how far this sensitiveness to the precise meaning of words can be taught. It should be possible to teach almost any intelligent human being not to write badly, though even this has not yet been done in spite of ten thousand schoolmasters. But to take an ordinary human being and teach him to write really well—that seems as impossible as to teach him to be a good painter. On the other hand, it ought to be possible to teach any human being of the docile age to be a better writer than he already is, and that is, perhaps, as much as any of the books of instruction on the art of writing aim at.

The chief school of good writing is literature itself. Those who write well are as a rule those who have read well in their most receptive years. Most of the writers of books have been brought up in an environment of books, or have at least lived in such an environment since their early teens. Their minds are steeped in literature. They are as intimate with the ways of words as a young country-bred naturalist with the ways of animals. They have absorbed a vocabulary from the vocabulary of the masters. It is, of course, only when genius or talent exists that this early association with books produces literature. But it is here that genius and talent find their best instruction.

To say this is not to belittle the work of teachers and of writers of books on the King's English. These are counsellors who have the power both to inspire and to warn even the elderly against the thousand pitfalls in the path of those who set out to write. There is probably not a writer alive, however expert, who is not guilty at times of blunders in the use of speech such as grammarians quote to their pupils as examples of bad English. Some years ago, in *Hail and Farewell*, Mr. George Moore did his best to tear to pieces the reputation of Cardinal Newman as a master of style. Newman wrote of 'the lessons which I gained in the experience of my own history in the past.' Mr. Moore protested that one does not 'gain' lessons. Newman wrote of a correspondence that 'took place' in 1834: Mr. Moore observed magisterially: 'A prize-fight takes place; a correspondence begins.' And so with phrase after phrase till 'the greatest master of lucid English' was made to look a mere muddler of words. Other critics, I think, have dredged Mr. Moore's own writings for errors in the use of English, and at least one critic has discussed at length the vices of the prose of Conrad. I am sure that errors of the same kind could be discovered in the work of every writer of good English from Addison down to W. H. Hudson. Human beings are fallible in the conduct of words as in the conduct of life, and the grammarians could find examples of most of the atrocities of language without going outside the works of the accepted masters.

No reasonable critic, however, condemns a good writer for an occasional blunder. There are good writers who have misused the words 'phenomenal' and 'individual'; who have written 'very interested' and have erred in their use of 'and which,' who have defied the laws of grammar and mixed their metaphors. It is a mere pedantry to emphasize the importance of such errors. A good writer must be allowed his quota of errors, and George Borrow may justly be forgiven mistakes that would be seriously criticized in a school essay. It is good to inculcate faultlessness in the young, but ultimately it is positive qualities rather than absence of faults that makes good writing. Even those who dislike the split infinitive—a dislike for which, I think, there is much to be said—would not deny genius to the prose of Ruskin because he occasionally split an infinitive.

There has during the past generation been a marked change in the attitude of those in authority to the split infinitive, 'averse to,' and various other things that a more pedantic age regarded as barbarities of speech. This was a natural reaction against the rule of the precisians, who regarded it as a sin against English to end a sentence with a preposition, and who would have tested the quality of a writer's prose by his use of 'which' and 'that.' Excellent a thing as it is, however, to have put an end to such pedantries, it seems to me that the reaction against pedantry is going too far. We have grammarians to-day who declare that 'It's me' is good English, and I should be surprised to learn that no one has yet justified 'different to.' After all, the meaning of 'different to' is perfectly clear, or at least clear enough, and thousands of Englishmen and women use the expression daily. If the living colloquial speech is to be the standard of good writing, there is much to be said for 'different to.'

Colloquial speech, however, can never be the standard of good writing, especially in a country like England. There are writers who are said to have an easy conversational style, but I have never yet heard one of them conversing in the same style in which he writes. The conversational style of writing may produce the effect of conversation, but it does not do this by imitating the method of conversation. It is careful where conversation is careless, and is more likely to be founded on the prose of Addison and Swift than on the locutions of the con- temporary suburban train. The literary language of the day draws part of its strength from the common speech of the day, but it draws its strength also from the traditional speech of the

*I

great writers. It is only through this acquaintance with the speech of the great writers that the modern author acquires tact in the use of the speech of his own time. It is from the great writers that he learns the good use of words, and, having done so, he learns to use even the slang phrases of his own time with literary effectiveness, as C. E. Montague did.

But no writer will ever become a master of prose unless his style is rooted in the past. It is in the acknowledged master-pieces of the past that the manners of writing are learnt, and it is through acquaintance with them that words come to have a rich burden of associations beyond their precise meaning. I doubt if it would be possible for any man who knew only the literature of his own time to write superlatively well. Shake-speare drew on the classics and on his predecessors; Bunyan knew the Bible almost by heart; Dickens had devoured the novelists of the eighteenth century. To-day a great deal of attention is paid in the schools to contemporary authors, and I am told that this has increased the interest of the young in literature. At the same time, in a complete education in reading and writing, a balance should be preserved between the old and the new. Literature, both in its matter and in its manner, hands down a tradition, and the writer who is not in touch with that tradition is likely to be a parvenu both in his use of words and in his judgment of contemporary work.

The truth is, literature, though more keenly conscious even than politics of the present, always looks back longingly on the past. Even in his use of words, the man of letters resents the continuous flood of new speech that threatens to swamp the language that has been handed down to him. Swift is sometimes derided for having objected to the use of the word 'snob,' but Swift in his day was right. All new words or phrases should be challenged until they can show certificates of naturalization. To-day, more than ever, the flood of new words is pouring into English—music-hall slang, cinema slang, and the jargon of new inventions and new sciences—and, though a small percentage of this will ultimately be absorbed into classical English speech, it is none the less important to challenge every new expression to prove its right to citizenship. The modern writer is 'up against it,' and it is 'up to him' to 'get busy' and to see that none of these modern locutions 'stay put' except such as have 'earned their keep.' There was probably never an age in which conversational speech was at greater enmity with literary speech than the present. That is why the young writer of to-day, while listening keenly to the conversation of his own time, should also be able to stand aloof and measure it by the standard of the good speech that has been handed down from times past.

Our Debt to Greece

(1945)

THE controversy about the value of the dead languages has broken out again, and letters from eminent men on both sides of the question have been appearing in *The Times*. It was, to me, a new and surprising thing to find two Latin masters expressing the opinion that teaching Latin is, for the most part, a waste of time. I can appreciate Frank Jones's sense of disappointment as he remembers the half-million or so boys and girls to whom he has taught Latin, and reflects that probably not one in a hundred of them has ever read Latin for pleasure after leaving school or the university. If the object of teaching Latin were to enable human beings—and, indeed, to persuade them—to read Horace and Tacitus in their spare time when the days of what is called their education are over, we should have to admit that the Latin class in schools and colleges has failed in its purpose and has been an unpardonable waster of time.

It seems to me, however, that the teaching of almost any subject can be proved to be a waste of time if put to so severe a test. The mathematics master, for example, might well feel that his teaching had been mostly a waste of time, if he faced the fact that, by middle age, only a minority of his pupils would be able to tell the difference between a surd and a quadratic equation. I certainly could not do so; though I know there is a difference, I could not explain it either to myself or to anybody else. Nor, in spite of the years I spent over the theorems and problems of Euclid, could I at the present day prove that the something of a hypotenuse of a right-angled triangle is equal to something else. Even arithmetic, after the division lesson, has proved useless to me in later life. I remember nothing of proportion but its name, and as I have never possessed a stock or a share, all that stuff about stocks and shares in the arithmetic book has long since slipped from my memory.

Yet once I was awarded a second prize for mathematics in a

large class—I thought at the time, and still am inclined to think, that the examiner must either have confused my papers with another boy's or have been unable to read my writing, and so have thought that my scrawls meant something different from what they did mean.

Useless as most of my mathematical instruction has been to me in later life, however, I do not think it is of no use to learn mathematics. After all, almost any subject can provide exercise for the brain. And the object of education, it seems to me, is to provide exercise for the brain, even more than to load the brain with knowledge that will last a lifetime.

If we turn from Latin and mathematics to history, I wonder whether we shall not find that this, too, is a subject the teaching of which is largely a waste of time. What proportion of middle-aged men and women in these days, do you think, could sit down to-morrow to a fairly simple examination paper in history, and earn even twenty-five marks in a hundred with their answer? Only a small minority, I fancy.

Not long ago a teacher in an East End slum maintained that the teaching of history—whether it was about King Alfred and the cakes, or about Hannibal and his elephants—to poor children was mostly useless and made no appeal to their imaginations; and he suggested that time would be more profitably spent in teaching them about evolution, and other such things, and that they would find this much more interesting. Well, evolution is a good subject, but I think that the life story of a great nation —or, indeed, of a little nation—is no less good. Whether a subject is interesting or not to children depends first on its being interesting to the teacher, and secondly on his being able to communicate this interest.

One might go through nearly all the subjects taught in schools, after the three Rs, and ask concerning them, one by one, of what use it will be in later life to have studied them. Of the pupils in the French class, how many will ever be able to speak French, and how many will read French poetry and novels in the original for pleasure? Only a minority and not a large minority. If we apply Mr. Jones's test of uselessness, teaching French, I am afraid, will have to be admitted to be largely a waste of time—not so great a waste of time as teaching Latin, perhaps, but still a waste of time.

As I have said, however, I do not accept Mr. Jones's test. It seems to me that the chief aim of education should be to discipline the mind and the character; and, with the help of a good master, this can surely be done in the Latin class as well as in any other. To banish Latin from the schools merely because most people do not read Virgil in later life would, to my mind, be as unreasonable as to banish English poetry from the schools because most people do not read Milton in later life. If much of the teaching is apparently wasted, so is much of the turnip seed that the farmer sows in his field. It is necessary for the farmer, one might say, to sow more seed than is necessary if he wishes to get a first-rate crop.

I confess, however, that I am prejudiced in favour of Latin and Greek. I fell in love with Latin when I first opened a grammar and saw the word 'mensa.' I do not, however, read Latin authors in the original for pleasure now. But I enjoy them all the more for taking an occasional glance at the original in one of the volumes of the Loeb Library in which Latin and the English translation are printed on opposite pages.

To know even a little of a language seems to me to make one appreciate more fully the masterpieces of its literature in translation. Mr. Jones justly praises Mr. Gilbert Murray's translations of the plays of Euripides. But I fancy that those who enjoy Mr. Murray's translations most are those who once learned a little Greek at school. Keats, with his imaginative genius, could get to the heart of Homer in Chapman's English version though he had never learnt Greek; but there has been only one Keats.

Hence I should like to see more and not less Latin and Greek taught. I do not think everybody should be compelled to learn them, but I think everybody should be given a chance to learn them, and be encouraged to learn them.

After all, the civilization of Europe has been moulded chiefly by three great peoples—the Greeks, the Romans, and the Jews; and one of the best ways to acquire a sympathetic understanding of the mind of a people is to study its language even for a year or two. For this reason I think it might be a good thing to teach a little Hebrew in schools as well as Latin and Greek.

I have just been reading *The Glory that is Greece*, edited by

Miss Hilda Hughes; and have been marvelling once more at the always astonishing sum of what we owe to the Greeks.

The book, to which many writers have contributed, is concerned largely with the glorious Greece of the present; but several fascinating chapters are devoted to the centuries-old Greek inheritance. In one of them Mr. Michael Holroyd tells us:

In poetry, the Greeks have taught us almost all we know. Epic and lyric, the drama (Tragedy and Comedy), the ode, and even the lampoon; the forms of poetic creation all come to us from Greece. Ballads from the north, satire from ancient Rome, the troubadour poetry from France and its Sicilian offspring, the sonnet; these alone of all the European verse forms derive from other sources.

As regards the other arts:

Our European sculpture and painting and architecture, even more than our poetry, have always been Greek in formal outline, Greek in method, and Greek in their fundamental life.

Turn to the article of Dr. A. P. Cawadias on Greek medicine, and you will read: 'The Greeks created medicine as a science.' Mrs. Naomi Mitchison and Mr. Frank Pakenham write with illuminating freshness of Plato and Aristotle, who still remain the highest peaks in the range of philosophic thought. The Greek contribution to political thinking, both practical and Utopian, is also a living influence even to-day.

The aim of Miss Hughes's book, however, is not to magnify the Greece of between two and three thousand years ago, so much as to emphasize the glory that is Greece to-day—the Greece that was never more glorious in its heroism than when it stood up to the invader in the war that has just ended [1945]. Not that the articles on modern Greece are written in the vein of the ecstatic panegyrist. To give information rather than to eulogize is their purpose; thus, Miss Nadine Pilcher writes on the women of modern Greece, Miss Tsouderos on the progress of modern Greece, Dr. Helle Lambridis on the modern Greek language, and Mr. Compton Mackenzie on the political and economic future of Greece. Travel in Greece is the subject of chapters by Miss Dilys Powell, Dr. C. M. Bowra, Mr. Marcus N. Tod, and Mr. Louis Golding.

Far from wishing us to over-idealize the modern Greeks, one of the writers, Demetrios Capetanakis, who died at an early age last year, pleads with us to remember that the Greeks are only human beings. 'The more educated an Englishman is,' he declares, 'the more difficult it is for him to see Greece to-day as she really is,' and he gives us an amusing picture of the embarrassment a Greek is often made to feel during a visit to England, where Greek scholars appear to expect him to be a combination of Aristotle and one of the athletic heroes of Pindar. On the other hand, the writer is careful to point out the equal error of those who go to the opposite extreme and think of the modern Greek as the rich, vulgar Smyrna merchant of whom Mr. T. S. Eliot has written.

An English writer, Mr. Miles Vaughan Williams, is also eager that we should remember that the Greeks are human beings. 'Greece,' he writes, 'is not a land of ruins, but of living people . . . enough of sightseers wrapping their heads in a cloud of sentimental worship of the past and failing to see the vivid originality and vitality of the living.'

Still, it is possible, and even probable, that Mr. Williams would never have visited Greece and discovered the glory that is there to-day, if he had not learnt something of the glory of the past in the Greek class at school. There is much to be said for the life-giving powers of the dead languages. A boy might waste his school years in many worse ways than in trying to learn at least two of them.

Arnold Bennett as Critic

(1945)

As I was searching along my disordered shelves for another book I caught sight of Arnold Bennett's *Books and Persons* and took it out, full of curiosity to see how far his literary judgment would be acceptable to-day—nearly forty years afterwards.

I remembered the eagerness with which many of us read these literary causeries as they appeared in that brilliant but unequal paper *The New Age*, then edited by A. R. Orage and Holbrook Jackson. There, week by week, over the pseudonym 'Jacob Tonson,' he made his quasi-papal pronouncements on books; and no literary columnist, as he would be called nowadays, has ever written with greater zest or with a greater air of authority.

He lacked the grace, the scholarly humaneness and the discipular devotion to the old masters that once charmed us in the causeries of Quiller-Couch in the *Speaker*. He was more inquisitive about the modern than about the ancient masterpieces, but he too loved good and great work, and to praise the few creative artists among his contemporaries was a luxury to him. He was also a stylist: he put life into the words he used, and his sentences were as expressive of his personality as the ties he wore and his cocky forelock.

On the whole, his comments on his contemporaries of thirty or forty years ago would still be regarded by most good judges as sound. We find him writing with just appreciation of Conrad, Galsworthy, Wells, Yeats, W. H. Hudson, and C. E. Montague. He did not foresee how good a novelist Mr. Masefield was to become, but at least he took his work seriously and wrote characteristically: 'Mr. Masefield is not yet grown up. He is always trying to write literature, and that is a great mistake. He should study the wisdom of Paul Verlaine:

> *Prends l'éloquence et tords lui son cou.*
> (Take literature and wring its neck.)

By the time he was writing in *The New Age* Bennett had outgrown his early enthusiasm for Kipling. The younger generation must find it difficult to realize the devotion that many of us in the nineties felt for Kipling, so that when he lay dangerously ill of pneumonia in New York we waited almost as anxiously for the latest bulletin about his condition as in later years we have waited for the news of the result of a battle. 'I remember,' says Bennett, 'giving a party with a programme of music in that fortnight, and I began the proceedings by reading aloud the programme, and at the end of the programme, instead of "God Save the Queen" I read "God Save Kipling," and everybody cheered.' There was no posturing in this—that was how we felt.

Like others, however, Bennett was estranged by Kipling's politics. 'Kipling's astounding manifestations, chiefly in verse,' he wrote, 'have shocked and angered me.' Even so, Bennett never became blinded—as I confess I did for a time—to the fact that Kipling was a true creative artist. 'Nevertheless,' he wrote after censuring his dethroned idol, 'I, for one, cannot, except in anger, go back on a genuine admiration. I cannot forget a benefit. If in quick resentment I have ever written of Kipling with less than the respect due to an artist who has once excited in the heart a generous and beautiful emotion and has remained honest, I regret it.' And he added: 'At his worst, Kipling is an honest and painstaking artist. No work of his but has obviously been lingered over with a craftsman's devotion.' That is nobly said.

Of all Bennett's judgments, the one that gave the greatest offence, perhaps, was his judgment on Henry James. I remember the outcry among the Jacobeans when Bennett declared flatly: 'Henry James lacks ecstasy, guts.' 'He seldom chooses themes of first-class importance,' he wrote, 'and when he does choose such a theme, he never fairly bites it and makes it bleed. Also, his curiosity is limited. He seems to me to have been specially created to be admired by super-dilettanti.' To admirers of Henry James, Bennett's imagery, his demand for guts and blood, seem to unfit him to be a critic of the master. At the same time Bennett's condemnation of James was tempered with eulogy. 'James,' he wrote, 'is a truly marvellous craftsman. He writes like an angel. Also he savours life with eagerness, sniffing the breeze of it like a hound.' What will puzzle most readers is how these last sentences can be reconciled with the opinion that

Henry James had no guts, and that he was merely an author for the super-dilettanti.

Among the criticisms in *Books and Persons* with which I for one did not agree is his criticism of Saintsbury. It used to be the fashion to belittle Saintsbury as a critic because of what was regarded as his atrocious style, and Bennett was merely in the mode when the wrote: 'No one who has any feeling for literature could possibly put down the style that Professor Saintsbury commits. His pen could not be brought to write it.' From this, especially, Bennett was led to maintain that Saintsbury had not 'the root of the matter' in him. 'He has not,' he declared boldly, 'comprehended that which he has been talking about.' As a matter of fact, Saintsbury, like Bennett himself, had a very individual style, not graceful or good to imitate, but full of vitality and of words used with gusto. Read *The Peace of the Augustans* and you will see this.

Bennett also blamed Saintsbury for his misjudgment of contemporary writers, but how many powerful minds, whether those of critics or those of creative artists, have never been guilty of such misjudgments? Even Sainte-Beuve sometimes nodded. The best criticism as a rule has been criticism of dead authors. The truth is, Bennett was prejudiced against professors. They stood largely for tradition and he was in revolt against tradition, being chiefly engrossed in the contemporary scene.

It is this revolt that explains his general indifference to the great nineteenth-century novelists. I remember his once saying, when Dickens was mentioned: 'Can't read him.' In one of his causeries he makes the sweeping statement: 'Between Fielding and Meredith, no entirely honest novel was written by anybody in England.' It all depends, as the saying is, on what you mean by honest. I should have said that *Pride and Prejudice* is as honest a novel as *Jude the Obscure* and that *The Pickwick Papers* is as honest a novel as *Sons and Lovers*.

Jane Austen and Dickens certainly left out things that you will find in the novels of Hardy and Lawrence, but then Hardy and Lawrence left out things that you will find in the novels of Jane Austen and Dickens. Each novelist makes his own selection from the infinite variety of the world he knows, and is to be judged, not by the material he discards, but by his success in creating characters and interest in them and in their story. If dishonest novelists can give us Mr. Collins, Mr. Pecksniff, Becky Sharp, and Mrs. Proudie, and a host of the most memorable characters in fiction, the logical conclusion would be that there is something to be said for dishonesty in novel writing. But dishonesty is the wrong word. It is a word used in haste merely as an expression of resentment at the nineteenth-century prudery which Dickens satirizes in Mr. Podsnap.

The statement I have quoted, however, is only one of a number of rash statements capriciously dashed off by Bennett. In another, speaking of the fairly comfortable middle class, he writes: 'I do not belong to this class by birth. Artists very seldom do. I was born slightly beneath it.' Surely, one reflects as one reads this, nearly all the great English writers from Shakespeare and Milton to Browning and Bridges were born in this class. This was only natural in a world in which the upper class for the most part had too much money and the working class had too little education. Bennett, however, was animated with hostility to the middle class, a hostility he frankly confesses. 'I am acquainted with members of it,' he wrote, 'and some are artists like myself; a few others earn my sympathy by honestly admiring my work, and the rest I like because I like them, but the philosopher in me cannot, though he has tried, melt away my profound and instinctive hostility to this class. Instead of decreasing, my hostility grows.'

It is all the more surprising to find Bennett writing of Galsworthy on another page:

As for John Galsworthy, the quality in him which may possibly vitiate his right to be considered a major artist is precisely his personal animosity to his class. Major artists are so seldom cruelly hostile to anything whatever, as Galsworthy is to this class. He does in fiction what John Sargent does in painting, and their inimical observation of their subjects will gravely prejudice them in the eyes of posterity.

And on yet another page Bennett writes of a book of Galsworthy's:

In the actual material of the book its finest quality is its extraordinary passionate cruelty towards the oppressors as distinguished from the oppressed. That oppressors should be treated with less sympathy than the oppressed is contrary to my own notion of the ethic of the creative art, but the result in Mr. Galsworthy's work is something very pleasing.

ARNOLD BENNETT

How inconsistent this is with Bennett's own hostility, and with his condemnation of other writers for their hostility to oppressors. The explanation is, I imagine, that Bennett's principles and antipathies did not always coincide.

Like Saintsbury, he was a good critic, not because he was a perfect law-giver, but because he was a remarkable human being with a remarkable brain and a remarkable way of saying exactly what he, at the moment, believed; but, like Saintsbury, with prejudices of a different kind, he was usually right in his praise at least, if not in his dislikes.

There are few collections of weekly literary criticism so readable after between thirty and forty years as *Books and Persons*. Incidentally, Bennett paid a fine tribute to Wilfred Whitten, the original 'John o' London;' when he stated 'formally and with a due sense of responsibility that he is one of the finest prose-writers now writing in English.' It is not often a creative writer pays so generous a tribute to a journalist as that.

In Praise of Anthologies
(1945)

Human beings make collections of most things—from postage stamps to jade ornaments. I wonder whether there is anybody to-day who is collecting anthologies. If there is, and if he has been at it for some time, he must need a good many shelves to contain his treasures. A man could form an imposing library out of anthologies alone.

Acidulated critics have condemned the modern appetite for anthologies, as though it arose from a desire to obtain a superficial acquaintance with as many authors as possible with as little trouble as possible. I do not agree with this view. I am sure that Q's anthology, *The Oxford Book of English Verse*, has been found more useful and delightful by readers who are steeped in literature than by those who are content with a nodding acquaintance with the great poets. To read it is comparable to walking through a picture gallery instead of concentrating on a one-man show.

There are many poets, moreover, whose good verse can all be had in an anthology, so that there is little need, except for the scholar, to consult their collected works—Lovelace and some of the other seventeenth-century poets, for example. Many readers after boyhood cease to read Sir Walter Scott's long narrative poems, but at the same time find constantly renewed pleasure in the best of his short lyrics. It is largely the anthologies that have kept the best work of such poets alive. It was in anthologies that most of us first discovered Webster and Campion and, indeed, Ben Jonson himself.

Another function of the anthology is to introduce the reader —especially the young reader—to poet after poet, exhibiting them at their best and most characteristic. If this is well done, the reader finds himself eager to come to a closer acquaintance with this or that poet—say Landor or Francis Thompson; and the anthology will prove to be as useful to him as a good guide-book to a traveller.

Anthologies of modern verse are, I imagine, particularly

valuable as guides to the young reader. Here he will find himself attracted or repelled by the work of a contemporary; and, if he is attracted, will be put on the road to further knowledge of it. He will come upon samples of Mr. W. H. Auden and Mr. Andrew Young, of Mr. Louis MacNeice and Mr. Frank Kendon; and these samples ought to be of some help to him in his choice of reading.

Mr. Richard Church and Miss M. M. Bozman, in their original and delightful anthology in Everyman's Library, *Poems of Our Time: 1900-1942*, suggest that a modern anthology should also give a poem a time-setting so that a poet should be shown as 'a living and developing creature of the century'; and they have arranged the poetry of the last forty years in four periods. 'We have,' they say, 'not been content merely to accept the accidents of chronology and to rank the poets according to their birthdays. That method has no meaning, and is a waste of the significance of the time-spirit.' They urge that their method enables us to follow the development of a poet, giving W. B. Yeats as an example. In point of fact, however, very few of the poets represented here have developed in the same degree in which Yeats did. And the development of Yeats can be shown equally well by a separate sequence of his poems chosen to illustrate his different periods.

I do not quarrel, however, with the plan preferred by any anthologist for compiling his book. I hold that all plans are good if the resultant anthology is a book of good poetry. I can forgive even those anthologists who withhold the names of the authors of the poems so that we have to turn to the end of the book to find out who wrote what. In regard to anthologies, one might adapt what Kipling said of tribal lays:

> There are nine-and-sixty ways of constructing tribal lays,
> And every single one of them is right.

As was to be expected, Mr. Church and Miss Bozman have given us a first-rate anthology. It surprises me to find them omitting Sir William Watson, Sir Henry Newbolt, and Sir John Squire, while including the work of a good many poets who seem to me to be of much smaller stature. Such differences of taste are inevitable, however, in regard to contemporary and all but contemporary work.

Nor do I complain that the compilers have not strictly adhered to their time plan. While they follow it closely enough to represent Bridges only by the work of his later years, they throw it overboard when they come to Yeats and admit several of his poems that belong to the nineties. On the subject of Yeats, I confess, my taste differs from theirs. They clearly prefer him in his early and late periods. I like him best in his late-early and middle period. If all tastes concurred, however, there would be no room for more than one anthology of the verse of any age.

Many readers when they take up an anthology of this kind are naturally driven to look for evidence as to the progress or retrogression of poetry in our time. Most of them, I fancy, will be inclined to doubt whether any of the younger poets has written anything so beautiful as Mr. Walter de la Mare's *Farewell*, with its memorable closing verse:

> Look thy last on all things lovely,
> Every hour. Let no night
> Seal thy sense in deathly slumber
>   Till to delight
> Thou have paid thy utmost blessing;
> Since that all things thou wouldst praise
> Beauty took from those who loved them
>   In other days.

Memorableness, delight, beauty—all these qualities of poetry seem to many readers to have faded somewhat in recent years.

Hardy's very pessimism has in it a soul of delight such as cannot be discerned in a great deal of modern work. We find this soul of delight in the work of such living poets as Mr. Young, Mr. Kendon, and Mr. Church himself, but not often in what may be called up-to-date poetry.

The obscurity, too, of some modern verse is baffling. Some enthusiasts deny that it is obscure, but they cannot deny that many people find it so. Take, for example, Mr. Alexander Comfort's *Hoc Est Corpus*:

> I who am nothing and this tissue
> steer, find in my servant still my maker,
> rule and obey, as flame to candle mated:
> whom bone has conjured, Banquo shall the Bard
> command, the marble rule Pygmalion.
> Did this tower build me then who am its garrison?

Strange that in me the shadow
moving the substance speaks: strange that such air
pulls the blue sinew, whom the blood maintains,
whom the heart's coming slight defection
shall spill, speaks now and holds
time like a permanent stone, its cold weight judging.

I see, or think I see, vaguely what the poet means; but I do
not understand:

whom bone has conjured, Banquo shall the Bard
command, the marble rule Pygmalion.

Nor do I know what the 'blue sinew' is that 'such air pulls.'

If poetry puzzles the wits like this, the reader is set asking
himself prosaic questions like a schoolboy translating a difficult
passage of Latin verse, and that is not the way to enjoy poetry.
Browning no doubt puzzled his readers in the nineteenth
century, but his most puzzling verse is not the verse of his that
has endured.

It would be grossly unfair, however, to suggest that all the
poets of the more or less modern mood are obscure.   Nothing
could be more lucid than Mr. A. S. J. Tessimond's admirable
imaginative poem, *Earthfast*:

Architects plant their imagination, weld their poems on rock,
clamp them to the skidding rim of the world and anchor them down
   to its core;
leave more than the poet's or painter's snail-bright trail on a friable
   leaf;
can build their chrysalis round them—stand in their sculpture's belly.

They see through stone, they cage and partition air, they crossrig
   space
with footholds, planks for a dance; yet their maze, their flying trapeze
is pinned to the centre.   They write their euclidean music standing
with a hand on a cornice of cloud, themselves set fast, earth-square.

Or take Mr. Edwin Muir's charming lyric, *The Bird*, with its
musical echoes of Hopkins and Bridges:

Adventurous bird walking upon the air,
Like a schoolboy running and loitering, leaping and springing,
Pensively pausing, suddenly changing your mind
To turn at ease on the heel of a wing-tip.   Where

> In all the crystalline world was there to find
> For your so delicate walking and airy winging
> A floor so perfect, so firm and fair,
> And where a ceiling and walls so sweetly ringing
> Whenever you sing, to your clear singing?
>
> The wide-winged soul itself can ask no more
> Than such pure, resilient and endless floor
> For its strong-pinioned plunging and soaring and upward and
> upward springing.

Mr. Muir, however, is perhaps not to be classed as a 'modern' poet in the usual sense of the word. Only a minority of the modern poets quoted in the anthology, indeed, are modern in this sense.

Here, then, is a book of plentiful delights—a choice of modern verse that will at once interest the literary controversialist and give pleasure to the lover of poetry.

Why we enjoy Sad Books
(1943)

IN a public lecture, Archbishop Temple said: 'If I am to be entertained, I must enjoy the outlook of the author and the company of the people to whom he introduces me.' This, no doubt, is true of Dr. Temple's experience, but I doubt whether it is true of the experience of all readers.

It is a nice question how far we must enjoy the outlook of an author in order that his work may give us pleasure. To fall under the spell of FitzGerald's *Omar Khayyám* it is obviously not necessary to be an agnostic. In fact, some of the original members of the Omar Khayyám Club were clergymen. Probably, none of them had ever sat underneath the bough in a wilderness with a book of verses, a jug of wine, a loaf of bread, and an *inamorata*; but, none the less, they were entranced by the poet's vision of the constituents of an earthly Paradise. Similarly, they cannot have regarded as anything but heretical the sentiments expressed in the verse:

> Oh, Thou, who Man of baser Earth didst make,
> And ev'n with Paradise devise the Snake:
> For all the Sin wherewith the Face of Man
> Is blacken'd—Man's forgiveness give—and take!

If such a sentiment had been expressed in ordinary prose every one who disagreed with it would have been repelled by it. Yet FitzGerald's words move us as the perfect expression of a mood—of an outlook with which we may vehemently disagree, yet which we know from our own experience is natural in a melancholy hour.

In later years A. E. Housman's *Shropshire Lad* was a book that gave pleasure to thousands of readers who did not share the poet's outlook. It was the perfect art of the verse on its own level, with its irony and its sense of the tragedy of life, that endeared to us a point of view from which many of us—perhaps most of us—dissented. Just as a member of parliament may enjoy a brilliant speech made by someone on the other side of

the House, so the reader can recognize a master even in a poet
or prose-writer whose outlook seems to him to be that of the
Father of Lies. Thus you will often find an agnostic reader
enjoying great religious literature, and a Christian reader enjoying
great sceptical literature. It is much the same in all the arts.
The religious Handel was the favourite composer of the agnostical
Samuel Butler, and one does not need to be an orthodox
Catholic to love the paintings of Fra Angelico or to be impressed
by the majesty of St. Peter's. Great art, expressive of an
outlook not our own, affects us more strongly than commonplace
art expressive of an outlook that we share.

I doubt whether, even in reading fiction, we always need to
'enjoy the outlook of the author and the company of the people
to whom he introduces' us in order to be entertained by him.
There is, I admit, a good deal to be said for the Archbishop's
view. As a general rule, it is probably true. Dickens is
infinitely re-readable largely because he introduced us to so
many characters, from Mr. Pickwick and Sam Weller onwards,
who never cease to be enjoyable company. But what about
such a novel as Meredith's *Egoist*? I cannot believe that any one
ever found Sir Willoughby Patterne good company. Robert
Louis Stevenson said somewhere that he read and re-read *The
Egoist* as a kind of moral discipline, like a man looking at his
reflection in the cruel mirror of truth. Most of us, however,
read *The Egoist*, not for self-discipline, but for entertainment;
and the fact is that we are entertained in literature by all sorts
of people whose company in real life we should find detestable.
Mr. Collins entertains us in *Pride and Prejudice*; but should we
not regard a week-end visit from him as purgatorial? Pew
entertains us in a terrifying way in *Treasure Island*, but who
would think of him as a good companion? Mr. Squeers and
Silas Wegg are good company in a book, but who would care
to be often in their company in real life? At the same time, it
must be admitted that those who most enjoy the novels of Jane
Austen, Dickens, and Stevenson do 'enjoy the outlook of the
author' even if some of their most enjoyable characters are
people for whom they feel no affection.

Possibly, indeed, the novelists whom we enjoy most are those
whose outlook we most fully share or at least most admire. I
can think of no great English novelist whose outlook has not

helped to popularize his genius. From Fielding to Scott, from Jane Austen to Hardy, a noble and courageous outlook on life has been a characteristic of great English fiction. Dr. Temple said:

I am disposed to say that among the worst books ever committed to paper is Hardy's great masterpiece, *Tess of the D'Urbervilles*, because to me it gives the impression that although Tess may no doubt be rightly described on the title-page as a pure woman, the net result of the novel is to produce the impression that it does not matter whether she was or was not, and that is much more disastrous than if she had been, quite frankly, an impure woman.

But surely the wealth of pity felt and expressed by Hardy for one for whom the world had little pity was the mark of a noble nature. Hardy's theories about the universe may have been mistaken; but the responses of his heart were generously noble.

I fancy that there must be some element of nobility of this kind in action to make it permanently readable. You will find it in Conrad's *Typhoon* and in Henry James's ghost story, *The Turn of the Screw*. Minor literature, such as the farce or the detective story, may manage without it; but they seldom become part of the literature that endures.

In modern times many people are moved largely by psychological curiosity in their preferences among novels. Psychology is one of the newest sciences, and there are novels that are studied almost like text-books on the subject. It is not certain, however, that the psychology of to-morrow will agree with the psychology of to-day; and no novel is likely to last that depends for its interest on the fashion of an hour.

In a sense, of course, all great literature is packed with psychology. Shakespeare was a psychologist long before the science of psychology was invented. After all, human nature is the material both of the imaginative writer and the psychologist. Some modern novelists, however, seem to approach human nature in the spirit of scientific analysts rather than of artists. This, I think, is a passing phase. Characters are more important in a novel than analysis of character.

Take, for example, that great psychological novelist, Dostoevsky, of whose novels Dr. Temple writes that they 'derive almost the whole of their power and value from the fact that they are interpretations of life in its heights and depths.' How

vividly we remember the characters in *Crime and Punishment!*
And yet I sometimes wonder whether in his portrayal of the
chief character, Raskolnikov, Dostoevsky's psychology is
altogether true to human nature.   Would a man of his character
have committed that particular murder in that particular way?
I doubt it.   But the characters somehow seem real.   One
accepts the murder too, as one accepts the incredible folly of
King Lear in the first act of the play, and all the rest follows
naturally.   But most people now agree that *The Brothers
Karamazov* is a greater novel than *Crime and Punishment.*   Here
one has no doubts that the characters, being what they are,
would have behaved as they are represented as behaving.

In speaking of books Dr. Temple drew a distinction between
books that entertain us and books that give us an interpretation
of life.   It is a useful distinction, since we read some books
merely for entertainment—the stories, for example, of Edgar
Wallace and Mr. P. G. Wodehouse.   At the same time, I should
prefer to divide books into those that are only entertaining and
those that, owing to their rich wisdom or at least thought about
life, are more entertaining (in the finest sense of the word)
still.   The very word 'play' suggests entertainment; yet it is
in poetical plays or entertainments, from those of Aeschylus to
those of Shakespeare, that we find the noblest understanding of
the heights and depths of human nature in secular literature.
The small gallery boy in the provincial theatre is enthralled by
Hamlet—a play packed with exciting incidents, that begins with
a ghost and ends with a duel—no less than the philosopher or
the university professor.   If you take to your bedside a light
novel and the plays of Shakespeare, you will probably on some
nights cease reading the light novel and turn to *Macbeth* simply
because it is so much more engrossingly enjoyable.

It is true that *Macbeth* does not fulfil Dr. Temple's requirements
as a literary entertainment since we can hardly be said to 'enjoy
the company of the people to whom the author introduces us.
Or, perhaps, in a measure we do; Macbeth and Lady Macbeth
speak such miraculous verse that their crimes lose something of
their foulness in our imaginations, and they become pitiable in
their doom.   Perhaps it is easier to sympathize with those who
perpetrate great crimes if they are sufficiently remote from us
in time or place, as Macbeth and Othello are.   Yet, however

we may pity Macbeth or Othello, Shakespeare's outlook never ceases to be that of a moralist.   We feel that it is just that Macbeth and Othello, having violently sinned, should perish violently. Shakespeare had an almost terrifying sense of justice, as he showed in that scene in which Henry V casts off Falstaff.

The books we enjoy most lastingly are those which excite in us most profoundly sympathy with our fellow creatures, love of the earth on which we live, and awe before the mystery of life. Thus tragedy is in a sense more enjoyable than comedy, because at its greatest it excites all these sympathies.   If Macbeth had survived to reign for twenty or thirty years after his crimes, we might regard him as an interesting figure, but interesting only on a low plane.   We should not have read his story again and again with pleasure.   Many good books and plays have happy endings—and there is much to be said for a happy ending if it is not false to life—but tragedy reaches down to greater depths in our imaginations.   Hence, paradoxically, as readers, we may be said to be happiest when we are saddest.   Sympathy is one of the chief needs of our nature, and it is in tragic literature that the sympathy of the reader becomes most complete and most profound.

Why we enjoy Criticism

(1945)

Mr. JAMES STEPHENS once made a (to me) rather startling remark in the *Sunday Times*. After saying that 'a time may come when you never wish to see a page of prose again,' he went on to make an exception in favour of criticism. Criticism, he declares, is a 'type of writing which can grow upon you and only fail with, say, your eyesight. Criticism, were there enough of it, would become one's finally treasured reading.'

I wonder whether there are many readers whose tastes change in this fashion with increasing years. So far as my experience goes men in their seventies who have enjoyed the prose of Jane Austen in earlier life continue to enjoy it with as much relish as ever. It was when he was growing old, I think, that Sir James G. Frazer edited the choice prose of two of his beloved authors, Addison and Cowper. I know a man of nearly seventy who still reads Gibbon through once a year.

At the same time, I agree that with the approach of age the appetite for reading becomes less voracious and less, if you will, healthily indiscriminate. Older readers, more easily than younger, can control the desire to read every newcomer among books that is praised by the critics as a masterpiece. They have had their own times of enthusiasm among new masterpieces, and their hunger for novelty is somewhat abated.

To them it has ceased to be a recommendation of a book that everybody else is reading it. Perhaps they no longer read works of fiction with the same earnestness with which they used to read them and most of the masterpieces in modern times are novels. Apart from this, they have long associations with a good many of the older books, and one of the great pleasures of reading is to re-read a good book with which one is familiar. I am not suggesting that the ordinary reader as soon as he reaches sixty loses his interest in contemporary literature. I think, however, that it has less magnetic power over him than it would have if he were forty years younger.

I hope you won't think, however, after what I have written, that I imagine the younger readers of to-day read mainly fiction. They seem to me, on the contrary, to be able to devour books on economics and politics with a gusto of which their elders are incapable.

There has probably—I should say certainly—never been so large and serious minded a body of young readers as exists to-day. If wisdom increased at the same pace as knowledge, we might well begin to cherish rosy hopes of so well educated a leaven in modern society. I doubt, however, whether the volumes of the economists would have been allowed the honourable title of books by Charles Lamb. Even the young do not read and re-read them as a rule for the flavour of their sentences.

As for criticism, that, like economics, is surely read in youth with even more zest than in age. In youth the world of literature is mainly unknown territory and we long for reports of those who have travelled in it and who can awaken the desire and the hope that we too may one day visit the same golden regions. Our opinions are still in process of formation and we sub-consciously search for the critic who can influence and shape them. We do not want a dictator of taste, but at least we want a leader. Some of us, on the other hand, who are born with the spirit of contradiction, rebel against the leaders set over us by tradition, and indulge, as we read, in the pleasures of disagreement.

At a later age we cease to be greatly concerned with the rightness or wrongness of the critics' opinions. We enjoy reading good criticism as we enjoy listening to a good con-versationalist. When conversing with a friend we do not expect him to agree with us in all our tastes. It was more entertaining to hear Arnold Bennett confessing that he could not read Dickens than it would have been to hear a man of less original mind saying the usual right things in praise of *The Pickwick Papers*. Dr. Johnson's opinions are enjoyable not only when they are just, but when they are so unjust as to be laughable. The eccentric or whimsical critic, however, must himself be interesting in mind or character in order that his wrong-headed-ness may be interesting and not merely irritating.

K

Thus we can read Macaulay's caricatureish account of Boswell and enjoy it as a delightful and original piece of writing, while feeling that he has missed realizing in what half of Boswell's genius consisted; but if a much smaller writer dogmatized so unjustly about, say, Oliver Goldsmith, we should think his stuff not worth reading.

I think it is partly because good criticism gives us something of the pleasure of discussion with an original mind that many of us find it so attractive.   Thackeray may not commend himself to modern taste with his critical opinions of some of the English humorists, but how readable he remains.

Robert Louis Stevenson offended a number of readers by some of his observations on Burns and Thoreau, but *Familiar Studies of Men and Books* is still a collection of literary essays well worth reading.   It was as moralists, however, not as aesthetic critics that Thackeray and Stevenson chiefly gave offence.   Still, morals and aesthetics cannot always be kept separate.

Mr. Stephens is opposed to those critics who allow the life and writings of an author to become too closely intertwined with criticism; he writes that there are certain ills about it. He enumerates these: 'That there isn't much of it is one,' he declares.   'That it is often not very well written is another, and then there are many critics who think that biography is a real part of their art and they will give you a sad lot of it.'

I cannot agree with this last judgment.   I like to read of the author as well as of his work; and I like if possible to see what relation his work bears to his life.   We all know, of course— or we all should know—that an author in his hours of inspiration is a different man in many respects from the same author fuming over a plate of under-cooked mutton or murmuring jealous disparagements of his rivals in the company of his friends.   An author in his hours of inspiration is a man purified from those gross and commonplace qualities which he shares with the uninspired or less inspired masses of mankind.   Turner's pictures were the creation of a part of him separate from his meanness and his other vices.   Even so, facts about an author may help to elucidate certain qualities in his work.   The fact that Words-worth had no sense of smell explains why his poetry is scentless in comparison with that of Shakespeare, or Shelley, or Keats. Pope's brilliant and bitter satire on Addison becomes more intelligible when we learn that Addison had offended Pope by preferring a rival.

On the other hand, there is one form of biographical criticism that, to me, is wearisome. This is criticism of the psycho-analytical sort which has been popular in the inter-war years. Author after author has been subjected to psycho-analytical tests, and, by comparing his life and his work, it has been easy to prove that his work bears the mark of a painful unresolved conflict in his nature. This has been done with Tolstoy and Dickens and Kipling. It is all rather mechanical; it is as though an oculist were to discover to his own satisfaction that all works of genius are the product of eyestrain.

Psycho-analysis, indeed, whatever virtues it may have in healing certain ailments, seems to me an instrument unsuited to literary criticism. I once read a book by a psycho-analyst who maintained that the horses in Browning's poems were sexual symbols. Another psycho-analyst made *Alice in Wonderland* look like the expression of a by no means pleasant subconscious. And the psycho-analyst has given us extraordinary analyses not only of authors but of the characters created by authors. Freud himself explains Hamlet's hesitation about killing his uncle by the assumption that Hamlet himself hated his father and would have liked to kill him, so that he could hardly blame his uncle for so desirable a murder. Take again a psycho-analyst on Ophelia. 'Ophelia,' he wrote some years ago, 'was a case of confusional psychosis. She had a subjective awareness of difficulty in concentration, an appearance of perplexity, an impairment of awareness of the environment, and a reduced and distorted awareness of temporal and spatial relationships.' I do not know whether this is to Ophelia's credit or not, for I cannot quite follow it.

Ordinary biographical criticism, however, is quite another matter. After all, Johnson's *Lives of the Poets* is not only the best, but the most readable, book of literary criticism published in the eighteenth century. Take Hazlitt's criticism, at a later date, and you will find that, when he criticizes his contemporaries his writing is enriched with the knowledge, not only of their books, but of themselves. Most of us, I am sure, re-read what he wrote about Coleridge and Lamb more often even than his admirable discourses on Shakespeare. Some people think it fortunate that we know so little about Shakespeare the man.

And that we can criticize his plays merely as literature without reference to his life. I cannot agree. Knowing so little about his life, the critics have given rein to their imaginations and have invented a man they call Shakespeare, who is probably as unlike the real Shakespeare as they themselves are. I remember how Frank Harris became temporarily famous as an interpreter of Shakespeare with a book in which he maintained that Shakespeare was a neuropath. The fact is, being neurotic himself, Harris made Shakespeare to a large extent in his own image. If a full biography of Shakespeare had existed, he would have pontificated less boldly.

I myself, I confess, can read almost any kind of criticism that is not too abstract and obscure. I can enjoy reading even the extravagant things that Swinburne has written about Shakespeare the dramatist. I can enjoy Samuel Butler's nonsense as a critic and Mr. Oliver Elton's sense. The life-giving quality in criticism, as in other parts of literature, is the individuality of the writing. This can ensure immortality to wisdom and capriciousness alike.

The Importance of Controversy

(1945)

W E should be grateful, it seems to me, to the creators of the new poetry and their followers for one thing, even if we cannot share their opinions. They have at least done a great deal to keep literary controversy alive; and controversy is not only enjoyable but often useful.

It is enjoyable even as a game, like receiving and hitting back a tennis ball, as everybody knows who has ever been a member of a debating society. Like tennis, it continues to be enjoyable to many men who have left their youth a long way behind them, as you would have seen if you had attended the Forum debates in Manchester, at the beginning of the century—do they still take place, I wonder? As you may see, indeed, in the House of Commons. The purpose of serious controversy, most of us would say, is to convert other people—even one other person— to what one believes to be the truth; and in this lies its chief usefulness. When we are young we imagine that it is possible to convert even an opponent by sound argument. As we grow older, however, we realize how difficult, how rare, this is. No arguments used by Mr. Churchill are likely to convert Mr. William Gallacher, and no arguments used by Mr. Gallacher are likely to convert Mr. Churchill.

Hence, when an eminent man argues with another eminent man in public, he does so in the hope, not of changing the other's opinion, but of changing the opinions of those who are listening to his words or who read them in a newspaper. There used to be occasional public debates between a champion of Christianity and a champion of atheism. Did the Christian ever believe, do you think, in the possibility of converting the atheist? Or did the atheist ever believe in the possibility of converting the Christian? I do not think that such a thing ever happened. Each man, I am sure, was bent, not on converting, but on knocking out his opponent, and the people he really

277

aimed at converting with his argumentative punches were the audience.

Even apart from its power of changing mass opinion, however, controversy has considerable uses.

The man who differs from you, if he has any ability, challenges you with his statements to think with greater energy about what you believe and why you believe it. If you hold your creed lukewarmly, he may raise your lukewarmth to a healthier temperature, though not, if you are wise, to boiling-point. If your mind is in a state of muzziness, he may tempt you to wish to clear it, in order to be able to explain, not only to him, but to yourself, why you believe such and such a thing. Whether this is that man's ancestry can be traced back with a missing link or so through vast periods of pre-human evolution, or that Milton is the English poet who comes next in stature to Shakespeare, most of us hold a good many of our opinions in a mood of languid orthodoxy. Hence, even a writer who wrote so much that was poisonous—so, at least, some of us think—as Nietzsche, may have performed great services, as well as great disservices, to his time by his provocations.

In the history of English literature there is an outstanding example of the good that may be done by controversial and provocative writing. Thomas Love Peacock published a brilliant essay entitled *The Four Ages of Poetry*, in which he most ingeniously attempted to deflate poetry by suggesting that it was a relic of barbarism. He wrote it, I imagine—it is a long time since I last read it—largely from a delight in paradox, but Shelley was stung by it into a frenzy of inspiration in which he composed that noble reply, *The Defence of Poetry*. If Peacock had not been so provocative we should not possess Shelley's skyey and lyrical masterpiece of prose.

I do not think that any other great piece of controversial literature about literature appeared during the nineteenth century. The literary idols of the past remained, for the most part, securely on their pedestals, till Mr. Shaw set about belabouring the statue of Shakespeare. There was a rather pointless argument for a time as to whether Pope was a poet or not, but no one became unduly heated over the matter. The gospel of 'Art for Art's Sake,' which became popular among the aesthetes, ought to have excited some first-rate controversy, but on the

whole the aesthetes wrote better in defence of their theory
than their critics could write against it.   The epilogue to Walter
Pater's *Studies in the Renaissance* is, in my opinion, the expression
of a false view of life, but no one with a truer view replied to
it on the same intellectual and imaginative level.   If the Victorians became excitedly partisan about literature it was usually
on moral rather than on artistic grounds, as some of them did
on the publication of Swinburne's first *Poems and Ballads* and
Hardy's *Tess of the D'Urbervilles*.

At the same time there were some lively arguments between
those who would nowadays be called highbrows and lowbrows
about the obscurity of Browning and Meredith.   But it was
seldom that those who praised Browning and those who attacked
him had any fundamental difference of opinion about what
poetry is.   They differed, not about the nature of poetry, but
about a particular poet and whether he came up to a standard
which both of them more or less accepted.

To-day, however, differences about poetry go deeper.   Those
who disagree on the subject of the new poetry seem to be
divided by as deep a gulf as the Reds and the Whites in the early
days of Bolshevism.   There are people, indeed, who associate
the new poetry with the left wing in politics.   They are under
the impression that novelty and progress in the arts are much
the same thing.   They say to the critics of the new poetry
'You dislike it because it is new'—which suggests that they like
it because it is new.

Chesterton, in one of his essays, pointed out that this belief
in the virtue of newness in the arts is itself nothing new.
He wrote:

When I read all this confident exposition about new methods that
must now supersede old methods; . . . I heave a sigh that is full of
old and tender memories.   I do not feel as if I were reading some
revolutionary proclamation of new anarchic hopes or ideals; I feel as
if I were reading Macaulay's essays.   I read Macaulay when I was a
boy and believed him because I was a boy. . . .   Progress, said
Macaulay, never stops.   'What was its goal yesterday will be its
starting point to-morrow.'   I believed that simple theory when I was
a boy.   But I am rather surprised by this time that the boys have not
found a new one.

At the same time, Chesterton admitted the necessity of

novelty. It is necessary because human beings are subject to fatigue and even the best literature and art can become fatiguing. 'If a man is made to walk twenty miles,' wrote Chesterton, 'between two stone walls engraved on each side with endless repetitions of the Elgin Marbles, it is not unlikely that by the end of his walk he will be a little weary of that classical style of ornament. But that is because the man is tired; not because the style is tiresome.'

Thus we grow tired of even a good poet like Tennyson when we have over-feasted on him. 'We may turn away from a good thing,' as Chesterton said, 'not because it is good, but because we have really had too much of a good thing.'

Thus new fashions are necessary even when they are not an improvement on the old—even, indeed, when they are inferior to the old. Pope was a great writer, but a revolt against his fashion of writing was needed as it became more and more monotonous and more and more exhausting to the ear. Hence, it is possible to put up a reasonable defence even of the extravagances of the new poetry.

The adherents of the new poetry, however, seem to me to have claimed too much for it. They have maintained that it is comparable in importance to the poetical revolution in which Wordsworth and Coleridge played historical parts. Undoubtedly some remarkable writers are to be found among the new poets —Chesterton himself, in his later years, paid a tribute to the chief of them, Mr. T. S. Eliot—but I doubt whether there are any poets of Wordsworthian bulk among them. As for the work of most of them, it lacks that union of sound and sense that is characteristic of good poetry. Chesterton explained this epigrammatically by saying: 'A union of sound and sense is a Marriage; and this is an age of Divorce.'

It seems odd to find poets, again, claiming that they write for specialists and that only specialists can understand them. I wonder whether any book written for specialists ever got into the gallery of literature? Books for specialists—medical textbooks, mathematical treatises, and so forth—are needed, but their value is not literature Poetry and science may embrace, but science, in order to become poetry, must be addressed to a wider audience than specialists.

You will remember that the editor of a magazine of new

poetry in Australia was taken in, some time ago, by two hoaxers whose meaningless rubbish he published, eulogizing it as wonderful poetry. When it became known that the thing was a hoax, some of the new poetry school at once declared that the fake poems were really good and that the hoaxers had been inspired by the genius of poetry in spite of themselves.

If this is an example of the way in which specialists can deceive themselves about poetry, the sooner poetry is taken out of the hands of specialists the better. Words should mean something, and the traditional good use of them should be followed even in the newest poetry. On the subject of the poet and his use of words let me quote Chesterton again. The fact remains, he declared, 'that since he has to use the words of some language, he has got the words from somewhere and learned them from somebody. And the words are in fact winged or weighted with the thoughts and associations of a thousand years. If they were not he would not use them; he might just as well say "grunk" or "quoggle."'

*K

Learning to like Poetry

(1944)

I ONCE received a letter from a reader who wrote:

'I have recently taken up poetry reading, and, in spite of my fifty-three years, am getting great pleasure and satisfaction from it.'

In his enthusiasm as a convert he continued: 'Now I'm trying to win a friend into imitating me. Would you, please, refer me to books or writings or articles, the reading of which would enthuse my friend—and myself—into believing that, in missing poetry, he is missing something great in life?'

That short letter raises an important question that has never been solved. How can one persuade other people that one's own ideals and pleasures are worth sharing? In youth, everybody of any energy of spirit wishes to convert his friends to his own beliefs and tastes. In politics, he becomes, say, a Socialist, and longs to persuade everybody he knows that a Utopia of equality is just round the corner if only everybody would take the right turning. In practice, however, he finds it extremely difficult to persuade other people of this. Certainly, at the end of the nineteenth century, most of the people with whom one argued stuck to their own opinion, with the counterargument: 'If you divided all the money into equal shares, some people would save it, and some people would spend it on drink, and, at the end of a year or two, you would have the same mixture of rich and poor as you have to-day.'

Conversion by argument is a very difficult thing. The most famous conversion in history—that of Saul on the way to Damascus—happened suddenly and was not the result of a logical statement of an opposite opinion. Conversion, I fancy, usually happens suddenly as if in a flash of lightning. One finds oneself believing one thing year after year, and then one finds oneself released into a new world of a different faith. The new world seems to be the only world worth living in, but how can one persuade other people of this?

282

The apostle Paul performed miracles of conversion, but even he preached to deaf ears by the thousand.   Yet he could reinforce his arguments with promises of eternal bliss and threats of eternal punishment.   None the less, he left the world largely unconvinced and as pagan as Hitler's Germany.

If religious conversion, with all its promises and threats, is so exceptional, how can we hope to convert our neighbours to our political and artistic beliefs where there are no such powerful sanctions?   In literature, for example, how can one persuade a sceptic that he would be happier if he read and re-read the first book of *Paradise Lost* as well as the football results, and that to read *Macbeth* is a more exciting experience than backing the winner of the Derby?

It may be that there are some people born with an incapacity to enjoy poetry, as there seem to be some people who are born with an incapacity to enjoy good music, good painting, and good architecture.   I doubt this, however.   I think we are all born with the gift for enjoying beautiful things, but that we are indifferent to many of them because our attention was never called to them in childhood.

In my own childhood, our attention was called to the intricacies of Latin grammar and algebra—excellent things in themselves—but seldom to the birds, flowers, and trees of the countryside in which we lived.   We were taught more about the Punic wars than about the nature that sang and blossomed at our doors.   As a result, we walked half deaf and half blind through the wealth of spring and early summer, so that I, for example, could not have named the song of the willow-wren till I was in my thirties.

Victorian business men might have asked 'What is the use of being able to recognize the song of the willow-wren?' and there is obviously nothing to be gained from it financially.   But, when once you take an interest in birds, you feel that to live for a brief time on the earth and to be unable to name the song-birds as they sing—nightingale, blackbird, thrush, hedge-sparrow, blue-tit, wren, white-throat, and tree-pipit—is to walk through the valley of life as a deaf man.   Every convert to the love of birds feels this, but how can he persuade those who are indifferent of how much they are missing?

In the same way, those who enjoy reading poetry wonder

how other people can contentedly go through life missing this great enjoyment. Here, they see, is a world of enchantment with wide-open doors; yet, for some reason or other, thousands of people will not enter. Even after long years of universal education, the majority of people never read a line of poetry after their schooldays. It is as if, being offered ambrosia, they chose pork pies. Not that I dislike pork pies, but life becomes doubly life with occasional ambrosia. How, then, to persuade the indifferent to enjoy this divine dish—this dish without money and without price? I do not know.

We are all born, it seems to me, with a taste for poetry. At school we make rhymes about multiplication and subtraction and about the number of days in the months of the year. I doubt whether any child was ever unresponsive to the charm of the rhymes in 'Jack and Jill,' 'Little Boy Blue,' and 'Old King Cole.' We are all poets at that age. Even during lessons at school, we used to respond to the rhythmic beat of 'An Arab's Farewell to His Steed' and 'Young Lochinvar.'

There are people who tell us that the reason why most boys, after leaving school, never or seldom read poetry again is that they were compelled to learn it in class and so acquired a distaste for it. I do not believe this. I can understand how some schoolboys get to dislike some particular poet because they associate him with the drudgery of the class-room. Tennyson, for example, declared that Horace was spoiled for him by being turned into a school book. At the same time, Tennyson can hardly be cited as an example of a boy who gave up reading poetry in disgust as a result of an unfortunate education.

Most boys, I am sure, are attracted rather than repelled by Scott, however pedantic their schoolmaster may be.

> The way was long, the wind was cold,
> The minstrel was infirm and old,

are lines that interest even the most sluggish imagination. Shakespeare, too, I always found one of the most enjoyable of school books, whether in *The Merchant of Venice*—which H. G. Wells surprisingly thinks the dullest of his plays—or in *Julius Caesar* with its magnificent oratory.

Even boys who never read poetry except in school books flocked to these plays when they came to the theatre. I knew only one schoolboy—he was nicknamed 'Smiler' and he looked perpetually happy—who refused to go to see a play by Shakespeare, giving as his excuse: 'In my opinion, Shakespeare's all rot.' Most small boys delight in Shakespeare on the stage, like the barefoot gallery urchin in Dublin who advised his friend to go and see *Hamlet*, as it was 'a grand play, with a ghost and a jool fight' (duel fight). Shakespearian performances in the provinces could pack the gallery in the theatre as well as the stalls for weeks on end. I am sure that touring Shakespearian companies, speaking the lines as poetry and not as an obscure kind of prose, would be the most effective of all instruments for spreading the love of poetry.

The ordinary man, I fancy, prefers poetry, not in purely lyrical form, but as part of an exciting story whether in a play or in narrative verse. Hence the enormous popularity of long narrative poems in comparison with collections of short pieces. Byron and Tennyson reached scores of thousands of readers through their narratives who would have been indifferent to a collection of their lyrics. In our own time, no other modern poetry has been read by such vast numbers of readers as the narrative masterpieces of Mr. John Masefield.

Hence I think the reader whom I have quoted would do well to give his friend a book of narrative verse as a present on his next birthday. Lord Wavell's anthology would be an excellent choice for this purpose, for Lord Wavell delights both in narrative and rhetoric—two of the easiest things to enjoy in poetry. I mean that they can be enjoyed by many people who find Shelley too ethereal and W. B. Yeats a little obscure.

Lord Wavell's own comments, too, have an infectious quality, and might well invite a beginner to come into the garden of poetry and enjoy himself—enjoy himself first with Kipling and Chesterton, proceeding from these to Browning, and, after that, who knows? Perhaps he will become sufficiently acclimatized to verse to be able to read Wordsworth and Shelley with pleasure —two poets who still remain outside the radius of even Lord Wavell's appreciation.

A good anthology of verse, it seems to me, is a better propagandist for poetry than any book or article on the subject. I can think of no other kind of book—at least, of no book in prose—which is likely to transform a grown-up man who cares nothing for poetry into a poetry lover. If poetry bores him, a book or an article about poetry is just as likely to bore him.

Is it possible, I wonder, to look forward to a world in which everybody, from the factory manager to the factory worker, from the lawyer to the farmer, from the publican to the book-maker, will find in poetry the solace and inspiration of his leisure hours? Or will poetry lovers always be in a minority, unable to convince their more prosaic fellows that they are missing one of the supreme pleasures of life?

Mr. James Agate once said that the British public had always preferred bad art to good and that he would regret to see the day when this ceased to be so. I gathered from this that he thought the cult of the arts has a weakening effect on the fibre of many human beings. We have recently seen, however, that a man can be a fairly tough soldier and yet live with poetry as his constant companion. The evidence that the love of poetry has no necessarily enfeebling effect on the character is as old as Alexander the Great, who slept with Homer beside his pillow.

Perhaps it would be a good thing in the interests of literary taste if someone wrote a short history of the great men of action who loved poetry—Wolfe of Quebec, for example. Such a book might convince the anti-'intellectual' that there may be something in poetry after all. It would be much more likely to influence an athletic boy than the divine arguments of Shelley.

But no one can be inveigled into a love of poetry by mere argument. To read poetry is not a duty but a pleasure, and the ordinary man does not like to miss one of the normal pleasures of men whom he respects. That is why Lord Wavell is so good a propagandist. He is respected by hundreds and thousands of people who do not know the difference between an elegy and an epic. The reader who set me writing this should try his book on his friend and see the result.

Reasons for Reading

(1944)

A READER'S letter sent me the other day to an almost, but not quite, forgotten book—Alexander Ireland's *Booklover's Enchiridion*, which is described on the title-page as:

> Thoughts on the Solace and Companionship of
> Books, and Topics Incidental Thereto, Garnered
> from Writers of Every Age for the Help and
> Betterment of All Readers.

A book of quotations on such a subject is bound to contain many enjoyable passages, and Ireland's collection is pleasant to dip into.

On the whole the writers quoted emphasize the profit rather than the entertainment to be got out of reading, and warnings against the wrong kind of reading come down to us from the beginning of the Christian era. Thus Seneca seems to have disapproved of what might be called aimless miscellaneous reading. 'The reading of many authors,' he wrote, 'and of all kinds of works, has in it something vague and unstable.' And again: 'It does not matter how many, but how good, books you have.' From Aulus Gellius a century or so later comes the doubtful assertion: 'The things which are well said do not improve the young so much as those that are wickedly said corrupt them.' I for one am inclined to think that bad books have done less to corrupt mankind than good books have done to improve it.

At the same time, if we have any respect for books we are bound to admit that they possess great powers both for good and for evil. After all, it was the reading of books that drove Don Quixote mad, and it was a fatal day for Germany when the sales of *Mein Kampf* began to exceed the sales of the Bible. The moralist, in his capacity as moralist, is not the ideal critic of literature; but he has a right to judge it from an ethical point of view, and to condemn as enervating many books that a more

287

purely aesthetic critic may think admirable. Even those who disagree with much of Tolstoy's *What is Art?* do not regret that he wrote it.

Among men of former ages the study of books had obviously something of a moral quality. Burton quotes Heinsius, the keeper of the library at Leyden, as saying:

> I no sooner come into the library but I bolt the door to me, excluding lust, ambition, avarice, and all such vices, whose nurse is idleness, the mother of ignorance, and melancholy herself; and in the very lap of eternity amongst so many divine souls I take my seat with so lofty a spirit and sweet content that I pity all our great ones and rich men that know not this happiness.

Milton's description of a good book as 'the precious life-blood of a master-spirit, embalmed and treasured up on purpose to a life beyond life' is a more famous utterance of the view that the chief end of literature is to provide us with something higher than aesthetic pleasure. To Isaac Barrow in the same century the reading of books was 'but conversing with the wisest men of all ages and of all countries.'

In modern times reading has become for the greater part of the public less of a moral effort and more of a pleasure. Even in the old days, however, thousands of people must have read new books for enjoyment rather than for edification. The Greeks probably enjoyed the plays of Aristophanes as light-heartedly as English people in the last generation or two have enjoyed the comic operas of Gilbert and Sullivan. In Rome the appreciators of the more Epicurean odes of Horace and, afterwards, of the anecdotes and amorous nonsense of Ovid were not moralists but pleasure-lovers. The moral tale, perfectly told by Aesop, which, we are told, originated before the amusing tale of the *Arabian Nights* kind, gradually became a medium of entertainment more than of instruction. Yet the great men who wrote about books continued for the most part to commend them as founts of virtue rather than as founts of pleasure.

Not many readers before Horace Walpole looked on reading as a pastime comparable to a game of cards. Horace Walpole thought of books less as character-builders than as sweetmeats. In one of his letters he says:

> I sometimes wish for a catalogue of lounging books—books that one takes up in the gout, low spirits, ennui, or when waiting for company.

Some novels, gay poetry, odd whimsical authors, as Rabelais, etc. A catalogue *raisonné* of such might be a good lounging book.

That, I think, is the first quotation Alexander Ireland gives suggesting that reading is a game for the idle, not always an occupation for the seeker after the eternal verities.

After Walpole came Goethe, who expressed the traditional view of the essential seriousness of literature. He would manifestly have been horrified by the development of the amusing kinds of writing that are now such sources of delight. 'I have never,' he said, for example, 'made a secret of my enmity to parodies and travesties. My reason for hating them is because they lower the beautiful, noble, and great.' Alexander Ireland tells us that George Eliot was equally intolerant of the literature of delightful ridiculousness. 'She carried this feeling to such a pitch,' he writes, 'that she even disliked a book like *Alice in Wonderland* because it laughed at the things which children had a belief in.' Writing of the modern love of burlesque, she said:

Let a greedy buffoonery debase all historic beauty, majesty, and pathos, and the more you heap up the desecrated symbols the greater will be the lack of the ennobling emotions which subdue the tyranny of suffering and make ambition one with virtue.'

We who read books for many reasons—sometimes for instruction, sometimes for the delight of meeting saints and seers who can translate us into worlds far above our common scope, and sometimes for the sheer delight of enjoying the comedy of life, will be reluctant to agree with a theory of literary appreciation which would forbid us to read some of the masterpieces of Sir Max Beerbohm and Mr. Hilaire Belloc.

Serious writers, however, warn us solemnly against taking our reading lightly. Goethe, whom I have already quoted, wrote of some of the popular literature of his time:

In the whirlpool of the literature of the day I have been dragged into the bottomless abyss of the horrors of the recent French romance literature. I will say in one word—it is a literature of despair. . . . Everything true—everything aesthetical is gradually and necessarily excluded from this literature.

One can imagine many a modern critic writing in much the same vein about the works of Hardy and Housman, of Proust and James Joyce.

And so the attack on bad reading goes on. Schopenhauer, who believed in toleration in everything except literary criticism, wrote:

It is the case with literature as with life; wherever we turn we come upon the incorrigible mob of humankind, whose name is Legion, swarming everywhere, damaging everything, as flies in summer. Hence the multiplicity of bad books, those exuberant weeds of literature which choke the true corn. Such books rob the public of time, money, and attention, which ought properly to belong to good literature and noble aims, and they are written with a view merely to make money or occupation. They are therefore not merely useless but injurious.

Ruskin in the Victorian age was equally anti-popular in his detestation of books that he thought would do their readers harm. Few noble writers have given stranger advice to their readers than he. For example:

Mrs. Browning's *Aurora Leigh* is, as far as I know, the greatest poem which the century has produced in any language. Cast Coleridge at once aside, as sickly and useless; and Shelley, as shallow and verbose; Byron, until your taste is fully formed, and you are able to discern the magnificence in him from the wrong. Never read bad or common poetry, nor write any poetry yourself; there is, perhaps, rather too much than too little in the world already.

Hazlitt, however, had already written eloquently of the goodness of reading for pleasure. Here we find the confessions of a man who resembles the reader of modern times. He was profoundly interested in philosophy and aesthetics, but he loved books, for purposes not chiefly of edification, but of delight. How we can all enter into his enjoyment of the old novels and romances:

The greatest pleasure in life is that of reading, and I have had as much of this pleasure as perhaps any one. I have had more pleasure in reading the adventures of a novel (and perhaps changing situations with the hero) than I ever had in my own. I do not think any one can feel much happier—a greater degree of heart's ease—than I used to feel in reading *Tristram Shandy*, and *Peregrine Pickle*, and *Tom Jones*, and *The Tatler*, and *Gil Blas of Santillane*, and *Werther*, and *Boccaccio*.

Nowadays most of us are Hazlittites in our reading. His and Charles Lamb's confessions make reading seem, not a duty, but a holiday. A book is to them a gate into a Utopia, not of instruction, so much as of imagination.

As one who, during most of his life, has read mainly for pleasure, I agree up to a point with Hazlitt and Lamb. At the same time, I remember how in youth I sought, not only pleasure, but wisdom in books—how I felt that I ought to be a better man after reading Emerson's essay on 'Self-reliance,' how I longed to be indifferent to the rubs of circumstance as I read Marcus Aurelius, how even the essays of Stevenson exhilarated me, not merely as delightful literary exercises, but as expressions of a philosophy of life.

Even to-day, though I read for the most part with no high moral purpose, I like those authors best who seem to me to be wise men. Wordsworth's verse is to my mind the supreme poetic achievement of the nineteenth century because he, more than any other poet, was a poet, not merely of the beauty of the world, but of permanent wisdom. In Chaucer, Shakespeare, and Browning wisdom, too, seems to be an essential ingredient of genius, as it is in the biographies of Plutarch and in the music of Handel and Mozart. There is wisdom mixed with unwisdom even in authors who are guilty of almost unpardonable errors—in Ruskin and Kipling, for example. As one reads them one sometimes thinks, 'How foolish!' and, a few pages later, 'How wise.'

After all, wisdom about life is an even more enjoyable dish than a two-hours' indulgence in excitement or fun. Probably the old writers quoted in the *Booklover's Enchiridion* were right. To read wisely is like dining wisely—and certainly not to regard the *hors-d'œuvres* and *pêches Melbas* as anything but minor dishes.

Picasso, Gladstone, Keats

(1946)

NOW that the battle of the critics over Picasso is ended—or, at least, suspended—I should like to join in, not as a fighter, but as a commentator on some aspects of the struggle. I am too ignorant of the technique of painting to be able to discuss the merits of pictures with much profit to other people, but the row about Picasso raised questions that are just as interesting in relation to books or music or architecture as in relation to pictures.

One thing that troubled me during the controversy was the way in which some of the champions of Picasso succeeded in bullying a large part of the intellectual public into dumbness, by an entirely false piece of reasoning. How many people there were who, if you asked them what they thought of the show, replied: 'Well, I keep an open mind. After all, even if you don't like the stuff, you have to admit that every forward movement in the arts has at first been denounced and jeered at.' Nowadays, the partisans of the latest thing in the arts again and again use this argument to quench hostile criticism, and they have used it so often that thousands of people have almost convinced themselves that any artist whose work is attacked during his lifetime is a genius.

This, I submit, is nonsense. The plain fact is that, in the arts as in politics, the leading figures as a rule get both a good deal of abuse and a good deal of praise. The abuse proves nothing one way or the other. Gladstone was abused, but so were many of the incompetents who have filled great political offices. Browning was mocked at, but no great poet was ever all but beaten to death as the poetaster Montgomery was by Macaulay. Macaulay's derisive onslaught, however, is not generally regarded as evidence that Montgomery was a genius.

When I first came to London the painters who chiefly roused the contempt of the critics were not the innovators but the Royal Academicians. If to be abused is the prerogative of genius, the Royal Academy of those days must have been stacked with men of genius.   How often did one hear the Royal Academy assailed as the home of everything that was poisonous in art!   I do not remember ever hearing a good word for Marcus Stone or Alma Tadema or even for Lord Leighton or Poynter.   As for Millais, ever since he sold his picture 'Bubbles' to be used as an advertisement for soap, he was spoken of with contempt as a lost soul.   Yet all these attacks on the Royal Academy and the Royal Academicians did not suffice to give Marcus Stone and Alma Tadema a place among the immortals.

Again, take the literature of the same period.   The two novelists who came in for the chief blasts of critical mockery were Hall Caine and Marie Corelli.   So badly did Marie Corelli suffer from the attacks of the critics that she forbade her publishers to send out copies of one of her novels to the reviewers. As for Hall Caine, every humorist in the country had a dig at him.   It is true that Thomas Hardy had also suffered at the hands of a number of critics when *Tess* and *Jude* appeared and had abandoned fiction in consequence; but he had an easy time among the critics in comparison with the later Hall Caine and Marie Corelli.   Kipling, on the other hand, was seldom attacked except by those who hated his politics; and I do not remember seeing any attacks on the newcomer, H. G. Wells, till he wrote *Ann Veronica*.

If Shaw's plays were attacked, this was only to be expected. He himself began the shindy.   He hit out at a huge section of the British public, and a huge section of the British public, articulate and semi-articulate, hit back.

As I have said, however, all this praise and blame prove nothing as regards the genius of the authors.   The attacks on Hall Caine and Marie Corelli—both of them writers with remarkable gifts, by the way—do not prove they were writers of genius—of greater genius than the generally praised Kipling and H. G. Wells.

There is no evidence, it seems to me, that on its first appearance genius as a rule gets more kicks than halfpence. Shakespeare was bitterly spoken of by a rival, but he appears to have had a fairly smooth passage to fame and fortune, and the tributes paid to him by Ben Jonson and Fletcher show in how high esteem he was held by the best of his contemporaries.

They did not, perhaps, realize how much greater he was than any of them, but at least they did not decry him.

If we come down to a later date we find Congreve sailing into fame when scarcely more than a youth and being hailed by Dryden as a second Shakespeare. It is true that he and his fellow dramatists of the Restoration stage were vehemently attacked by Jeremy Collier, but this was on moral grounds; and on moral grounds there is a good to be said, I think, for Jeremy Collier. There has certainly never been a more flippant view of life exhibited on the stage than at that time.

In a later generation Pope undoubtedly had many enemies; but possibly, like Shaw, it was he who began the hostilities. He himself certainly became the most effectively venomous hostile critic in the history of English literature; and in *The Dunciad* he spoke as ill of some of the bad poets of his time as Mr. D. S. MacColl has spoken of Picasso. I wonder whether his victims said at the time: 'Men of genius have always been abused in their lifetime,' and consoled themselves with the thought. They have certainly become immortal. They have been immortalized, however, not as good poets, but as bad ones; and, if Pope had not attacked them, even the names of most of them would have been forgotten.

The poet who is usually called in as witness by the 'genius-is-always-mocked-at' school is Keats. I have more than once pointed out that Keats had a much better reception from his critical contemporaries than is generally realized. He had some violent things said about him by Byron and De Quincey and *Blackwood's* and the *Quarterly Review*; but among those who praised him were Leigh Hunt and Lamb and Hazlitt, and the *Edinburgh Review* spoke well enough of him to infuriate Byron.

There is one interesting difference, however, between the lot of writers who were attacked in previous ages and that of the writers who are attacked in ours. The men of genius of old not only suffered detraction but found merely a tiny public for their work. To-day, writers who are attacked seem as often as not to flourish on hostility, and their critics no less than their champions advertise them into fame. There is nothing to beat controversial criticism as an aid to publicity. Poets may be abused to-day; but they no longer—at least, those of them who are most energetically criticized—starve.

And it is the same, I imagine, with painters.   A picture that has been violently criticized seems to have as good a chance of being sold at a high price as a picture that has earned nothing but praise.

Hence it seems to me to be absurd for the champions of any new school of art to resent criticism.   At least, it would be absurd of the rest of us to take their resentment seriously.   Let me repeat that it would also be absurd to accept their suggestion that new genius is always persecuted, or their implication that this 'persecution' is evidence of the possession of genius by the artist 'persecuted.'

Do not then allow yourselves to be bullied into accepting new pictures or books as works of genius merely because a number of voluble critics attack them, or into remaining silent about your doubts, if any, when your opinion of them is asked. Keep an open mind, certainly; but keep for a better reason than this.

Another misleading argument used in the recent controversy by the admirers of Picasso was that his latest paintings must be good because, when he painted more conventionally, he showed that he could beat the conventional painters at their own game. In other words, they argue that because an artist once painted well he must remain a good painter till the end of his life. This is, of course, ridiculous.   Take Sir John Millais, for example—Millais who has actually been named by the pro-Picasso school as a man of genius whose early work was abused by the critics.   Millais, no doubt, preserved certain good qualities till the end; but many critics who admire his early work deplore his later.

In literature we have a number of instances of writers whose later work seems to belong to a different world from their earlier.   James Joyce, for example, began his career as a prose-writer with the lucid *Dubliners* and *Portrait of the Artist as a Young Man*.   He then shocked the world with the less lucid *Ulysses*.   Finally, he bewildered all but the faithful few—and I fancy he bewildered even them—with the unintelligible *Finnegans Wake*.   What should we think of a critic who tried to browbeat us into praising *Finnegans Wake* by reminding us that Joyce showed in *Dubliners* that he could write straightforward prose as well as most of the best of his contemporaries?   To say this would not prove that *Finnegans Wake* was anything but a philologic freak concocted by a man of genius.

May it not be that, just as there were two Joyces, there may be two Picassos and that one of them may deserve praise and the other may deserve something less than praise or may deserve condemnation?

If Picasso's later work is to be praised, it should be praised for its own qualities and not commended to us on the ground that it is likely to possess genius because many critics have denounced it, or because the painter's earlier work was masterly.

After all, many men of genius—Wordsworth among them—have done bad work as well as good. I do not say—as I did not see the pictures—that the later work of Picasso is bad. But many good critics have thought it is, and why should any one get angry with them for saying so?

Poetry versus Prose

(1946)

I WAS amazed the other day, when looking for something else in the complete edition of Tennyson's works, edited by his son, to come on a note on *Ulysses*—a poem which, we are told, Carlyle especially admired.

Edward FitzGerald, in recording this, says that Carlyle had probably read nothing of Tennyson before the volume containing *Ulysses* appeared, 'being naturally prejudiced against one whom every one was praising, and praising for a *Sort* of Poetry which he despised.' 'But,' adds FitzGerald, 'directly he saw, and heard, the Man, he knew there was A Man to deal with: and took pains to cultivate him; assiduous in exhorting him to leave Verse and Rhyme, and to apply his genius to Prose and *Work*.'

No odder advice can ever have been given to a poet of genius. Here was Carlyle telling Tennyson in effect that his poetry was so good he should waste no more time on it. It was as though, like some schoolmasters, he regarded the writing of verse chiefly as a good preparation for the writing of prose. Schoolmasters of this kind, however, do not expect their pupils to write verse of genius, but recommend verse-writing merely as good exercise in the choice and economy of words. Carlyle, on the other hand, though he had included the poet among his Heroes, seems to have looked on poetry as an inferior kind of writing to prose—more or less, indeed, as a toy.

Carlyle, however, is not the only writer who has spoken belittlingly of the art of poetry. One of the most entertaining and wrong-headed critical essays in English literature is Thomas Love Peacock's *Four Ages of Poetry*, in which he denounced poetry as a survival from the ages of barbarism. His essay, no doubt, was written partly as a joke, and reminds one of the brilliant sophistries of a clever undergraduate debating for debating's sake and supporting a side in which he does not in the depth of his heart believe.

Peacock argued that the materials of poetry no longer exist in the civilized world. On this point he wrote:

In the origin of perfection of poetry, all the associations of life were composed of poetical materials. With us it is decidedly the reverse. We know, too, that there are no Dryads in Hyde Park nor Naiads in the Regent's Canal. But barbaric manners and supernatural interventions are essential to poetry. Either in the scene, or in the time, or in both, it must be remote from our ordinary perceptions. While the historian and the philosopher are advancing in, and accelerating, the progress of knowledge, the poet is wallowing in the rubbish of departed ignorance, and raking up the ashes of dead savages to find gewgaws and rattles for the grown babies of the age.

He gave examples of this from the poetry of his own time:

Mr. Scott digs up the poachers and cattle-stealers of the ancient border. Lord Byron cruises for thieves and pirates on the shores of the Morea and among the Grecian islands. Mr. Southey wades through ponderous volumes of travels and chronicles, from which he carefully selects all that is false, useless, and absurd, as being essentially poetical; and when he has a commonplace book full of monstrosities, strings them into an epic. Mr. Wordsworth picks up village legends from old women and sextons; and Mr. Coleridge, to the valuable information acquired from similar sources, superadds the dreams of crazy theologians and the mysticisms of German metaphysics, and favours the world with visions in verse, in which the quadruple elements of sexton, old woman, Jeremy Taylor, and Emmanuel Kant are harmonized into a delicious poetical compound.

Peacock summed up the case against the modern poet in a fine burst of undergraduate eloquence:

A poet in our times is a semi-barbarian in a civilized community. He lives in the days that are past. His ideas, thoughts, feelings, associations, are all with barbarous manners, obsolete customs, and exploded superstitions. The march of his intellect is like that of a crab, backwards. . . . The highest inspirations of poetry are resolvable into three ingredients: the rant of unregulated passion, the whining of exaggerated feeling, and the cant of factitious sentiment, and can therefore serve only to ripen a splendid lunatic like Alexander, a puling driveller like Werter, or a morbid dreamer like Wordsworth.

Sticklers for the exact truth might deplore the publication of such near-nonsense; but after all, Peacock was a wit and a humorist; and a still better justification of his essay is that it

produced in reply Shelley's inspired *Defence of Poetry*. There
is something to be said for provocative writing, however
perverse, when a man of intellect is the writer.

Mockery of poets, however, has for long been a sport of the
mischievous. To be a 'spring poet,' as it was called, was in
my schooldays to court derision. The 'spring poet' was the
butt of many an easy jest in *Comic Cuts* and *Chips* and other
laughter-providers for the young. But mockery of poets has
never been confined to schoolboys. De Quincey, in his literary
reminiscences, tells us how Lamb on one occasion revelled in
making fun of Coleridge. De Quincey at the time was a youth
under twenty years old, and the intensity of his enthusiasm for
Coleridge may be measured from his remark: 'We have heard
in the old times of donkeys insulting effete or dying lions by
kicking them, but in the case of Coleridge and Wordsworth it
was effete donkeys that kicked living lions.'

Lamb could not resist the temptation to pull the leg of a
youth so ecstatic in his enthusiasm. De Quincey tells us:

At length, when he had given utterance to some ferocious canon of
judgment, which seemed to question the entire value of the poem, I
said, perspiring (I dare say) in this detestable crisis—'But, Mr. Lamb,
good heavens! How is it possible you can allow yourself in such
opinions? What instance could you bring from the poem that would
bear you out in these insinuations?'

'Instances!' said Lamb; 'oh, I'll instance you, if you come to that.
Instance, indeed! Pray, what do you say to this:

> The many men so beautiful,
> And they all dead did lie?

So beautiful, indeed! Beautiful! Just think of such a gang of Wapping
vagabonds, all covered with pitch, and chewing tobacco; and the old
gentleman himself—what do you call him?—the bright-eyed fellow?'

What more might follow [says De Quincey] I never heard; for,
at this point, in a perfect rapture of horror, I raised my hands—both
hands—to both ears; and, without stopping to think or to apologize,
I endeavoured to restore equanimity to my disturbed sensibilities by
shutting out all further knowledge of Lamb's impieties.'

More than once I have heard railleries of a comparable sort
at the expense of poets. I have a friend—himself a devout
lover of poetry—maintaining out of love of paradox that poetry
was largely an excuse for writing what would be recognized as

nonsense if it were written in prose.   He gave as an example
the opening of Shelley's 'Skylark':

> Hail to thee, blithe spirit!
> Bird thou never wert.

'Imagine a prose-writer addressing a skylark,' he would say,
'and telling it that it wasn't a bird.   A prose-writer who wrote
such twaddle would not be praised as a man of genius, but
would be ridiculed.'   And he argued that Wordsworth was
equally defiant of common sense when, in addressing the cuckoo,
he wrote:

> O cuckoo, shall I call thee bird
> Or but a wandering voice?

In the first place he said it is unnatural to address a bird as
'O this!' or 'O that!'; and in the second place it is so obvious
that a cuckoo is both a bird and a wandering voice that it is
childish to suggest that it must be called either the one thing
or the other.

Perhaps we who have tried to write good poetry and have
failed are a little jealous of the poets.   That, at least, is one
possible explanation of the ridicule to which the poets have
often been subjected.

Another partial explanation may be that the poets have at
times claimed rather too much for themselves, as though they
alone among writers were inspired from on high.   Some of
them have gone so far as to maintain that it is verse alone that
gives immortality to the heroism of the soldier and to women's
beauty.   Such extravagant claims invite a retort from prose-
writers who do not like to have it rubbed into them that they
are practising an inferior art.

The truth is that it is absurd to praise one art to the detriment
of another.   To say that music is a greater art than painting,
or that architecture is a nobler art than sculpture, is as foolish
as to say that the sea is more beautiful than mountains or that
rivers are lovelier than cornfields.   There is room in the world
for all these things, and the excellence of the one does not
diminish the excellence of the others.

There is, it may be conceded at once, nothing greater in
literature than the greatest poetry.   But the greatest poetry
could all be housed on a single shelf in a library.   The wisest

thing, to my mind, is not to praise the one art at the expense of the other, and not to criticize one of the arts for not being the other, any more than we should criticize the wild rose for not being the honeysuckle.

Carlyle's identification of prose with work, with the implication that verse is play, seems to me to be an almost incredible piece of unintelligence on the part of a great writer. And, after all, in his advice to Tennyson, he overlooked one thing—the fact that good poets can no more be sure of being able to write good prose than good prose-writers can be sure of being able to write good poetry. A few men of genius, from Shakespeare and Milton to Meredith and Hardy, have written both; but there is no rule in the matter. Writers in either art need not envy or disparage the art of the other. After all, only a very few of them will be readable a hundred years after they are dead.

What Use is History?

(1946)

MR. HENRY FORD has been credited with the forcible remark: 'History is bunk.' I have been told either that Mr. Ford never said this, or that, if he did say it, he did not mean what everybody thought he meant—I forget which. Whether he said it or not, however, the sentence probably expresses what a good many people believe.

He could certainly make out a plausible case for the view that history is of little or no use to us. History is a record of the experience of mankind, and how little we learn even from our own experience! And how much less we learn from the experience of our forefathers or of nations that are known to us only by name!

In the hour of disaster the Hebrews listened to their prophets and called on the Lord for help, but no sooner did they feel safe than they forgot their dependence on heaven, and thus brought their nation to ruin again and again. As a result, they plunged back into disaster, and only then did they once more begin to accept the lessons of history that their prophets taught them. I sometimes wonder whether one of the chief lessons of history is not that the feeling of safety is more dangerous to a people than the sense of danger. Men are corrupted by ease no less than by disease—not a very cheerful thought.

At the same time, it seems to me that if history is no use, that is not the fault of history, but of ourselves who will not learn the lessons that it teaches us. The lessons are there, but, either because we are too comfortable, or because they would put a check on our ambitions, we prefer to ignore them. In modern times it has become the custom to belittle historical analogies and historical parallels and comparisons between a contemporary situation and something that happened in ancient Greece and Rome or even in eighteenth-century France. I myself believe that such comparisons may be useful. 'History does not repeat itself. Historians repeat each other,' said a famous wit. I agree only with the second half of the epigram.

I remember some time before the last war writing an essay in which I pointed out that in Livy's story of Hannibal and the Second Punic War one could find reasons for believing that Hitler could not succeed in a *blitzkrieg* against England. Hannibal, Livy tells us, promised the Carthaginians a lightning war that would end in victory, and based his confidence on the view that the Romans had become decadent and unwarlike. If I could find my essay, I could quote the various arguments by which I forecast the defeat of Hitler—a more faithless and cruel Hannibal —but when could I ever find a book on my shelves when I wanted it?

One of my critics argued that it was the English, not the Germans, who were comparable to the Carthaginians. It seemed to me, however, that of the two peoples the English bore the closer resemblance to the Romans, both in their situation and in their character, and I was confirmed in this opinion when I recently took down by chance a volume of Livy in the Loeb Library translation. Here I found a rather English speech made by Scipio to his army after the Romans had suffered reverses in Spain in which his father and uncle had fallen.

'It is a lot assigned to us by some fate,' said Scipio, 'that in all the great wars we have been first defeated and then victorious.' How often has the same thing been said about the English— the nation that, according to an extreme statement, always loses every battle except the last!

The story even of Scipio's departure for Spain reads like an episode in English history—in English history as recent as the last war. At the time he left, you may or may not remember —I confess I had forgotten it, if I ever knew it—Rome was in deadly peril and the Carthaginians had reached the gates of the city 'with no one preventing.' They were all the more ashamed, Livy tells us, 'to find themselves so scorned that, while they were sitting before the walls of Rome, out of another gate marched a Roman army bound for Spain.' Here surely we have a recognizable parallel with the conduct of the English in the recent war, when England was (in the phrase of the time) a besieged fortress and yet was sending troops and guns that she could ill spare to Egypt and badly needed aeroplanes and other munitions of war to Russia.

Parallels of this kind are educative. They help to fortify the will like a great example. And other parallels are equally educative as warnings to those who take notice of them. If Hitler had read Livy to good purpose he would have realized that ruthlessness does not always pay in the end. He would have pondered over Livy's account of the ruthlessness of Hannibal which estranged the peoples of Italy.

Naturally inclined to greed and cruelty, his temperament favoured despoiling what he was unable to protect, in order to leave desolated lands to the enemy. That policy was shameful in the beginning, and especially so in the outcome. For not only were those who suffered undeserved treatment alienated, but all the rest as well; for the lesson reached larger numbers than did the suffering.

Again, the fact that Hannibal, though he encamped for a time only three miles from Rome, was never able to take the city, might have caused a modern aggressor to reflect that a people with the Roman spirit might to-day, as of old, evade the grasp of a seemingly victorious tyrant. How magnificently the Romans of those days refused to admit even the possibility of defeat! This refusal played a considerable part, we are told, in depressing the hopes of Hannibal:

The important thing was that he heard that, although he was sitting armed before the walls of the city of Rome, soldiers had set out under their banners to reinforce Spain. And the important circumstance was that he learned from a prisoner that about that time the land on which he had his camp chanced to have been sold, with no reduction of price on that account. But it seemed to him so arrogant and such an indignity that a purchaser should have been found at Rome for the ground which he had seized in war and was himself its occupier and owner, that he forthwith summoned a herald and ordered the bankers' shops which were round the Roman Forum to be sold.

How much more impressive such a symbolic act of an unconquerable people is than a repeated cry of 'We will never capitulate.' Some people will probably say, however, that the Romans, like the English, were unimaginative people who didn't even know when they were beaten.

History, educative though it is, however, may be misleading if read only in scraps. Dr. G. M. Trevelyan, in his lecture to a

National Book League audience, *History and the Reader*, quotes a passage in which Professor Butterfield, of Cambridge, speaks of the dangers of misreading history:

Nations do remember one thing and another in the past. And so terrible are the evils of a little history that we must have more history as quickly as we can. And since one of the most dangerous devices of propaganda at the present day—by far the neatest trick of the year —is to narrate what the foreigner once did, while withholding everything in the nature of historical explanation, we must have more of the kind of history which is not mere narrative but exposition—the history which takes account of the differences between the centuries, between stages of intellectual development, even between types of social structure. The study of history matters, not because it turns men into statesmen . . . but because in every genuine victory it gains it is contributing to the growth of human understanding.

Dr. Trevelyan himself, admitting that the Americans know more of English history than the English know of American history, tells us that even here a danger comes from 'learning bits of past history without bringing the story up to recent and present times!'

The Americans, for example, tend to think of England as she was long ago, as a monarchical and aristocratic country. Their knowledge of our past is greater than their knowledge of our present. A few months ago, a friend and intelligent American officer said to me that when he first came over to England for this war he expected to find a land of castles with serfs tilling the soil for the benefit of a feudal aristocracy. I told him that his historical knowledge of England would have been suitable if he had come over to lend a hand in the *earlier* part of the Hundred Years War.

Dr. Trevelyan, however, is not chiefly intent on proving that a little history is a dangerous thing. His chief purpose is to counter the theory of Bury and other nineteenth-century historians that history is a science—just that and nothing more. He rightly contends that it is both a science and an art, and that, if it were not an art, no one but a small minority of experts would read it.

The scientific theory of history was natural enough as a protest against the rather biased narratives of such 'artistic' historians as Macaulay and Froude. But the fact remains that twenty people can read Macaulay and Froude for one who can read the

L

more scientific Gardiner or Bury himself. Most of the great historians have been biased—Tacitus and Gibbon among them— but they interest the common man in history and in pursuing the quest of historical truth. Hence a biased man of imagination may serve the cause of truth better than a more impartial dry-as-dust.

Livy himself, it is said, wrote with bias—bias in favour of the Republic and against the Empire, and bias against the Carthaginians. At the same time he gave enough credit to the virtues and achievements of the Carthaginians to win a good deal of sympathy for them from posterity.

He wrote, however, deliberately to magnify his own people —an admirable object within reason. Now that England has ceased to be the boastful country of the end of the last century there is room for an English Livy as a reaction against those who are inclined to see only the virtues of foreign nations and the crimes and faults of their own. Such a book would be full of warnings, but also full of encouragements—a book that would increase national self-respect without pandering to national self-satisfaction. Dr. Trevelyan himself has already written English history of this fine temper, and it would be well if it could now be brought down to the year 1945. After all, English history, with all its black pages, is the most remarkable that the world has seen since Rome perished.

'Poetry is Valueless'

(1944)

I HAVE had a letter from a reader asking an opinion on that very old question about poetry as about many other things: 'What use is it?' The question arose, he tells me, in the course of a 'fight' with a friend about Keats's *Ode to a Nightingale*, the friend maintaining that it is purely sensuous, and denying, therefore, that it has any value.

That is surely to take an extremely ascetic view of life. If the pleasures we derive from the senses are to be contemned and rejected, we shall never eat turkey at Christmas or offer a child even a first helping of plum pudding. It is difficult to imagine why we were given our five senses if we were meant merely to let them become atrophied.

Apart from this there is no reason to think that the pleasures of the senses are useless, even on the most prosaic level. Dieticians tell us that the pleasure of taste is an aid to digestion. Again, why should we regard the sense of smell as useful when it enables us to detect a gas escape but dismiss it as useless when we are inhaling the fragrance of honeysuckle or roses? Smelling honeysuckle or roses is from several points of view a useless occupation; but it heightens the enjoyment of life at the moment in a not always enjoyable world and, indeed, is one of the multitude of things that make life seem worth living and that probably increase one's mental health.

Even the great Puritans never proposed to banish the pleasures of the senses from the Commonwealth. Milton declared that poetry should be simple, sensuous, and passionate, and no man can ever have taken greater delight in the music of instruments and the music of words. With his sensuous speech he enchants the ear even of those who dislike him as a man and who are antipathetic to his creed. Christian poets, painters, and musicians, indeed, invite us to the enjoyment of sensuous pleasures no less than the pagan masters of the arts. The pleasures of the senses, it is clear, cannot be kept separate from what may be

called spiritual pleasures, but merge into them and enable us
to express them more intently.   Consider, for example, Handel's
Messiah—a sensuous as well as a spiritual masterpiece.

I do not wish to magnify the importance of the pleasures
of the senses.   To over indulge in them is no wiser than to
reject them altogether.   But if you had said to Socrates that a
thing that was sensuous was necessarily useless, I think he would
have asked you to define the word 'useless'—a most difficult
thing to do.

It would be easier to understand the point of view of someone
who objected to the *Ode to a Nightingale* on the ground that it is
morbid than the point of view of someone who holds that,
being sensuous, it is of no value.   For the mood it expresses is
certainly morbid, if it is morbid to long for death as for a drug
and to think of the world merely as a place 'where men sit and
hear each other groan.'

Even in regard to this, however, it should be remembered
that Keats's *De Profundis* was a cry of suffering—suffering over
the prospect of a beloved brother dying of consumption, over
the uncertainty of his own life and of Fanny Brawne's love for
him.   We cannot with justice call any literature morbid that
reveals the anguish of which the human heart is capable.

Apart from this, the final impression the 'ode' leaves on most
readers is an impression, not of morbidity, but of the beauty of
the earth in which nightingales sing through the darkness; the
pain is the pain of ecstasy wrung from despair.   The line:

> Being too happy in thine happiness

is only the beginning of joyous utterances that break through
the gloom of a black night in a black world.   The most famous
verse in the poem is in essence praise of life, not praise of death!

> Thou wast not born for death, immortal Bird!
> No hungry generations tread thee down;
> The voice I hear this passing night was heard
> In ancient days by emperor and clown:
> Perhaps the selfsame song that found a path
> Through the sad heart of Ruth, when, sick for home,
> She stood in tears amid the alien corn;
>   The same that oft-times hath
> Charm'd magic casements, opening on the foam
> Of perilous seas, in faery lands forlorn.

Let it be admitted that Keats was enthralled by the senses to a much greater degree than Wordsworth or Shelley; but how divine a use he made of his servitude!

My correspondent's friend, however, was not content with attacking the sensuousness of Keats. He went on to question the value of literature, painting, and music in general. 'These things,' he argued, 'are only of value for about two per cent of the population; therefore, what good are they?'

I do not think a Gallup Poll has ever been taken of the percentage of people to whom Shakespeare, Bach, and Titian are inexhaustible sources of pleasure; but I have no doubt devotees of poetry and the other arts are a minority. That seems to me to be evidence, however, not that the arts are useless, but that the human race is still very badly educated and no more than half civilized. Obviously it requires a certain amount of education of the right sort fully to appreciate any of the arts. That education may be the result either of a bookish and artistic environment at home or of contact with an inspiring teacher at school. Occasionally it is the result of a natural aptitude developed in inauspicious surroundings. At the same time, even at an early stage of civilization the ordinary human being feels the need of the arts. The mother sings her child to sleep with lullabies that are certainly works of art; the music of the dance, the music of soldiers on the march, the music of grief, are as much part of the language of life as the spoken word. Old men tell stories round the fire in the evening, and every village has its Grimm, if not its Homer.

Even at a later stage of civilization, the common man is more sensitive to beauty, I think, than is generally believed. You need only go to Twickenham on a day on which Wales is playing England at Rugby football to realize that in Wales music is the possession, not of a minority, but of the majority. Take another of the arts—architecture. Not many of us, perhaps, are experts in our appreciation of architecture, but I am certain that graceful buildings are a substantial source of enjoyment to ordinary men and women. If, on a fine Sunday, you walk along one of the old London streets where the houses have the charm both of age and of design you will notice how often people stop to admire and explain about some building. Nor is the ordinary man indifferent to poetry, even though he may seldom read it. Let

Mr. Churchill, however, end one of his broadcasts, at a crisis
in his country's history, with a quotation of noble verse, and
even the most stolid listeners are moved. How profoundly he
enunciated the hope coming from America when he quoted the
last verse of Clough's best-known poem:

> And not by eastern windows only,
> When daylight comes, comes in the light,
> In front, the sun climbs slow, how slowly,
> But westward, look, the land is bright.

I did hear of a solicitor who said he wished that Mr. Churchill
would stop quoting poetry. 'There is no need to,' he said;
'Churchill is just as great a master of English as Shakespeare.'
Mr. Churchill knows better, however, and with poetry he
helped to steel men's souls.

The truth is men's souls hunger for beauty, and the beauty of
the arts and the beauty of nature help to satisfy this hunger.
Even the week-end flights to the country and the sea, with all
their ugliness of litter-throwing and overcrowding, are imperfect
attempts to satisfy this hunger.

My correspondent's friend, however, maintains that the
enjoyment of landscape is like the enjoyment of a man who
drowns his sorrows in beer.   Well, beer, they say, is best; but
I would point out that very few of the people who drink beer
do so in order to drown their sorrows. They drink beer
because they like it and because of the company in which they
drink it. In the same way, we do not go out and look at a
landscape in the hope of stupefying ourselves. We go out
because we enjoy such things as a child enjoys playing games.

But, says our ascetic, it is 'an insult to suffering humanity
to get joy from such things.'   At this point I begin more than
ever to suspect that my correspondent's friend is a bit of a leg-
puller. Arguments such as his are in nine cases out of ten
meant to tease rather than to persuade. Assuming that he is
perfectly serious, however, one is inclined to ask: 'Are not
most of us part of this suffering humanity? And does he really
believe that we are insulting ourselves by enjoying a walk in the
country?' Even if we are fortunate enough to be free from
anxiety, free from pain, free from suffering in any form, what
conceivable good can we do to others less fortunate, by refusing

to enjoy the beauties of nature or the beauties of poetry? Many of those who care most for nature and poetry are also those who suffer most. The existence of literature would be justified, indeed, if by nothing else, by the solace it has brought to countless thousands of suffering men and women. After all, the great writers themselves have mostly been men who suffered more than the common lot. Even so happy a book as the *Essays of Elia* is the work of a writer who has plumbed the depths of suffering. We know little of the life of Shakespeare; but who can read the plays and believe them to be the work of a man who lived in perpetual sunshine? Great literature, far from being something the enjoyment of which is an insult to suffering humanity, is itself one of the finest creations of suffering humanity.

I confess I have little sympathy with people who suggest that it is wrong for any one to enjoy himself whilst others are suffering. No one is nobler than the saint who sacrifices all pleasures in order to devote himself to the mitigation of suffering; but few of us have the genius of the saints. We enjoy a cup of tea even in the world of 1944, and we feel that the world is all the better because so many people can still enjoy a cup of tea. And the world is also surely all the happier because so many men and women enjoy books. Soldiers at the front and prisoners of war cry out, we are told, for more and more books, and they would be surprised if they were told that they were insulting suffering humanity—in other words, themselves—by reading them.

How any one can argue that it would be better for humanity if we all became illiterate savages, I find it hard to understand. Perhaps my correspondent's friend can explain.

Fictitious Biography

(1943)

SOME people have an antipathy to historical novels. They like history to be history and fiction to be fiction, and can get no pleasure from reading a book in which it is impossible to tell what is fact and what has been invented by the author. I have known other people who have the same prejudice—among them that brilliant novelist and biographer, Ethel Colburn Mayne. If you sent her an historical novel to review, she would condemn it out of hand on the ground, not that it was bad of its kind, but that all historical novels were unreadable.

Having as a schoolboy loved the novels of Sir Walter Scott even more than penny dreadfuls, and having found in *The Three Musketeers* and *The Vicomte de Bragelonne* entertainment so exciting that I went on reading them in bed by candlelight till my eyes ached, I could not agree with her. Perhaps the reason was that I was not particularly interested in facts.

Facts were such things as the length of the Yangtsekiang, the height of Ben Nevis, and the name of the woman whom George III married. How much more enjoyable was a blend of fact and fiction in which D'Artagnan, Alan Breck, and Sydney Carton intruded into the dry-as-dust wastes of history!

And, after all, the people who dislike historical novels forget that all the early historians were in some measure writers of fiction. The Greek and Roman historians felt at liberty to invent speeches, for example, which they put into the mouths of famous statesmen and soldiers. One of the greatest speeches in literature—the funeral speech of Pericles—may, for all we know to the contrary, be an invention of Thucydides. Some modern scholars tell us that Livy's history is to a great extent fiction, and that the character of Hannibal in it is based not on fact but on the prejudices of an imaginative writer. Whether Livy was right or wrong in his view of Hannibal I do not know. But there is no denying that the historians of ancient times claimed

312

much more of the licence that has since been enjoyed by the historical novelists.

Biography, too, in Greek and Roman times was composed of a mixture of fact and fiction. Who can tell how much of the Socrates we know was invented by Plato? It is quite incredible that Plato could have memorized all those intricate discussions that he claims to record in the *Dialogues*.

In the modern world the distinction between fact and fiction has become sharper. At least, it had done so until the first quarter of the present century. Macaulay and Froude seemed to many of their critics to be unduly imaginative, but, at least, they kept to historical facts so far as their prejudices permitted them to do so. Then came a new school of historical biography in which the writers invented conversations as freely as the ancient Romans, so that when you read a life of Napoleon you never knew whether the page you were reading was fact or fiction. This, I confess, I found exasperating. I can enjoy historical novels; but semi-fictitious biography has always irritated me. I would much rather read a straightforward life of Shelley than such a piece of semi-fiction, charming though it is, as M. André Maurois's *Ariel*.

The rise of the new school of biographical fiction is obviously due to the fact that this is an age of novel readers, and that for one person who will read a book called a biography there are ten or twenty who will read a book called a novel. A few years ago, for example, there appeared a novel—a hostile novel about Charles Dickens, and it created a hundred times the stir that greeted a new edition of Forster's biography. Another biographical novel that caused considerable excitement was Morley Roberts's novel about George Gissing. I remember how one critic accused the author of being a ghoul. But possibly the book by its candour would have given the same offence even if it had been an unfictitious biography of a writer not long dead.

Novels about men and women recently dead—men and women, many of whose friends are still living—will always raise questions of taste in the minds of their readers. I am myself in this matter on the side of reticence. I do not like to see someone whom I have met and admired made a character in fiction, with secrets revealed that should have been kept hidden till they had become part of the world of the dead. Hence it

* L

was with some prejudice that I began to read a new novel, *Daughter of Time*, described as 'the Life of Katherine Mansfield in novel form.' It seemed to me rather shocking to take a woman of beautiful genius and her sorrows and to put into her mouth sentences some of which must wound people still living.

After reading the book, however, I confess most of my prejudices disappeared. Mrs. Nelia Gardner White, the author, has undoubtedly written some pages that will cause pain to the living; but at the same time she has painted a deeply moving portrait of Katherine Mansfield, and members of the Mansfield group have already been so outspoken in their accounts of themselves that they obviously do not share the common taste for reticence.

There is no need, for example, to be reticent about D. H. Lawrence, who is one of the principal characters in this novel. Lawrence has already been exposed to the glare of publicity beyond any writer of our time. It is strange to think of the spell he cast on those who were most intimate with him and how none of his friends have been able to communicate this spell to the outside world. In *Daughter of Time*, where he appears as T. L. Davies, he will strike most readers as a half-mad egotist. His treatment of his wife was abominable, as it is presented here, and we are told that one of the bitter sorrows of Katherine's life was due to Lawrence's domination over her husband.

Lawrence, however, is merely a minor character in the book compared with Katherine. Katherine wins the heart from the time when we first meet her as a sensitive and imaginative child in New Zealand—a creature of spirit born to a destiny of genius and unhappiness. When one thinks of that child with the fast-beating heart, one feels that Byron's lines might have been set on her tomb as an epitaph:

> For the sword outwears its sheath,
> And the soul wears out the breast,
> And the heart must pause to breathe,
> And love itself have rest.

It is not surprising that, when she came to Europe, one of the books she brought with her was Marie Bashkirtseff's journal. She had the same avid and beautiful nature, longing to get from

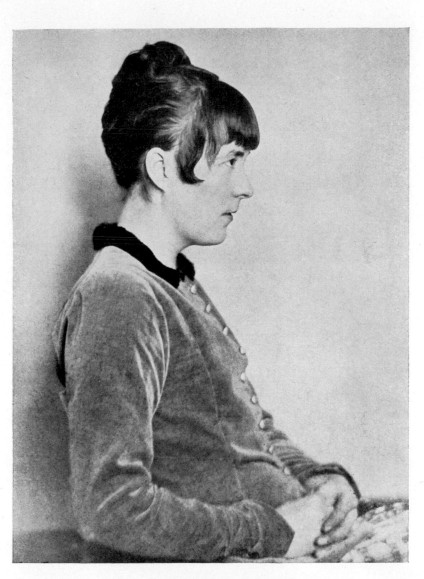

KATHERINE MANSFIELD

experience more than experience could give. She had the moth's desire for the star and the moth's doom of suffering in the candle flame.

It was this reckless feeling that an artist must have what is called experience that led her into strange adventures. One can only describe as reckless the life that brought her a dead baby and that married her to a man whom she left four days later. With an enormous capacity for happiness, she seems always to have let happiness escape her. Even the supreme love of her life—the love of that Aaron, as he is called in the novel, who afterwards became her husband—brought her heartbreak as well as bliss. She had her moments, her exaltations, however, till the hour of her death when, after flying for salvation to the Forest Philosophers of Fontainebleau, she was filled with radiant joy by the coming of Aaron, only to die of a sudden haemorrhage.

I do not know what readers who cannot identify the various characters introduced will make of *Daughter of Time*. I fancy, however, that even they will be moved to deep sympathy with the character of Katherine. I wish that the author had given us a chapter revealing Katherine as the soul of good company— an incarnation, when she chose, of the comic spirit. As it is, she has given us the tragic story of an artist—an artst who died believing that her best books were still unwritten.

The characterization in the novel seems to me to be good in spite of the rather bookish quality of some of the dialogue. I doubt whether Katherine Mansfield ever talked as we are asked to believe that she talked to Dorian about New Zealand:

'People think it's an uncivilized place, that it's full of savages and volcanoes and suchlike things! And perhaps it is uncivilized beside England. But there is life there, Dorian. *Life*. It hasn't all been passed out by schools and traditions. For instance, you could paint there. Oh, I was anxious to get away from it once. I thought that the traditions were more important, and I thought that an artist had to be where other artists are. Well, I know better now. But perhaps one has to stand off awhile and look back to know. Now I know you can be an artist anywhere where there is love and sensitivity. There are a lot in England who know the last without the first. But New Zealand—well, you get the feeling of life beginning, not ending, as you often do here. In England the story seems all told, and if you try to make it seem new and beautiful again they lift their brows at you and realize you came from a wild island in the Pacific.'

That reads more like a passage from a letter than a piece of conversation.

At the same time Mrs. White has done her work well—well enough to have removed the prejudice against the biographical novel from the mind of at least one of her readers.

Quotations and Poetry

(1943)

THE longer I live, the more I feel inclined, when I see a quotation, to challenge it. At school, in the writing class, I used to agree with all the copy-book maxims which I wrote down again and again in semi-legible script—such as 'Birds of a feather flock together,' 'No gains without pains,' 'Discretion is the better part of valour,' and a score of other sentences that appeared to be solidifications of the traditional wisdom of mankind. As I grew older, however, I began to wonder whether some of these pithy sayings were as true as they looked. From all I could gather from my observation of birds and my reading about them, it seemed to me that birds of a feather were by no means certain to flock together. Male chaffinches are said to flock together during winter, but after St. Valentine's Day they separate into married couples. Robins certainly do not flock together, nor, so far as my experience goes, do wood wrens.

As for 'No gains without pains,' is it so certain that wealth is acquired merely by toil? I have known men who bought land for a song and who afterwards found it turned into a gold-mine as a result of its being brought nearer the heart of a city by a new tram-line. Gains and pains, I am afraid, are not always such a pair of Siamese twins as the proverb suggests. One could go through most of the proverbs in this way, questioning them and finding that, though they contain a considerable amount of truth, it is usually only a half truth. 'Discretion is the better part of valour' is a useful warning against the waste of valour through recklessness; but 'the better part'—what an exaggeration it is! The sentence is, when closely examined, as non-sensical as: 'Genius is an infinite capacity for taking pains.'

Perhaps I was born with an instinct for contradiction, or, perhaps, the discovery of the fallacies contained in my copy-book influenced me unduly; but, for some reason or other, I seldom see a short sentence quoted without wondering, not whether it is partly true, but exactly how true it is. I was inspired—if you can call it so—with this doubt again and again as I read Miss Edith Sitwell's *A Poet's Notebook*, a large part of which consists of quotations about poets and poetry. On the very first page, for example, which deals with 'the poet's nature' I found this quotation from Blake:

'What,' it will be Question'd, 'when the Sun rises, do you not see a round disk of fire somewhat like a guinea?' 'Oh, no, no, I see an Innumerable Company of the Heavenly Host crying Holy, Holy, Holy, is the Lord God Almighty.' I question not my Corporeal or Vegetative Eye any more than I would Question a Window concerning a Sight. I look thro' it and not with it.

That is a noble and beautiful saying; but it seems to me to be fallacious to compare the eye with a window. After all, the eye sees, but the window does not. The window is a dead thing: looking out from a room, one sees the same swallows dipping their breasts in the pond whether the window is shut or open. Shut the eye, on the other hand, and one no longer sees the same world that one saw when one's eyes were open. Blake's saying was true, I think, in so far as it described the nature of his own genius, but I do not think it expressed a universal truth. Wordsworth looked at the daffodils, for example, not only through the eye, but with it. Shakespeare was equally a slave of the eye as he saw 'daisies pied and violets blue, and lady-smocks all silver white.' At the same time, if one had to choose between Blake's emphasis on the function of the imagination and poetry that is merely descriptive of what the eye sees, one would be enthusiastically on the side of the half truth of Blake.

Miss Sitwell tells us that her note-book is a private note-book and we naturally expect to find in it much that has meant a great deal to her, but that will not, out of its context, convey the same meaning to the ordinary reader. Take, for instance, this quotation from Baudelaire:

The poetic idea which disengages itself from the movement, in the lines, would seem to postulate the existence of a vast being, immense, complicated but of harmonious proportion—an animal full of genius, suffering and sighing all sighs and all human ambitions.

That, I think, will puzzle a good many readers as much of the later nineteenth-century poetry puzzled Tolstoy when he was writing *What is Art?* In its context, the postulated 'animal of genius, suffering and sighing all sighs and all human ambitions' may throw some light on the nature of poetry; but, isolated from its context, the phrase simply puzzles the ordinary poetry lover's mind.

It is, unfortunately, impossible to give any clear and indisputable definition of the nature of poetry. A sonnet by Shakespeare explains itself as no critic or commentator can explain it. This does not mean that criticism is useless, but the critic is useful only to those in whose imagination he happens to strike a spark. Thus, Miss Sitwell finds illumination in Cocteau's warning that 'the raw elegance of the lion is dangerous,' and in another statement of his that 'we become drunk with a strong honey, and that honey must sometimes be gathered from the paw of a young bear.' To Philistines such phrases will be so obscure as to be meaningless, and to a good many people who are not Philistines. They are none the less interesting to us, however, since they have meant something to a woman of Miss Sitwell's genius and may illuminate the imaginations of other readers in the same way.

As one begins to read *A Poet's Notebook*, one gets the impression that Miss Sitwell holds a religious view of the nature of poetic inspiration—that she regards the poet as a prophet with a vision of things divine. Many of her quotations are of a transcendentalist kind; and it is a pleasure to see her taking pleasure in the wisdom of that great outmoded seer, Emerson. Whitman, too, another prophetic voice, is among her idols.

Those who are especially interested in the technique of poetry will take particular pleasure in her analysis of a number of poetical passages and her explanation of the technical devices by which the poet makes his vision delightful to the reader. The ordinary reader enjoys poetry without asking himself why he enjoys it. He reads *Paradise Lost* without observing consciously how Milton varies the caesura and does not know how much he owes to this constant variation. It is one of Miss Sitwell's purposes to make us conscious of the means by which the poet gives us pleasure—to point out how much we owe to him for not only his vision and the choice of the right word, but the choice of the right consonants and vowels.   Take, for example, one of her comments on Christopher Smart's *Hymn to David*:

The saint in him pierced down to the essence of all things seen— and that essence was light, with all its variations of warmth, richness, piercingness, glow.   It is impossible to know how he produces that quintessence of light.   But if, for instance, we take verse lxv,

> For Adoration, beyond match,
> The scholar bulfinch aims to catch
> The soft flute's ivory touch;
> And, careless on the hazel spray,
> The daring redbreast keeps at bay
> The damsel's greedy clutch,

we shall see how in the lovely softening from the *fl* of flutes to the *i* of ivory, the change from the fullness of the one-syllabled word 'flutes' to the long warm *i* of 'ivory' with the quavering two syllables that follow, in that word—the transposition of the *ulf* of 'bulfinch' to the *flu* of 'flutes'—the actual sound seems to echo the warmth, the very glow, of the scholar bulfinch's and the daring redbreast's sweet bosoms.

That is a small example of the thoroughness and ingenuity with which Miss Sitwell investigates the secrets of the verbal music of the poets.   Probably no great poet ever constructed a poem deliberately as a pattern of consonant and vowel sounds. Poets of genius mind their p's and q's instinctively, and their words owe less to cold craftsmanship than to fiery imagination. At the same time, a scientific study of the elements in verse that please the ear and so establish a communication between the imagination of the poet and the imagination of the reader is interesting; and Miss Sitwell's analysis of the music of a number of passages from Shakespeare, though it may not help readers to enjoy Shakespeare more, will enable many of them to understand more fully one of the reasons why they enjoy Shakespeare.

Ordinary readers, however, will be rather overwhelmed by the microscopic enthusiasm with which Miss Sitwell examines the use of the alphabet by the great poets.   For example:

In the lines with which Cleopatra's speech begins:

> 'Giue me my Robe, put on my Crowne; I haue
> Immortall longings in me; Now no more,'

—the first line has the same two long dissonantal *o*'s as in the first line of Lady Macbeth's

'And fill me from the Crowne to the Toe, top-full
Of direst Cruelties; make thicke my blood'

—but the place of the dissonances is reversed, and the effect is utterly different. This is due, in part, to the hard *t*'s of Lady Macbeth's lines, and to the *k* and *ck* of 'make thicke.' Also, in the second line of Lady Macbeth's, the vowels are not deep, dark, and rich as are those in the second line of Cleopatra's. In

'Giue me my Robe, put on my Crowne; I haue'

the long magnificence of the *o*'s, the first being rich and deep, but not dark, the second effulgent with brightening jewels—these darken to the splendour of the *o*'s in the second line—that in 'immortall' being the deepest; that in 'longing,' in spite of the *g* which gives it poignancy, is soft because of the *n*.

This to me seems a little fanciful and extravagant. It makes one wonder how much, after all, Shakespeare owes to the mere sound of his words. A vast amount, every one will agree; yet we have also to admit that Shakespeare is as greatly idolized a poet in German and Hungarian translations as in the English original. The English version of the Psalms is another example of the way in which the words of great poets can remain great poetry in the different music of another language. Homer's genius reached the imagination of Keats through the English rhymes of Chapman.

Shelley (whom Miss Sitwell quotes on the subject, not with entire agreement) believed the translation of great verse to be impossible. But I think Shelley was wrong.

Lucidity

(1930)

In C. E. Montague's *A Writer's Notes on His Trade* there is an interesting and provocative section entitled 'Only Too Clear.' Steeped in the poets, Montague realized that clearness is not everything—that Shakespeare could not write *Coriolanus* in the lucid sentences of a journalist describing the arrest of a man suspected of murder—that the visions of a mystic cannot be set down so accurately as the events of a football match—and, in a mood of revolt against materialists who suggest that everything that is worth saying can be said clearly, he pointed out that, 'if you are going to stand for clearness at any price, then you are going to shut yourself out from a good many things.'

Montague's indictment of lucidity was as specious as the most brilliant of lawyers could have made it. He instanced the 'insipid veracity' of Crabbe's lines:

> Something had happened wrong about a bill
> Which was not drawn with true mercantile skill.
> So, to amend it, I was told to go
> And seek the firm of Clutterbuck and Co.

And he went on to suggest that literature may be 'clear as an election poster is clear,' and that this clearness may be due to a deficiency of the imagination.

It is easy to understand Montague's protest against excessive simplicity. If immediate intelligibility is everything, then how can one defend the language of the later Shakespeare, Coleridge's 'Ancient Mariner,' or the lyrics in Mr. Yeats's *Wind Among the Reeds*? When 'The Ancient Mariner' first appeared in *Lyrical Ballads* Wordsworth believed that it injured the volume containing it, since 'the old words, and the strangeness of it, have deterred readers from going on,' and it must be admitted that the story of a case of shop-lifting, reported in a newspaper, has a more easily apprehended plot. The truth is, the schoolboy finds it easier to write clearly in his first exercises than some men of genius in their masterpieces. The nine-year-old dunce

who translates 'Balbus built a wall' into Latin writes Latin of
which the meaning is more immediately apparent than Horace
achieved in several of his greatest odes.

To say this, however, is only to acknowledge that good writing
is something more than a statement of bald facts. It is the
presentation of facts, ideas, feelings, visions in such a way as
will bring them home most fully and effectively to the reason
or imagination or both. Great literature attempts to express a
great many things that language is incapable of expressing except
by necessarily vague suggestion. If nothing but plain common
sense were admitted, we should have had little or no great
poetry. This, however, does not constitute a defence of
obscurity. The obscurity of many of the great writers is often
due to something in the reader's mind—to the inability of an
ordinary man to take sustained flights into the imaginative
world of a writer of genius.

There is, however, a considerable amount of literature in
which the obscurity is due to the author rather than to the
defect of the reader. Donne's capacity of expression, great
though it was, for instance, was unequal to the subtlety of his
emotion and perception; and in the result his work is full of
difficulties even for the most intelligent reader. Browning's
obscurity, again, is due to the fact that, though he was one of
the most imaginative poets since Shakespeare, he attained only
here and there a perfect mastery of language. Then there have
been deliberately obscure writers, as Meredith was in some of
his work—writers who regarded it as a virtue to set their
readers rock-climbing after their meaning. The obscurity of
Henry James was due to other causes. It was the obscurity of
a writer who had perfected the instrument of language for the
expression of the finest of fine shades and, in doing so, had ruined
it for the purpose of expressing much else, so that in the end
he found it impossible to say that a man died or that it was a
wet day without using a meaningless paraphrase. At the height
of the cult of a great writer, many of his admirers invariably
praise his obscurities. They take a genuine pleasure in over-
coming difficulties, and they also enjoy the sense of belonging
to a select society cut off from the vulgar mass which is incapable
of appreciating the master.

As time goes on, however, it becomes evident that obscurity

is, after all, not a virtue in the works of the great writers. Browning is still read, but not for his obscure work—'Sordello' and the later poems—but for 'Men and Women' and other poems which are scarcely more difficult to understand than 'The Idylls of the King.'   Similarly, Meredith's fame does not rest on the obscure *One of Our Conquerors* or on the opening pages of *The Egoist*, but on his more lucid writings—*The Egoist* as a whole, *Richard Feverel*, and *Harry Richmond*.   I imagine that Henry James's fame will ultimately be preserved not by the tortured obscurities of his later work, but by the simpler work of his earlier and middle periods.   If it is so, we are safe in concluding that, as a general rule, a writer is greatest when he is least obscure, or, at least, that inspiration plus lucidity are greater aids to immortality than an equal amount of inspiration plus obscurity.   This, indeed, is so obvious as to be hardly worth saying, but there can be no harm in emphasizing the fact—in reply to Montague's paradox—that it is the first duty of a writer to be as lucid as he can possibly be.   It is especially important to emphasize this to-day when all kinds of silly experiments are being made with prose and when prose that nobody can understand is being hailed as a new and desirable development in literature.

The plain truth is, obscurity is a vice in literature, whether it is due to woolliness of mind or to pretentious play with language.   The object of a writer is to get into as full communion as possible with his readers, and obscurity of expression is no more praiseworthy than mumbling in conversation.   There are some writers nowadays who, when they do not understand a new book, take it for granted that the fault is their own, and treat the book with unusual deference.   Such humility is unnecessary.   If an author has not conveyed his meaning somehow or other to an intelligent reader, the fault is the author's. It is manifestly a critic's duty to make a serious attempt to understand an author who at first sight may be obscure, but if the author continues to be obscure at a third or fourth reading, he has so far failed as a writer.

Lucidity, however, is something more than the absence of profound obscurity.   There is a great deal of prose that is quite easy to understand and that, at the same time, cannot be called lucid.   It is seldom that a political speech is made which is perfectly unintelligible, but it is also seldom that a political speech is made in prose as lucid as that of Swift or Cobbett. There is as much difference between the prose of an ordinary speech and good prose as there is between slightly muddy water and clear water from a spring. The logic does not flow smoothly from sentence to sentence. Words are used half accurately. Clichés that have lost half their meaning through over-use are introduced. In the end, the speech, when it is printed, proves to be half ineffective because the speaker has not taken the trouble to make his meaning clear. The great objection to jargon and to woolly language of all kinds is that they tend to dim and dull the meaning of what is being said. It is true that when a journalist, describing a Rugby football match, says, not that 'So-and-so kicked a goal,' but that 'So-and-so added the major points,' every one understands what has happened. But there is more lucidity in the plain statement than in the round-about expression; and, if there is a tiny loss of lucidity in one sentence after another the cumulative effect of all these losses is a great loss of lucidity in the writer's article as a whole.

The chief objection to bad grammar again is that it makes little by little for the loss of lucidity. The man who writes 'different from' both sees and presents his meaning more clearly than the man who writes 'different to.' He is clearer in his mind about the exact meaning of the word 'different,' and the writer who most clearly understands the exact meaning of every word he uses is the best writer. Our grammar, like our manners, is largely a matter of good form, and arises from custom. But we may take it that good form does not exist for itself alone. Our grammar and our manners are merely means of making communication between one human being and another as easy as possible. It is because they instinctively know that grammar is an aid to lucid communication, that good writers respect the laws of grammar. Yoy will see how much we owe to grammar for lucidity if you read an ungrammatical four-page letter. The effect is one of semi-unintelligibility.

It is, however, as I have said, the sense of the precise meaning of words that most of all makes for lucidity in writing. Young writers intoxicated with words often find themselves using them vaguely and choosing a musical sentence that does not convey their precise meaning rather than a less musical sentence that would do so.　It is only after years of experience that some writers learn to resist the temptation of the music of the meaningless and realize that, musical though it seems at first, the music does not last.　Many a writer, looking back on his earliest prose, is startled to find how what once seemed golden eloquence now reads like a parody of empty verbiage.　The safe rule in writing is to say what one precisely means, even if it appears to destroy the shape of the sentence.　If the sense does not give the sentence good shape, then all the high-sounding words in the dictionary will not do so.

ROBERT LYND, 1947
from a drawing by Henry Lamb

Choosing what to Read

(1945)

'As books multiply to an unmanageable degree,' wrote De Quincey nearly a hundred years ago,

selection becomes more and more a necessity for readers. And the power of selection more and more a desperate problem for the busy part of readers. The possibility of selecting wisely is becoming continually more hopeless as the necessity for selection is becoming continually more pressing.

As I was reading this the other day, I could not help wondering whether it was true a hundred years ago and whether it is true even in an age so prolific of printed matter as ours. Selection among books is, no doubt, a necessity, but is the problem of selection so desperate as De Quincey affirms? Complaining of the vast number of books is an old practice. Long before the invention of printing, a sage bemoaned the fact that of the making of many books there is no end. Yet he lived in an age that to a modern reader, I am sure, would seem a time of book famine.

That there is a superfluity of books everybody must agree. But there has never been a superfluity of great books. Even to-day when—during peacetime at least—the masterpeces of the past are being continually reprinted and when every civilized and semi-civilized country is pouring out an annual flood of new literature, a small room would hold all the great books ever written; and all the books that were good without being great could be housed in the British Museum. As for the innumerable other books, the problem of selection among them scarcely exists. They are read by that enormous number of readers who merely want a love story or a detective story to while away the time and for whom one fairly good love story or detective story will do as well as another. Books like these are consumed as children consume sweets, and reading them is a pastime rather than a pleasure comparable with the pleasure of reading a great book.

Greatness in literature, however, is not a common quality as readableness is. Almost any middling clever man or woman can turn out something that is readable, and the rest of us can enjoy it and be grateful for it. But as a rule it would be no great loss not to have read it, as it would be a great loss not to have read Wordsworth's *Ode on the Intimations of Immortality*. To have missed this would be to have missed one of the supreme pleasures to be got from reading. One feels permanently richer for having read it, as one feels for having seen a noble prospect in nature or for having been in the company of a man of noble character.

I doubt, however, whether the ordinary reader finds much difficulty in acquainting himself with such masterpieces. Posterity, that excellent critic, has made a selection of the great books of the past, and most of us in our youth have been largely guided by its verdicts. I do not mean that we accepted all its opinions; but we were led by them in the direction of famous books in order to see whether they were to our liking. We might quarrel with the position given by posterity, say, to Dryden's verse; but that might be our fault and not Dryden's.

Posterity, no doubt, is fallible like every other good critic. Like other critics, it is a prey to the irrational fickleness of fashion. Posterity thought little of Euripides, for a time, and buried Ronsard in long and deep oblivion. On the whole, however, its choice of masters and masterpieces has been reasonably constant. Some years ago a few young men who thought themselves posterity, attempted to dethrone Milton; but they turned out not to be posterity at all. Posterity still guards Milton on his pedestal.

At the same time, every age has its own preferences among masterpieces, and there is something to be said for De Quincey's pronouncement in the sentence:

Every great classic in our native language should from time to time be reviewed anew, and especially if he belongs in any considerable extent to that section of the literature which concerns itself with manners, and if his reputation originally or his style of composition is likely to have been much influenced by the transient fashions of his own age.

The present time, for example, takes up an entirely different attitude from the Victorian era to the Restoration Dramatists. It would have been impossible, I fancy, for Congreve's *Love for*

Love to have had a long run in the theatre in the days of Thackeray. I doubt whether a Victorian censor would have passed it for production, yet to-day not only is it produced but it escapes the entertainment tax on the ground that it is educational. A change in modern manners—whether for better or for worse is a matter on which there are two opinions—has brought Congreve back into public liking; and he has to be, in De Quincey's phrase, 'reviewed anew.' In the same way books that, in my schooldays, were kept in locked cases in the local library lest they should corrupt the young, are now published in Everyman's Library without a protest.

Even though many Victorians disliked various things in Congreve and Fielding, however, they did not deny their importance as literary figures. At school we were taught respect for their genius and indeed were examined in their lives and writings, despite the fact that we were not encouraged to read them.

De Quincey, in the sentence I have quoted, was referring not to literature supposed to be deficient in certain moral qualities but to literature deficient in genius. He held that it was the duty of critics continually to inspect the literature of the past, 'searching and revising until everything spurious has been weeded out from among the Flora of our highest literature and until the waste of time for those who have so little at their command is reduced to a minimum.'

'The public,' he wrote,

cannot read by proxy as regards the good which it is to appropriate, but it *can* as regards the poison which it is to escape, and thus as literature expands becomes continually more of a household necessity, the duty resting upon critics (who are the vicarious readers for the public) becomes continually more urgent—of reviewing all works that may be supposed to have benefited too much or too indiscriminately by the superstition of a name. The praegustatores should have tasted of every cup and reported its qualities before the public call for it; and above all they should have done this in all cases of the higher literature—that is of literature properly so called.

This seems to me to imply that a selection of great literature can be made which should be accepted as all that is worth reading by intelligent men and women alike. I do not think it is possible to make such a selection. One reader will have his imagination illuminated by Keats's *Endymion*; to another, however devoted to Keats he may be, reading *Endymion* is an ungrateful and unprofitable task.

Much the same thing is true of a good deal of the work of nearly every great poet. One man's food is another man's boredom. There is no canon of literature that will not include things that will fail to inspire many intelligent readers and that will not exclude things that inspire many others. Even Charles Lamb is not loved by everybody. Mr. Somerset Maugham finds in his essays merely the maudlin sentimentality of a drunkard. Obviously then it is no use recommending Lamb to Mr. Maugham; in regard to the essays he suffers from one of those 'imperfect sympathies' of which Lamb wrote. And we all have our imperfect sympathies. Some able modern critics have—incredible as it may seem—felt a strong distaste for Jane Austen. Many people cannot get through *Tristram Shandy*. Even Shakespeare has his detractors.

Few of us, I am sure, wish to be dictated to in the matter of what is best in literature. We like to make our own choice. This is shown by the fact that we are not content to possess only a selection of the supposedly best work of a great poet. Much as we enjoy Matthew Arnold's selection of Wordsworth in the Golden Treasury series, we must also have a complete Wordsworth on our shelves containing the rubbish as well as the gold. We even insist on having a complete Coleridge though the greater part of his verse reveals little of his genius and would have perished long ago but for the magic of his name. Selections of the best of a poet's writing are all very well for an educational course, but the general reader wants the whole landscape of his works, barren as well as fertile, choked with weeds as well as rich with grain. He does not really lose much time in discovering the good among the bad. As a reader he has instincts like those of a bee searching for honey in a garden.

Nor is he content to live exclusively among the greatest masterpieces. If the Elizabethan and Jacobean drama has cast a spell on him he will read with delight plays that by a severe standard of criticism would have been confined to oblivion long ago. Interest in the novel may make it worth his while to read Mackenzie's *Man of Feeling* and Lewis's *Monk*, though to a reader with little time to spare, reading either book would be a waste of that little. To say this, however, is to suggest that time spent in reading anything but the greatest literature is wasted, and that would be a hard saying. Greek and Latin scholars do not spend all their time with Sophocles and Virgil. They relax occasionally on the lesser heights of Parthenius and Apuleius; the more new books are published, the more minor classics are read, if it is only in the Loeb translations.

The discovery of great books is, it seems to me, no more difficult now than it has ever been. The great names are as conspicuous as Everest and Mont Blanc, and there is plenty of time to read them for most of those with a taste for them. We have time, indeed, to read not only these but hundreds of things that De Quincey would have warned us against as spurious and as weeds in the flower beds of literature.